EXPERT RESUMES for
People Returning
to Work

Wendy S. Enelow and
Louise M. Kursmark

JIST Works

AUG   2003

Expert Resumes for People Returning to Work

© 2003 by Wendy S. Enelow and Louise M. Kursmark

Published by JIST Works, an imprint of JIST Publishing, Inc.
8902 Otis Avenue
Indianapolis, IN 46216-1033
Phone: 1-800-648-JIST   Fax: 1-800-JIST-FAX   E-mail: info@jist.com

Visit our Web site at **www.jist.com** for information on JIST, free job search tips, book chapters, and ordering instructions for our many products!

See the back of this book for additional JIST titles and ordering information. Quantity discounts are available for JIST books. Please call our Sales Department at 1-800-648-5478 for a free catalog and more information.

Acquisitions and Development Editor: Lori Cates Hand
Cover Designer: Katy Bodenmiller
Interior Designer and Page Layout: Trudy Coler
Proofreaders: Cheri Clark, Jeanne Clark
Indexer: Larry Sweazy

Printed in the United States of America
06 05 04 03 02   9 8 7 6 5 4 3 2 1

Library of Congress Cataloging-in-Publication Data is on file with the Library of Congress

We have been careful to provide accurate information in this book, but it is possible that errors and omissions have been introduced. Please consider this in making any career plans or other important decisions. Trust your own judgment above all else and in all things.

Trademarks: All brand names and product names used in this book are trade names, service marks, trademarks, or registered trademarks of their respective owners.

ISBN 1-56370-911-2

CONTENTS AT A GLANCE

ABOUT THIS BOOK ....*x*

INTRODUCTION ....*xii*

PART I: Resume Writing, Strategy, and Formats **1**

CHAPTER 1: Resume Writing Strategies for People Returning to Work *3*
   The top nine resume strategies for getting noticed and getting interviews; plus format and presentation standards.

CHAPTER 2: Writing Your Resume *19*
   Write your resume following the steps in this chapter.

CHAPTER 3: Printed, Scannable, Electronic, and Web Resumes *53*
   Learn the techniques for using technology effectively in your job search. Choose the best resume type for your situation.

PART II: Sample Resumes for People Returning to Work **63**

CHAPTER 4: Resumes for People Returning to Work After Raising Children *65*
   Use a functional format to deemphasize your time out of the workforce.

CHAPTER 5: Resumes for People Returning to Work After Divorce, Death of Spouse, or Financial Reversal *81*
   A sudden change in circumstances can dictate the need to find work—fast.

CHAPTER 6: Resumes for People Returning to Work with Extensive Volunteer Experience *91*
   Highlight your volunteer experience that supports your current career goals.

CHAPTER 7: Resumes for People Returning to Work After Serving as a Caregiver 103

Tending to aging parents, disabled children, or others who need full-time care requires an absence from the workforce for many.

CHAPTER 8: Resumes for People Returning to Work After Illness 111

It's important not to let your recent absence or any disabilities overshadow your real qualifications.

CHAPTER 9: Resumes for People Returning to Work After Incarceration 123

Focus on skills and experience; save discussion of your circumstances for the interview.

CHAPTER 10: Resumes for People Returning to Work After a Sabbatical..137

Avoid any "red flags" from large gaps in employment and highlight the sabbatical experience as a key qualification.

CHAPTER 11: Resumes for People Returning to Work After Relocating..145

Moving to a new area (or a new country) can present employment challenges for a "trailing" corporate spouse, military spouse, or immigrant.

CHAPTER 12: Resumes for People Returning to Work After Retirement..159

Whether financially strapped or simply bored, retirees returning to work need to deal with a period of unemployment as well as the possibility of appearing "too old."

CHAPTER 13: Resumes for People Laid Off, Downsized, or Otherwise Out of Work for More Than Six Months......................173

Your period of unemployment might be due to a tight job market or a lack of opportunity because of serious downsizing in your area.

CHAPTER 14: Resumes for People Returning to Work After Additional Education...195

Choose the most compelling information to present on your resume, so that both education and experience are appropriately emphasized.

CHAPTER *15: Resumes for People Returning to Work*
After an Entrepreneurial Venture..............................*209*

Present multifaceted entrepreneurial experience so that your
resume is focused on a specific area of expertise.

APPENDIX: *Internet Career Resources* *231*

Where to go on the Web for help with your job search: general
job search advice, career information, resume key words,
company information, interviewing tips, and salary information.

GEOGRAPHIC INDEX OF CONTRIBUTORS *240*

How to contact the professional resume writers who contributed
to this book.

INDEX *249*

TABLE OF CONTENTS

ABOUT THIS BOOK ....*x*

INTRODUCTION ....*xii*

PART I: Resume Writing, Strategy, and Formats 1

CHAPTER 1: *Resume Writing Strategies for People Returning to Work* 3

Resume Strategies 4

    Resume Strategy #1: Who Are You and How Do You Want to Be Perceived? 4

    Resume Strategy #2: Sell It to Me...Don't Tell It to Me 5

    Resume Strategy #3: Use Key Words 6

    Resume Strategy #4: Use the "Big" and Save the "Little" 8

    Resume Strategy #5: Make Your Resume "Interviewable" 9

    Resume Strategy #6: Eliminate Confusion with Structure and Context 9

    Resume Strategy #7: Use Function to Demonstrate Achievement 10

    Resume Strategy #8: Remain in the Realm of Reality 10

    Resume Strategy #9: Be Confident 10

There Are No Resume Writing Rules 10

    Content Standards 11

    Presentation Standards 15

    Accuracy and Perfection 17

CHAPTER 2: *Writing Your Resume*................................*19*

Recommended Resume Formats for Returning-to-Work
Job Seekers...19

Resume Format #1: Functional/Skills Resume......................20

Resume Format #2: Educational-Emphasis Resume................22

Resume Format #3: Experience-Emphasis Resume.................25

Why Format Is So Important...27

Step-by-Step: Writing the Perfect Resume.............................31

Contact Information...32

Career Summary...33

Education, Credentials, and Certifications..........................36

Professional Experience..38

The "Extras"..42

Writing Tips, Techniques, and Important Lessons.................47

Get It Down—Then Polish and Perfect It...........................47

Write Your Resume from the Bottom Up.............................47

Include Notable or Prominent "Extra" Stuff in Your
Career Summary...48

Use Resume Samples to Get Ideas for Content, Format,
and Organization..48

Include Dates or Not?...48

Always Send a Cover Letter When You Forward Your
Resume...50

Never Include Salary History or Salary Requirements
on Your Resume...51

Always Remember That You Are Selling..............................51

CHAPTER 3: *Printed, Scannable, Electronic, and*
Web Resumes...53

The Four Types of Resumes..53

The Printed Resume...53

The Scannable Resume..54

The Electronic Resume..54

The Web Resume...56

The Four Resume Types Compared...60

Are You Ready to Write Your Resume?...62

PART II: Sample Resumes for People Returning to Work 63

CHAPTER 4: *Resumes for People Returning to Work After Raising Children*...65

CHAPTER 5: *Resumes for People Returning to Work After Divorce, Death of Spouse, or Financial Reversal*.................81

CHAPTER 6: *Resumes for People Returning to Work with Extensive Volunteer Experience*.................................91

CHAPTER 7: *Resumes for People Returning to Work After Serving as a Caregiver* 103

CHAPTER 8: *Resumes for People Returning to Work After Illness*...111

CHAPTER 9: *Resumes for People Returning to Work After Incarceration*...123

CHAPTER 10: *Resumes for People Returning to Work After a Sabbatical*...137

CHAPTER 11: *Resumes for People Returning to Work After Relocating*..145

CHAPTER 12: *Resumes for People Returning to Work After Retirement*...159

CHAPTER 13: *Resumes for People Laid Off, Downsized, or Otherwise Out of Work for More Than Six Months*................173

CHAPTER 14: *Resumes for People Returning to Work After Additional Education*...195

CHAPTER 15: *Resumes for People Returning to Work After an Entrepreneurial Venture*....................................209

APPENDIX: *Internet Career Resources*....................231

GEOGRAPHIC INDEX OF CONTRIBUTORS.................240

INDEX..249

ABOUT THIS BOOK

If you're reading this book, you're most likely one of the tens of thousands of people who are returning to work after an extended absence. It may be that you've made this decision because of any of the following reasons:

- You've raised your children, they're in school, and you're ready to start or continue your career.

- You've been through a divorce or your spouse has passed away, and your financial situation dictates that you find a job.

- You've cared for a sick family member or friend for an extended period, and now that those obligations are finished, you're ready to resume your career.

- You're bored with retirement or need extra money and feel the need to return to work.

- You've just completed an extensive volunteer project and are now ready for a paying job.

- You've owned your own business for years and are now ready to work for someone else.

- You've just been released from prison and it's time to get on with your life.

These are just a few of the reasons you might be returning to work. There are many other reasons, and you'll find resumes that are applicable to all of them in this book.

Well, here's the good news: You've selected the perfect time to launch your search campaign! Despite the economic concerns that we are facing, believe it or not, it's a great time to look for a job.

According to the Bureau of Labor Statistics of the U.S. Department of Labor, the employment outlook is optimistic. Consider these findings:

- Total employment is projected to increase 15 percent between 2000 and 2010.

- Service-producing industries will continue to be the dominant employment generator, adding more than 20 million jobs by 2010.

- Goods-producing industries will also experience gains in employment, although not as significant as those in the service sector.

In chapter 1, you can read more interesting statistics, all of which will reinforce the fact that you've made the right decision to launch your search campaign today.

To take advantage of all of these opportunities, you must first develop a powerful, performance-based resume. To be a savvy and successful job seeker, you must know how to communicate your qualifications in a strong and effective written presentation. Sure, it's important to let employers know essential details, but a resume is more than just your job history and academic credentials. A winning resume is a concise yet comprehensive document that gives you a competitive edge in the job market. Creating such a powerful document is what this book is all about.

We'll explore the changes in resume presentation that have arisen over the past decade. In the past, resumes were almost always printed on paper and mailed. Today, e-mail has become the chosen method for resume distribution in many industries. In turn, many of the traditional methods for "typing" and presenting resumes have changed dramatically. This book will guide you in preparing resumes for e-mail, scanning, and Web-site posting, as well as the traditional printed resume.

By using *Expert Resumes for People Returning to Work* as your professional guide, you will succeed in developing a powerful and effective resume that opens doors, gets interviews, and helps you land your next great opportunity!

INTRODUCTION

This book, the fourth in the *Expert Resumes* series, has been the most challenging to write so far because it includes such a large and diverse audience. Compare it to the previous books in the series:

- ***Expert Resumes for Manufacturing Careers.*** The entire book focuses exclusively on the manufacturing industry, from production laborers to CEOs, from engineers to supply-chain managers.

- ***Expert Resumes for Teachers and Educators.*** This book was written for people in the education industry, from the kindergarten teacher to the university administrator, media specialist, and corporate trainer.

- ***Expert Resumes for Computer and Web Jobs.*** This book is for techies: programmers, Web-site designers, project managers, IS managers, and technology-company executives.

Then we decided to tackle *Expert Resumes for People Returning to Work,* for which there was no single category of people to write for, no single focus on just one profession or just one industry. Rather, this book presents a diverse portfolio of resumes, from chapter 4's focus on returning to work after raising children, to chapter 9's focus on returning to work after incarceration, and chapter 15's concentration on returning to the "traditional" workforce after an entrepreneurial venture.

There are, however, several common denominators facing every individual who is returning to the workforce after an extended absence. In fact, these will be the greatest issues and the most difficult challenges you will face as you prepare yourself either to re-launch your previous career or to seek a job that is new and different from what you've done in the past.

If you fall into the returning-to-work category, the critical questions you must ask yourself about your resume and your job search are the following:

- ***How* are you going to account for the time that you have been unemployed?** Are you going to share your entire "story," only certain parts, or none at all? What is the best way to communicate your history?

- ***What* resume format are you going to use?** You need to present your previous employment experience without immediately drawing attention to the fact that you have been out of the workforce for a while.

- ***Where* are you going to look for a job?** What types of jobs interest you, what types of companies, and what industries?

When you can answer the how, what, and where, you'll be prepared to write your resume and launch your search campaign. Use chapters 1 through 3 to guide you in developing the content for your resume and selecting the appropriate design and layout. Your resume should focus on your skills, achievements, and qualifications, demonstrating the value and benefit you bring to a prospective employer. The focus is on you, not your period of unemployment.

Then review the sample resumes in chapters 4 through 15 to see what other people have done—people in similar situations to yours and facing similar challenges. You'll find interesting formats, unique skills presentations, achievement-focused resumes, project-focused resumes, and much more. Most importantly, you'll see samples written by the top resume writers in the U.S., Canada, and Australia. These are real resumes that got interviews and generated job offers. They're the "best of the best" from us to you.

What Are Your Career Objectives?

Before you proceed any further with writing your resume, you'll need to begin by defining your career or job objectives—specifically, the types of positions, companies, and industries in which you are interested. This is critical because a haphazard, unfocused job search will lead you nowhere.

KNOW THE EMPLOYMENT TRENDS

One of the best ways to begin identifying your career objectives is to look at what opportunities are available today, in the immediate future, and in the longer-term future. And one of the most useful tools for this type of research and information collection is the U.S. Bureau of Labor Statistics (www.bls.gov).

In December 2001, the Bureau released its employment projections for the next decade. Here are some major findings that you'll find interesting and potentially relevant when selecting your industry and job targets:

- Total employment is projected to increase 15% between 2000 and 2010, 2% lower than the previous decade.

- Service-producing companies will continue to be the dominant employment generator, adding 20.5 million jobs by 2010, a gain of 19%.

- Goods-producing companies (manufacturing and construction) will contribute modest employment gains of only 3%.

- Health services, business services, social services, engineering, and other services are projected to account for almost one of every two non-farm jobs added to the U.S. economy over the next 10 years.

- Professional and related occupations and service occupations are projected to increase the fastest and add the most jobs—7 million and 5.1 million, respectively. This will account for more than half of the total job growth over the next decade.

- Transportation and material-moving occupations are projected to grow 15% (the average for most occupations).

- Office and administrative-support occupations are projected to grow more slowly than average, reflecting the need for fewer personnel as a result of the tremendous gains in office automation and technology.

- Production-related occupations are also projected to grow more slowly as manufacturing automation and technology reduce the need for specific types of employees.

- Eight of the 10 fastest-growing occupations will be in the computer, technology, Internet, and related professions.

- The 10 fastest-growing industries, from #1 in growth to #10, are computer services, residential care, health services, cable and pay television services, personnel supply services, warehousing and storage, water and sanitation, business services, equipment rental and leasing, and management and public relations.

- Occupations with the largest job growth are food preparation and service workers (#1), customer service representatives, registered nurses, retail salespersons, and computer-support specialists.

These facts and statistics clearly demonstrate that there are numerous employment opportunities across diverse sectors within our economy, from advanced technology positions to hourly wage jobs in food service and cable television. Although most industries may not be growing at double-digit percentages as in years past, companies continue to expand, and new companies emerge every day. The opportunities are out there; your challenge is to find them and position yourself as the "right" candidate.

MANAGE YOUR JOB SEARCH AND YOUR CAREER

To take advantage of these opportunities, you must be an educated job seeker. That means you must know what you want in your career, where the hiring action is, what qualifications and credentials you need to attain your desired career goals, and how best to market your qualifications. It is no longer enough to have a specific talent or set of skills. Whether you're a teacher, attorney, engineer, customer-service representative, PC technician, office manager, or any one of hundreds of other occupations, you must also be a strategic marketer, able to package and promote your experience to take advantage of this wave of employment opportunity.

There's no doubt that the employment market has changed dramatically from only a few years ago. According to the U.S. Department of Labor, you should expect to hold between 10 and 20 different jobs during your career. No longer is stability the status quo. Today, the norm is movement, onward and upward, in a fast-paced and intense employment market. And to stay on top of all the changes and opportunities, every job seeker—no matter the profession, no matter the industry—must proactively control and manage his career.

What's more, everyone reading this book is faced with the extra challenge of overcoming the bias that you might encounter because of your period of unemployment. Now you're faced with a competitive employment market, skills that might be outdated, and a gap in your work history. All of this can make your job search even more difficult than that of the more "traditional" job seeker who moves from one position to another without an extended period of unemployment.

And that is precisely why this book is so important to you. We'll outline the strategies and techniques that you can use to competitively position yourself against other candidates, creating a resume that highlights your skills and qualifications, while effectively minimizing the effect of your extended leave of absence.

Job Search Questions and Answers

Before we get to the core of this book—resume writing and design—we'd like to offer some practical job search advice that is valuable to virtually every job seeker who falls into the returning-to-work category.

WHAT IS THE MOST IMPORTANT CONSIDERATION FOR A RETURNING-TO-WORK CANDIDATE?

As outlined previously, the single most important consideration is how you are going to account for the time you have not been working. It goes without saying that you must be completely honest. However, that does not mean you have to tell the "entire story." Some information might be confidential and extremely personal. You should feel obligated to share only enough information to give an accurate account of why you haven't been working and what you've been doing with your time.

For some of you, the fact that you've been recently unemployed might not be a big obstacle to overcome. A prime example of this is the professional who resigns her position to enter graduate school and earn an MBA. Upon graduation, she's ready to re-launch her career and is in quite an advantageous position, now able to offer both experience and an advanced degree.

For others of you, this might be a much more significant challenge. If you've been a stay-at-home parent for 10 years, re-entering the workforce might take a bit of time to find just the right opportunity. Or consider individuals who have recently been released from prison or a mental-health institution. If you fall into these categories, your job search has an entirely different set of obstacles you'll have to overcome and explain.

Whatever your situation or obstacles, when preparing your resume you should keep in mind one critical fact:

Your resume is a marketing tool written to sell YOU!

HOW DO YOU ENTER A NEW PROFESSION?

In any industry or profession, your employment experience, education, and credentials are the keys to entry and long-term success. It is difficult to obtain a position in any new industry or profession without some related work experience, training, credentials, or relevant education. Here are a few pointers:

- **If you have work experience but want to transition into a different industry,** focus your resume on your professional experiences in a somewhat "generic" presentation that sells your experience and not the product or industry. Demonstrate how your skills relate to the industries you're currently pursuing.

- **If you're just starting to plan and build your career,** consider a four-year degree. Once you've earned your initial degree or completed your training, keep your sights focused on continuing your education as you move forward in your career. In many organizations, continuing education will be a prerequisite for long-term career advancement.

WHAT IS THE BEST RESUME STRATEGY FOR RE-ENTERING A FIELD?

If you already have experience in a particular field, remember that your resume must *sell* what you have to offer:

- **If you're a teacher or educational administrator,** *sell* the fact that you created new curricula, designed new instructional programs, and acquired innovative teaching materials.

- **If you're a computer professional,** *highlight* the new applications and new technologies you designed, implemented, or supported.

- **If you're an accountant,** *sell* the fact that you reduced operating costs by a certain percentage and contributed to a specific gain in net profitability.

When writing your resume, your challenge is to create a picture of knowledge, action, and results. In essence, you're stating "This is what I know, this is how I've used it, and this is how well I've performed." Success sells, so be sure to highlight yours. If you don't, no one else will.

WHERE ARE THE JOBS?

The jobs are everywhere—from multinational manufacturing conglomerates to the small retail sales companies in your neighborhood; from high-tech electronics firms in Silicon Valley to 100-year-old farming operations in rural communities; from banks and financial institutions to hospitals and health-care facilities in every city and town. The jobs are everywhere.

HOW DO YOU GET THE JOBS?

To answer this question, we need to review the basic principle underlying job search:

Job search is marketing!

You have a product to sell—yourself—and the best way to sell it is to use all appropriate *marketing channels* just as you would for any other product.

Suppose you wanted to sell televisions. What would you do? You'd market your products using newspaper, magazine, and radio advertisements. You might develop a company Web site to build your e-business, and perhaps you'd hire a field sales representative to market to major retail chains. Each of these is a different *marketing channel* through which you're attempting to reach your audience.

The same approach applies to job search. You must use every marketing channel that's right for you. Unfortunately, there is no exact formula that works for everyone. What's right for you depends on your specific career objectives—the type of position you want, the type of industry you're targeting, geographic restrictions, salary requirements, and more.

Following are the most valuable marketing channels for a successful job search. These are ordered from most effective to least effective:

1. **Referrals.** There is nothing better than a personal referral to a company, either in general or for a specific position. Referrals can open doors that, in most instances, would never be accessible any other way. If you know anyone who could possibly refer you to a specific organization, contact that person immediately and ask for their assistance.

2. **Networking.** Networking is the backbone of every successful job search. Although you might consider it an unpleasant or difficult task, it is essential that you network effectively with your professional colleagues and associates, past employers, past co-workers, suppliers, neighbors, friends, and others who might know of opportunities that are right for you. Another good strategy is to attend meetings of trade or professional associations in your area to make new contacts and expand your network. And particularly in today's nomadic job market—where you're likely to change jobs every few years—the best strategy is to keep your network "alive" even when you're *not* searching for a new position.

3. **Responding to newspaper, magazine, and periodical advertisements.** Although, as you'll read later, the opportunity to post job opportunities online has reduced the overall number of print advertisements, they still abound. Do not forget about this "tried and true" marketing strategy. If they've got the job and you have the qualifications, it's a perfect fit.

4. **Responding to online job postings.** One of the most advantageous results of the technology revolution is an employer's ability to post job announcements online and a job seeker's ability to respond immediately via e-mail. It's a wonder! In most (but not all) instances, these are bona fide opportunities, and it's well worth your while to spend time searching for and responding to appropriate postings. However, don't make the mistake of devoting too much time to searching the Internet. It can consume a huge amount of your time that you should spend on other job-search efforts.

To expedite your search, here are the largest and most widely used online job-posting sites—presented alphabetically, not necessarily in order of effectiveness or value:

http://careers.lycos.com
http://careers.msn.com
http://careers.yahoo.com
www.123usahire.com
www.americanjobs.com
www.careerbuilder.com
www.careerpath.com
www.careerweb.com
www.dice.com
www.employmax.com
www.flipdog.com
www.hirediversity.com
www.hotjobs.com
www.hotresumes.com
www.looksmart.com
www.monster.com
www.net-temps.com
www.sixfigurejobs.com
www.wantedtechnologies.com

5. **Targeted e-mail campaigns (resumes and cover letters) to recruiters.**
Recruiters have jobs, and you want one. It's pretty straightforward. The only
catch is to find the "right" recruiters who have the "right" jobs. Therefore,
you must devote the time and effort to preparing the "right" list of recruiters.
There are many resources on the Internet where you can access information
about recruiters (for a fee), sort that information by industry (such as banking,
sales, manufacturing, purchasing, transportation, finance, public relations, or
telecommunications), and then cross-reference it with position specialization
(such as management, technical, or administration). This allows you to identify
the recruiters who would be interested in a candidate with your qualifications.
What's more, because these campaigns are transmitted electronically, they are
easy and inexpensive to produce.

When working with recruiters, it's important to realize that they *do not* work
for you! Their clients are the hiring companies that pay their fees. They are not
in business to "find a job" for you, but rather to fill a specific position with a
qualified candidate, either you or someone else. To maximize your chances of
finding a position through a recruiter or agency, don't rely on just one or two,
but distribute your resume to many that meet your specific criteria.

6. **Posting your resume online.** The Net is swarming with reasonably priced (if
not free) Web sites where you can post your resume. It's quick, easy, and the
only *passive* thing you can do in your search. All of the other marketing channels require action on your part. With online resume postings, once you've
posted, you're done. You then just wait (and hope!) for some response.

7. **Targeted e-mail and print campaigns to employers.** Just as with campaigns to recruiters (refer to item 5), you must be extremely careful to select just the right employers that would be interested in a candidate with your qualifications. The closer you stick to "where you belong" in relation to your specific experience, the better your response rate will be. If you are targeting companies in a technology industry, we recommend that you use e-mail as your preferred method for resume submission. However, if the companies you are contacting are not in the technology industry, we believe that print campaigns (paper and envelopes mailed the old-fashioned way) are a more suitable and effective presentation—particularly if you are a management or executive candidate.

8. **In-person "cold calls" to companies and recruiters.** We consider this the least effective and most time-consuming marketing strategy. It is extremely difficult to just walk in the door and get in front of the right person, or any person who can take hiring action. You'll be much better off focusing your time and energy on other, more productive channels.

WHAT ABOUT OPPORTUNITIES IN CONSULTING AND CONTRACTING?

Are you familiar with the term "free agent"? It's the latest buzzword for an independent contractor or consultant who moves from project to project and company to company as the workload dictates. If you have particular expertise within a specific industry (for example, new product development, business turnaround, corporate relocation, or ad campaign design), this is an avenue that you might want to consider.

According to an article in *Quality Progress* magazine (November 2000), 10 years ago less than 10 percent of the U.S. workforce was employed as free agents. Currently, that number is greater than 20 percent and is expected to increase to 40 percent over the next 10 years. The demand for free agents is vast, and the market offers excellent career opportunities.

The reason for this growth is directly related to the manner in which companies are now hiring—or not hiring—their workforces. The opportunity now exists for companies to hire on a "per-project" basis and avoid the costs associated with full-time, permanent employees. Companies hire the staff they need just when they need them—and when they no longer need them, they're gone.

The newest revolution in online job search has risen in response to this demand: job-auction sites where employers bid on prospective employees. Individuals post their resumes and qualifications for review by prospective employers. The employers then competitively bid to hire or contract with each candidate. Also, employers can post projects that they want to outsource and prospective employees can bid on them. One well-established job-auction Web site is www.freeagent.com. Check it out. It's quite interesting, particularly if you're pursuing a career in consulting or contracting.

Conclusion

Career opportunities abound today, even for the returning-to-work candidate. What's more, it has never been easier to learn about and apply for jobs as it is now with all the Internet resources available to us. Your challenge is to arm yourself with a powerful resume and cover letter, identify the best ways to get yourself and your resume into the market, and shine during every interview. If you're committed and focused, we can almost guarantee that you'll make a smooth transition back into the workplace and find yourself happily employed.

PART I

Resume Writing, Strategy, and Formats

CHAPTER 1: Resume Writing Strategies for People
Returning to Work

CHAPTER 2: Writing Your Resume

CHAPTER 3: Scannable, Electronic, and Web Resumes

Resume Writing Strategies for People Returning to Work

If you're reading this book, chances are you haven't worked in a while. Maybe you've been away from work only six months, or maybe for years and years. Regardless of the length of time and the reason for your absence from the workforce, you are faced with some unique challenges in your job search and, more specifically, in how you write your resume. What can you do to capture employers' attention, impress them with your qualifications and achievements, and not be put "out of the running" if you haven't worked for a while?

Before we answer those questions and many others, let's talk about who this book was written for—a unique collection of people representing just about every profession and industry imaginable. The *only* thing that they have in common is the fact that they haven't been working recently. Consider this book an excellent resource if you are returning to work after

- Staying at home to raise children

- Being a stay-at-home wife/husband/partner

- The death or divorce of your spouse/partner or another close family member

- A change in your financial situation that forces you to seek an income

- Earning a college degree, advanced degree, or other type of educational training and/or certification

- An academic, research, or personal sabbatical

- A layoff or an extended period of unemployment (six months or more)

- Owning a business

- Retirement

- A long-term volunteer assignment

- An extended illness or serious accident

- Caring for someone who was ill and required a full-time caregiver

- Relocating

- Moving to the United States from a foreign country

- Incarceration

For every job seeker—those currently employed and those not currently working—a powerful resume is an essential component of the job search campaign. In fact, it is virtually impossible to conduct a search without a resume. It is your calling card that briefly, yet powerfully, communicates the skills, qualifications, experience, and value you bring to a prospective employer. It is the document that will open doors and generate interviews. It is the first thing people will learn about you when you forward it in response to an advertisement, and it is the last thing they'll remember when they're reviewing your qualifications after an interview.

Your resume is a sales document, and you are the product! You must identify the *features (what you know* and *what you can do)* and *benefits (how you can help an employer)* of that product, and then communicate them in a concise and hard-hitting written presentation. Remind yourself over and over, as you work your way through the resume process, that you are writing marketing literature designed to sell a new product—YOU—into a new position.

Your resume can have tremendous power and a phenomenal impact on your job search. So don't take it lightly. Rather, devote the time, energy, and resources that are essential to developing a resume that is well-written, visually attractive, and effective in communicating *who* you are and *how* you want to be perceived.

Resume Strategies

Following are the nine core strategies for writing effective and successful resumes.

RESUME STRATEGY #1: Who Are You and How Do You Want to Be Perceived?

Now that you've decided to look for a new position, the very first step is to identify your career interests, goals, and objectives. *This task is critical,* because it is the underlying foundation for *what* you include in your resume, *how* you include it, and *where* you include it. You cannot write an effective resume without knowing, at least to some degree, what type or types of positions you will be seeking.

There are two concepts to consider here:

- **Who you are:** This relates to what you have done professionally and/or academically. Are you/were you a teacher, sales associate, metalworker, engineer, banker, or senior executive? Did you return to college after a successful career to now pursue new opportunities? Were you bored and unhappy being retired, and now want to get back into your original career track? Who are you?

- **How you want to be perceived:** This relates to your current career objectives. Consider the following scenario: You're been a stay-at-home mom for eight years and done a great deal of volunteer and fund-raising work. Prior to having children, you were a loan officer with a major banking institution. Now you want to pursue a career in special-events planning and public relations. Rather than focus your resume on your banking career, focus it on the skills you've acquired through your volunteer efforts. Include information about the special events you've planned, marketed, and managed; about teams of people you've supervised; about advertisements and promotions you've designed; about logistics you've coordinated; about VIP relations you've handled. Don't allow yourself to think that just because your recent experience has all been volunteer, it doesn't have value. To the contrary; it has tremendous value in positioning you for the type of job you are seeking today.

  Here's another example: Three years ago you resigned your position to take care of your aging parents, who have subsequently passed away. You're now ready to return to your previous career in the manufacturing industry. Rather than focus on your chronological work experience, which will quickly point out that you haven't worked in three years, highlight your career successes and achievements. Of course, you'll need to include, at a minimum, a listing of your work history, but you should include that information at the end. Allow the beginning of your resume to focus on all that you've accomplished and the value you bring to a new employer.

The strategy is to connect these two concepts by using the *Who You Are* information that ties directly to the *How You Want to Be Perceived* message to determine what information to include in your resume. By following this strategy, you're painting a picture that allows a prospective employer to see you as you want to be seen—as an individual with the qualifications for the type of position you are pursuing.

> **WARNING:** If you prepare a resume without first clearly identifying what your objectives are and how you want to be perceived, your resume will have no focus and no direction. Without the underlying knowledge of "This is what I want to be," you do not know what to highlight in your resume. As a result, the document becomes a historical overview of your career and not the sales document it should be.

RESUME STRATEGY #2: *Sell It to Me...Don't Tell It to Me*

We've already established the fact that resume writing is sales. You are the product, and you must create a document that powerfully communicates the value of that product. One particularly effective strategy for accomplishing this is the "Sell It to Me...Don't Tell It to Me" strategy, which impacts virtually every word you write on your resume.

If you "tell it," you are simply stating facts. If you "sell it," you promote it, advertise it, and draw attention to it. Look at the difference in impact between these examples:

Tell It Strategy: Supervised construction of 2-acre chemical manufacturing facility.

Sell It Strategy: Directed team of 42 responsible for $2.8 million construction of 2-acre manufacturing facility. Delivered project at 20% under budget.

Tell It Strategy: Coordinated all secretarial, clerical, and administrative functions for medical office.

Sell It Strategy: Implemented a series of process improvements that reduced staffing requirements 20%, increased daily productivity 30%, and reduced billing errors 14% for a high-volume medical office. Full responsibility for all secretarial, clerical, and administrative functions.

Tell It Strategy: Set up PCs for newly hired sales and service staff.

Sell It Strategy: Installed more than 100 PCs and implemented customized applications to support nationwide network of sales and service staff for one of the world's largest insurance companies. Provided ongoing troubleshooting and technical support that reduced PC downtime by 38% over a 6-month period.

What's the difference between "telling it" and "selling it"? In a nutshell...

Telling It	Selling It
Describes features.	Describes benefits.
Tells what and how.	Sells why the "what" and "how" are important.
Details activities.	Includes results.
Focuses on what you did.	Details how what you did benefited your employer, department, team members, students, and so on.

RESUME STRATEGY #3: Use Key Words

No matter what you read or who you talk to about searching for jobs, the concept of key words is sure to come up. Key words (or, as they were previously known, buzz words) are words and phrases that are specific to a particular industry or profession. For example, key words for the manufacturing industry include *production-line operations, production planning and scheduling, materials management, inventory control, quality, process engineering, robotics, systems automation, integrated logistics, product specifications, project management,* and many, many more.

When you use these words and phrases—in your resume, in your cover letter, or during an interview—you are communicating a very specific message. For example, when you include the word "merchandising" in your resume, your reader will most likely assume that you have experience in the retail industry—in product selection, vendor/manufacturing relations, in-store product display, inventory management, mark-downs, product promotions, and more. As you can see, people will make inferences about your skills based on the use of just one or two specific words.

Here are a few other examples:

- When you use the words **investment finance,** people will assume you have experience with risk management, mergers, acquisitions, initial public offerings, debt/equity management, asset allocation, portfolio management, and more.

- When you mention **sales,** readers and listeners will infer that you have experience in product presentations, pricing, contract negotiations, customer relationship management, new product introduction, competitive product positioning, and more.

- By referencing **Internet technology** in your resume, you convey that you most likely have experience with Web site design, Web site marketing, metatags, HTML, search-engine registration, e-learning, and more.

- When you use the words **human resources,** most people will assume that you are familiar with recruitment, hiring, placement, compensation, benefits, training and development, employee relations, human resources information system (HRIS), and more.

Key words are also an integral component of the resume-scanning process, whereby employers and recruiters electronically search resumes for specific terms to find candidates with the skills, qualifications, and credentials for their particular hiring needs. Over the past several years, key-word scanning has dramatically increased in popularity because of its ease of use and efficiency in identifying prime candidates. Every job seeker today must stay on top of the latest trends in technology-based hiring and employment to ensure that their resumes and other job search materials contain the "right" key words to capture the interest of prospective employers.

In organizations where it has been implemented, electronic scanning has replaced the more traditional method of an actual person reading your resume (at least initially). Therefore, to some degree, the *only* thing that matters in this instance is that you have included the "right" key words to match the company's or the recruiter's needs. Without them, you will most certainly be passed over.

Of course, in virtually every instance your resume will be read at some point by human eyes, so it's not enough just to throw together a list of key words and leave it at that. In fact, it's not even necessary to include a separate "key word summary" on your resume. A better strategy is to incorporate key words naturally into the text within the appropriate sections of your resume.

Keep in mind, too, that key words are arbitrary; there is no defined set of key words for a secretary, production laborer, police officer, teacher, electrical engineer, construction superintendent, finance officer, sales manager, or chief executive officer. Employers searching to fill these positions develop a list of terms that reflect the specifics they desire in a qualified candidate. These might be a combination of professional qualifications, skills, education, length of experience, and other easily defined criteria, along with "soft skills," such as organization, time management, team building, leadership, problem-solving, and communication.

> **NOTE:** Because of the complex and arbitrary nature of key-word selection, we cannot overemphasize how vital it is to be certain that you include in your resume *all* of the key words that represent your experience and knowledge!

How can you be sure that you are including all the key words, and the *right* key words? Just by describing your work experience, achievements, educational credentials, technical qualifications, and the like, you will naturally include most of the terms that are important in your field. To cross-check what you've written, review online or newspaper job postings for positions that are of interest to you. Look at the precise terms used in the ads and be sure you have included them in your resume (as appropriate to your skills and qualifications).

Another great benefit of today's technology revolution is our ability to find instant information, even information as specific as key words for hundreds of different industries and professions. Refer to the appendix for a listing of Web sites that list thousands of key words, complete with descriptions. These are outstanding resources.

RESUME STRATEGY #4: Use the "Big" and Save the "Little"

When deciding what you want to include in your resume, try to focus on the "big" things—new programs, special projects, cost savings, productivity and efficiency improvements, new products, technology implementations, and more. Give a good, broad-based picture of what you were responsible for and how well you did it. Here's an example:

> Supervised daily sales, customer service, and maintenance-shop operations for a privately owned automotive repair facility. Managed a crew of 12 and an annual operating budget of $300,000 for supplies and materials. Consistently achieved/surpassed all revenue, profit, quality, and production objectives.

Then, save the "little" stuff—the details—for the interview. With this strategy, you will accomplish two things:

- You'll keep your resume readable and of a reasonable length (while still selling your achievements).

- You'll have new and interesting information to share during the interview, rather than merely repeating what is already on your resume.

Using the preceding example, when discussing this experience during an interview you could elaborate on your specific achievements—namely, improving productivity and efficiency ratings, reducing annual operating and material costs, improving employee training, strengthening customer relations, increasing sales volume, and managing facility upgrades.

RESUME STRATEGY #5: Make Your Resume "Interviewable"

One of your greatest challenges is to make your resume a useful interview tool. Once the employer has determined that you meet the primary qualifications for a position (you've passed the key-word scanning test or initial review) and you are contacted for a telephone or in-person interview, your resume becomes all-important in leading and prompting your interviewer during your conversation.

Your job, then, is to make sure the resume leads the reader where you want to go and presents just the right organization, content, and appearance to stimulate a productive discussion. To improve the "interviewability" of your resume, consider these tactics:

- Make good use of Resume Strategy #4 (Use the "Big" and Save the "Little") to invite further discussion about your experiences.

- Be sure your greatest "selling points" are featured prominently, not buried within the resume.

- Conversely, don't devote lots of space and attention to areas of your background that are irrelevant or about which you feel less than positive; you'll only invite questions about things you really don't want to discuss.

- Make sure your resume is highly readable—this means plenty of white space, an adequate font size, and a logical flow from start to finish.

RESUME STRATEGY #6: Eliminate Confusion with Structure and Context

Keep in mind that your resume will be read *very quickly* by hiring authorities! You may agonize over every word and spend hours working on content and design, but the average reader will skim quickly through your masterpiece and expect to pick up important facts in just a few seconds. Try to make it as easy as possible for readers to grasp the essential facts:

- Be consistent: for example, put job titles, company names, and dates in the same place for each position.

- Make information easy to find by clearly defining different sections of your resume with large, highly visible headings.

- Define the context in which you worked (for example, the organization, your department, and the specific challenges you faced) before you start describing your activities and accomplishments.

RESUME STRATEGY #7: Use Function to Demonstrate Achievement

When you write a resume that focuses only on your job functions, it can be dry and uninteresting and will say very little about your unique activities and contributions. Consider the following example:

> Responsible for all aspects of consumer lending at the branch level.

Now, consider using that same function to demonstrate achievement and see what happens to the tone and energy of the sentence. It becomes alive and clearly communicates that you deliver results:

> Processed and approved over $30 million in secured and unsecured consumer loans for Wachovia's largest branch operation in Memphis, Tennessee. Achieved and maintained a less than 2% write-off for unrecoverable loans (18% less than the industry average).

Try to translate your functions into achievements and you'll create a more powerful resume presentation.

RESUME STRATEGY #8: Remain in the Realm of Reality

We've already established that resume writing is sales. And, as any good salesperson does, one feels somewhat inclined to stretch the truth, just a bit. However, be forewarned that you must stay within the realm of reality. Do not push your skills and qualifications outside the bounds of what is truthful. You never want to be in a position where you have to defend something that you've written on your resume. If that's the case, you'll lose the opportunity before you ever get started.

RESUME STRATEGY #9: Be Confident

You are unique. There is only one individual with the specific combination of employment experience, qualifications, achievements, education, and special skills that you have. In turn, this positions you as a unique commodity within the competitive job-search market. To succeed, you must prepare a resume that is written to sell *you* and highlight *your* qualifications and *your* success. If you can accomplish this, you will have won the job-search game by generating interest, interviews, and offers.

There Are No Resume Writing Rules

One of the greatest challenges in resume writing is that there are no rules to the game. There are certain expectations about information that you will include: principally, your employment history and your educational qualifications. Beyond that, what you include is entirely up to you and what you have done in your career. What's more, you have tremendous flexibility in determining how to include the information you have selected. In chapter 2, you'll find a wealth of information on each possible category you might include in your resume, the type of information to be placed in each category, preferred formats for presentation, and lots of other information and samples that will help you formulate *your* best resume.

Although there are no rules, there are a few standards to live by as you write your resume. The following sections discuss these standards in detail.

CONTENT STANDARDS

Content is, of course, the text that goes into your resume. Content standards cover the writing style you should use, items you should be sure to include, items you should avoid including, and the order and format in which you list your qualifications.

Writing Style

Always write in the first person, dropping the word "I" from the front of each sentence. This style gives your resume a more aggressive and more professional tone than the passive third-person voice. Here are some examples:

First Person

> Manage 22-person team responsible for design and market commercialization of a new portfolio of PC-based applications for Marley's $100 million consumer-sales division.

Third Person

> Mr. Reynolds manages a 22-person team responsible for the design and market commercialization of a new portfolio of PC-based applications for Marley's $100 million consumer-sales division.

By using the first-person voice, you are assuming "ownership" of that statement. You did such-and-such. When you use the third-person, "someone else" did it. Can you see the difference?

Phrases to Stay Away From

Try *not* to use phrases such as "responsible for" or "duties included." These words create a passive tone and style. Instead, use active verbs to describe what you did.

Compare these two ways of conveying the same information:

> Responsible for all marketing and special events for the store, including direct mailing, in-store fashion shows, and new-product introductions and promotions.

OR

> Orchestrated a series of marketing and special-event programs for Macy's Reston, one of the company's largest and most profitable operating locations. Managed direct-mailing campaigns, in-store fashion shows, and new-product introductions and promotions.

Resume Style

The traditional *chronological* resume lists work experience in reverse chronological order (starting with your current or most recent position). The *functional* style de-emphasizes the "where" and "when" of your career and instead groups similar experience, talents, and qualifications regardless of when they occurred.

Today, however, most resumes follow neither a strictly chronological nor strictly functional format; rather, they are an effective mixture of the two styles usually known as a "combination" or "hybrid" format.

Like the chronological format, the hybrid format includes specifics about where you worked, when you worked there, and what your job titles were. Like a functional resume, a hybrid emphasizes your most relevant qualifications—perhaps within chronological job descriptions, in an expanded summary section, in several "career highlights" bullet points at the top of your resume, or in project summaries. Most of the examples in this book are hybrids and show a wide diversity of organizational formats that you can use as inspiration for designing your own resume.

Resume Formats

Resumes, principally career summaries and job descriptions, are most often written in a paragraph format, a bulleted format, or a combination of both. Following are three job descriptions, all very similar in content, yet presented in each of the three different writing formats. The advantages and disadvantages of each format are also addressed.

Paragraph Format

Business Manager   1989 to 2003

Smith Ag Production Company, Garnerville, Arkansas

Purchased run-down, debt-ridden farming operation and transformed it into a near showplace, honored as one of the best commercial Angus operations in southern Arkansas. Developed a far-reaching network throughout the agricultural industry and with leaders in state government, banking, and commercial lending.

Held full management authority for cattle and alfalfa production generating 2,500+ tons of hay per year and running up to 500 stock cows. Hired, trained, and supervised all employees. Managed budgets of $750,000 annually and over $2 million in operating lines of credit. Directed the sale/purchase of all commodities to support business operations. Gained an in-depth knowledge of the commercial agricultural industry and its unique financial, economic, and operating challenges.

Advantages

Requires the least amount of space on the page. Brief, succinct, and to the point.

Disadvantages

Achievements get lost in the text of the paragraphs. They are not visually distinctive, nor do they stand alone to draw attention to them.

Bulleted Format

Business Manager   1989 to 2003

Smith Ag Production Company, Garnerville, Arkansas

- Purchased run-down, debt-ridden farming operation and transformed it into a near showplace, honored as one of the best commercial Angus operations in southern Arkansas.

- Developed a far-reaching network throughout the agricultural industry and with leaders in state government, banking, and commercial lending.

- Held full management authority for cattle and alfalfa production generating 2,500+ tons of hay per year and running up to 500 stock cows.

- Hired, trained, and supervised all employees.

- Managed budgets of $750,000 annually and over $2 million in operating lines of credit.

- Directed the sale/purchase of all commodities to support business operations.

- Gained an in-depth knowledge of the commercial agricultural industry and its unique financial, economic, and operating challenges.

Advantages

Quick and easy to peruse.

Disadvantages

Responsibilities and achievements are lumped together, with everything given equal value. In turn, the achievements get lost and are not immediately recognizable.

Combination Format

Business Manager   1989 to 2003

Smith Ag Production Company, Garnerville, Arkansas

Held full management authority for cattle and alfalfa production generating 2,500+ tons of hay per year and running up to 500 stock cows. Hired, trained, and supervised all employees. Managed budgets of $750,000 annually and over $2 million in operating lines of credit. Directed the sale/purchase of all commodities to support business operations.

- Purchased run-down, debt-ridden farming operation and transformed it into a near showplace, honored as one of the best commercial Angus operations in southern Arkansas.

- Developed a far-reaching network throughout the agricultural industry and with leaders in state government, banking, and commercial lending.

- Gained an in-depth knowledge of the commercial agricultural industry and its unique financial, economic, and operating challenges.

Advantages

Our recommended format. Clearly presents overall responsibilities in the introductory paragraph and then accentuates each achievement as a separate bullet.

Disadvantages

If you don't have clearly identifiable accomplishments, this format is not effective. It also may shine a glaring light on the positions where your accomplishments were less notable.

You'll find numerous other examples of how to best present your employment experience in the resume samples that follow in chapters 4 through 15. Chapter 2 discusses formats you can use to highlight your skills and achievements more prominently than your work history. In many returning-to-work situations, this approach is critical to get yourself noticed and not passed over.

E-Mail Address and URL

Be sure to include your e-mail address prominently at the top of your resume. As we all know, e-mail has become one of the most preferred methods of communication between employers and job seekers. If you don't yet have an e-mail address, visit www.yahoo.com, www.hotmail.com, or www.netzero.com, where you can get a free e-mail address that you can access through the Web.

In addition to your e-mail address, if you have a URL (Web site address) where you have posted your Web resume, be sure to also display that prominently at the top of your resume. For more information on Web resumes, refer to chapter 3.

PRESENTATION STANDARDS

Presentation regards the way your resume looks. It relates to the fonts you use, the paper you print it on, any graphics you might include, and how many pages your resume should be.

Typestyle

Use a typestyle (font) that is clean, conservative, and easy to read. Stay away from anything that is too fancy, glitzy, curly, and the like. Here are a few recommended typestyles:

Tahoma	Times New Roman
Arial	Bookman
Krone	Book Antiqua
Soutane	Garamond
CG Omega	Century Schoolbook
Century Gothic	Lucida Sans
Gill Sans	Verdana

Although it is extremely popular, Times New Roman is our least preferred typestyle simply because it is overused. More than 90 percent of the resumes we see are typed in Times New Roman. Your goal is to create a competitive-distinctive document, and, to achieve that, we recommend an alternative typestyle.

Your choice of typestyle should be dictated by the content, format, and length of your resume. Some fonts look better than others at smaller or larger sizes; some have "bolder" boldface type; some require more white space to make them readable. Once you've written your resume, experiment with a few different typestyles to see which one best enhances your document.

Type Size

Readability is everything! If the type size is too small, your resume will be difficult to read and difficult to skim for essential information. Interestingly, a too-large type size, particularly for senior-level professionals, can also give a negative impression by conveying a juvenile or unprofessional image.

As a general rule, select type from 10 to 12 points in size. However, there's no hard-and-fast rule, and a lot depends on the typestyle you choose. Take a look at the following examples:

Very readable in 9-point Verdana:

Won the 1999 "Employee of the Year" award at Chrysler's Indianapolis plant. Honored for innovative contributions to the design and manufacturability of the Zodiac product line.

Difficult to read in too-small 9-point Gill Sans:

Won the 1999 "Employee of the Year" award at Chrysler's Indianapolis plant. Honored for innovative contributions to the design and manufacturability of the Zodiac product line.

Concise and readable in 12-point Times New Roman:

Training & Development Consultant specializing in the design, development, and presentation of multimedia training programs for hourly workers, skilled labor, and craftsmen.

A bit overwhelming in too-large 12-point Bookman Old Style:

Training & Development Consultant specializing in the design, development, and presentation of multimedia training programs for hourly workers, skilled labor, and craftsmen.

Type Enhancements

Bold, *italics*, <u>underlining</u>, and CAPITALIZATION are ideal to highlight certain words, phrases, achievements, projects, numbers, and other information to which you want to draw special attention. However, do not overuse these enhancements. If your resume becomes too cluttered with special formatting, nothing stands out.

> **NOTE:** Resumes intended for electronic transmission and computer scanning have specific restrictions on typestyle, type size, and type enhancements. We discuss these details in chapter 3.

Page Length

For most industries and professions, the "one to two page rule" for resume writing still holds true. Keep it short and succinct, giving just enough to entice your readers' interest. However, there are many instances when a resume may be longer than two pages. For example:

- You have an extensive list of technical qualifications that are relevant to the position for which you are applying. (You may consider including these on a separate page as an addendum to your resume.)

- You have extensive educational training and numerous credentials/certifications, all of which are important to include. (You may consider including these on a separate page as an addendum to your resume.)

- You have an extensive list of special projects, task forces, and committees to include that are important to your current career objectives. (You may consider including these on a separate page as an addendum to your resume.)

- You have an extensive list of professional honors, awards, and commendations. This list is tremendously valuable in validating your credibility and distinguishing you from the competition.

If you create a resume that's longer than two pages, make it more reader-friendly by carefully segmenting the information into separate sections. Your sections may include a career summary, work experience, education, professional or industry credentials, honors and awards, technology and equipment skills, publications, public-speaking engagements, professional affiliations, civic affiliations, technology skills, volunteer experience, foreign-language skills, and other relevant information you want to include. Put each into a separate category so that your resume is easy to peruse and your reader can quickly see the highlights. You'll read more about each of these sections in chapter 2.

Paper Color

Be conservative. White, ivory, and light gray are ideal. Other "flashier" colors are inappropriate for most individuals unless you are in a highly creative industry and your paper choice is part of the overall design and presentation of a creative resume.

Graphics

An attractive, relevant graphic can really enhance your resume. When you look through the sample resumes in chapters 4 through 15, you'll see some excellent examples of the effective use of graphics to enhance the visual presentation of a resume. Just be sure not to get carried away... be tasteful and relatively conservative.

White Space

We'll say it again—readability is everything! If people have to struggle to read your resume, they simply won't make the effort. Therefore, be sure to leave plenty of white space. It really does make a difference.

ACCURACY AND PERFECTION

The very final step, and one of the most critical in resume writing, is the proofreading stage. It is essential that your resume be well-written, visually pleasing, and free of any errors, typographical mistakes, misspellings, and the like. We recommend that you carefully proofread your resume a minimum of three times, and then have two or three other people also proofread it. Consider your resume an example of the quality of work you will produce on a company's behalf. Is your work product going to have errors and inconsistencies? If your resume does, it communicates to a prospective employer that you are careless, and this is the "kiss of death" in job search.

Take the time to make sure that your resume is perfect in all the little details that do, in fact, make a big difference to those who read it.

CHAPTER 2

Writing Your Resume

For many job seekers, resume writing is *not* at the top of the list of fun and exciting activities! How can it compare to developing a new product, writing an ad campaign, streamlining administrative affairs, cutting costs, reducing product-failure rates, or closing your first major sales contract? In your perception, we're sure that it cannot.

However, resume writing can be an enjoyable and rewarding task. When your resume is complete, you can look at it proudly, reminding yourself of all that you have achieved. It is a snapshot of your career and your success. When it's complete, we guarantee you'll look back with tremendous self-satisfaction as you launch and successfully manage your job search.

As the very first step in finding a new position or advancing your career, resume writing can be the most daunting of all tasks in your job search. If writing is not one of your primary skills or a past job function, it might have been years since you've actually sat down and written anything other than notes to yourself. Even for those of you who write on a regular basis, resume writing is unique. It has its own style and a number of peculiarities, as with any specialty document.

Recommended Resume Formats for Returning-to-Work Job Seekers

In the following section, you will find three resume formats that are designed for specific returning-to-work situations. We recommend that you identify which category is appropriate for you, based on your particular situation, and then use that specific format as a template for your resume.

It is very unlikely that you will find a format that exactly "matches" your life, experience, and educational credentials. Use the template as the foundation for your resume, customizing and reformatting as necessary to create your own winning resume.

After we present the three formats, we'll follow with a detailed discussion of each of the key resume components (the Career Summary, Professional Experience, Education, Technical Qualifications, Professional Memberships, and Volunteer Experience sections).

RESUME FORMAT #1: Functional/Skills Resume

This format is recommended for the following situations:

- Stay-at-home moms, wives, and partners

- After an extended illness, serious accident, death of a spouse or child, divorce, or a dramatic change in financial situation

- After being a full-time caregiver

- After retirement

- After a long-term volunteer assignment or an extended period of travel and adventure

- After a period of incarceration

    NOTE: We are assuming that you've been unemployed for at least one year, a long enough period of time to warrant changing your resume's format from a chronological style (the most common and preferred format, focusing on past employment experience) to a more functional style (focusing on skills and qualifications).

Resume Focus

The focus of Resume Format #1 is on your skills, qualifications, project highlights, and achievements. You want to draw your readers' attention to the experience, knowledge, and value you can bring to their organization. At the same time, it's beneficial to downplay (at least at the beginning of your resume) your previous work experience so that you're not drawing attention to the fact that you haven't worked for years.

Primary Resume Components

- A detailed Career Summary (the cornerstone of Resume Format #1)

- A consolidated listing of employment experience

- Education

ELLYN PARKER

2 Bronxville Road, Apt. 2D
Yonkers, NY 10709
home/msg.: (914) 779-4638
mobile: (914) 912-2630
e-mail: EParker95@aol.com

OBJECTIVE

Receptionist/Office Assistant. Qualified by extensive administrative experience in professional settings.

SKILLS SUMMARY

Customer Service   **Administration**
Oral & Written Communication   **Microsoft Word**
Proofreading & Editing   **Problem Solving**
Research & Analysis   **Shorthand**

CAREER HIGHLIGHTS

- Answered calls and scheduled appointments for a busy dental office. Listened to and addressed concerns of patients.
- Communicated with freight forwarders, chemical inspectors, overseas affiliates, and foreign vendors to ensure that Exxon's bulk chemical shipments were delivered on time.
- Created a charting system to track international shipments of bulk chemicals for Exxon.
- Coordinated orders and bills of lading for bulk chemicals.
- Ensured that current shipping regulations for countries were updated in an International Documentation Handbook.
- Reduced risk of late-payment fees with prompt processing of domestic and international bills.
- Converted international currency into U.S. dollars to accurately determine invoice amounts from overseas vendors.
- Prepared export documentation and reports.
- Established and maintained department filing system.
- Managed two high school reunions: found missing classmates, arranged radio and newspaper announcements, chose location and menu, and updated database.

WORK HISTORY

Receptionist (P/T), Dr. Terry Geller, Yonkers, NY (2 years)

Assistant Manager—Accounts Receivable, Exxon Corporation, New York, NY (6 years)

International Traffic Coordinator, Exxon Corporation, New York, NY (11 years)

Secretary, Exxon Corporation, New York, NY (7 years)

An example of Resume Format #1 (resume written by Kirsten Dixson).

RESUME FORMAT #2: Educational-Emphasis Resume

This format is recommended for the following situations:

- After earning a college degree, advanced degree, or other type of educational training and/or certification

- After a sabbatical or other type of academic or research leave of absence

Resume Focus

The focus of Resume Format #2 is on your recent academic, training, and educational experiences. These are your greatest selling points to a prospective employer, so you must be sure to bring them to the forefront of your resume.

Primary Resume Components

- Brief Career Summary

- Education, training, and related experiences (the cornerstone of Resume Format #2)

- Professional employment experience

ROXANNE LOWE

249 Marlborough Street
Boston, MA 02116

rolowe@attbi.com

Home: 617-823-4949
Mobile: 617-300-4004

MARKETING

PRODUCT MANAGEMENT ▶ PRODUCT DEVELOPMENT ▶ PACKAGING

Track record of revenue growth, profit enhancement, and successful product-line management during 9 years in progressively challenging marketing-management roles. Strong foundation in market research and technology paired with creativity and the ability to innovate. Talent for leading and inspiring teams to top performance.

▶ **Set new business directions** by recognizing and seizing market opportunities.

▶ **Improved performance in all products and brands managed;** grew revenues, cut costs, developed unique retailer programs and packages, and improved brand image.

▶ **Effectively prioritized multiple projects** to align results with business objectives.

EDUCATION

2002 **MBA** — Concentration: Marketing Management   Babson College, Wellesley, MA

▶ **Key Projects:**
—**Case Study / Marketing Strategy for Delta Airlines,** identifying marketing opportunities in a post-9/11 travel environment. Pinpointed competitive issues, market advantages, and financial strengths. *(Project Leader)*
—**Balanced Scorecard Study:** Analysis of corporate culture and practical application of balanced-scorecard system to the 4 business perspectives. *(Capstone Class Project)*

▶ **Graduate Research Assistant / Teaching Assistant**
—Taught Marketing Research to undergraduate business students, bringing real-world perspective to theoretical class learning.

2000 **BS** — Computer Information Systems   Suffolk University, Boston, MA

1990 **BSBA** — Concentration: Management   Boston College, Chestnut Hill, MA

EXPERIENCE

CORE CORPORATION, INC., Woburn, MA   1995–1999
($180MM public company manufacturing and marketing consumer comfort products. Marquee brand is HappyFeet; key accounts include Wal-Mart, Federated, and other national retailers.)

SENIOR MARKETING MANAGER, 1997–1999

Drove marketing strategy and programs for 3 product lines totaling $150MM sales. Held P&L accountability and coordinated the efforts of design, product development, manufacturing, and other departments to deliver products for seasonal deadlines. Managed $2MM marketing budget. Also directed the development of sales brochures and marketing materials; developed and gave sales-force presentations on seasonal product lines; and managed national sales meetings for upper management and national sales organization.

Increased sales and profitability in all 3 brand segments:

▶ **Value Brands:**
—Boosted profit margins from **25%** to **39%** through continuous improvement efforts that removed cost from every point of production — sourcing, production, packaging, distribution.
—Grew Wal-Mart program from **$3MM** to **$7MM** by identifying and capitalizing on sales trends and market opportunities.

▶ **HappyFeet™:**
—Identified growth opportunity, then created and launched Premier Collection with high-end retailers. Increased brand-segment sales **60%** — **$5.8MM** to **$9.3MM.**

(continues)

An example of Resume Format #2 (resume written by Louise Kursmark).

▸ **HappyFeet™,** continued
  —Initiated licensing partnership and developed proposal that included entrée into nontraditional markets and projected **100%** increase in men's product line.
  —Spearheaded redesign of product displays to accommodate **20%** more product without increasing costs.

▸ **CoreComfort™:** Challenged to redesign product packaging to improve visual appeal and create distinct brand image. Worked with designers on new packaging and with manufacturing on technology-based line restage; spurred **31%** increase in product sales.

▸ **Additional Business Contributions:**
  —Developed new packaging that increased inventory flexibility and saved **$95K** in first year of implementation.
  —Managed the company's market-research function, critical to product-line development, and increased understanding of industry dynamics, competition, and target customers.
  —Stepped in as interim Visual Manager for 8 months and managed a complete packaging restage from concept through implementation. Worked with outside agencies on the development of new packaging line, displays, and advertising.

PRODUCT MANAGER, 1995–1996

Recruited to join newly strengthened marketing team tasked with improving performance of both private-label and branded products.

▸ Contributed to record sales performance, 1996: **$148MM, 9%** growth over prior year.
▸ Developed POP sales program that increased retail space by more than **200%.**
▸ Spearheaded a packaging restage that generated **$8.1MM** in incremental sales, reduced packaging costs **15%,** and improved packaging image and brand identification.

LOWELL FIBERS, Lowell, MA   1990–1995
$50MM apparel and materials manufacturer.

ASSISTANT PRODUCT MANAGER, 1992–1995

Promoted to manage more than $11MM in private-label and branded products for accounts such as JC Penney and Sears, with responsibility for pricing, promotions, advertising, forecasting, and product/packaging development. Performed yearly budgeting/planning activities for private-label and branded product lines.

▸ Spurred **40%** year-over-year sales increase for product lines under management.
▸ Instrumental in developing new markets for an existing single-market product line that has become the company's signature product and currently generates **55%** of total revenue.
▸ Aggressively pursued a key catalog retailer (Lands' End), spearheading product development, product-mix selection, and pricing and working collaboratively with Lands' End buyers to develop what became one of its best-selling catalog promotions ever — and was the first step in a key business relationship that culminated in Lowell being selected as the primary supplier for a major new Lands' End line (today an **$18MM** account).

MARKETING ASSISTANT, 1990–1992

Recruited out of college based on strengths in statistics, mathematics, and analysis.

▸ Created a forecasting system that, for the first time, included sales history, inventory turns, and planned account expansion. Increased forecasting efficiency and improved on-time/complete shipping from **89%** to over **95%.**

AFFILIATION

American Marketing Association
Board Member (professional chapter) — Event Chair (student chapter)

RESUME FORMAT #3: Experience-Emphasis Resume

This format is recommended for the following situations:

- After a layoff or extended period of unemployment (six months or longer)
- After owning a business
- After relocating
- After moving to the United States from a foreign country

Resume Focus

The focus of Resume Format #3 is on your work experience. Just as with resumes you have seen for people who are currently employed, the #1 selling point you offer to a prospective employer is your work experience, even though it might not be current. Don't be intimidated into thinking you have to "cover up" a great work history just because you're not currently working. If your situation is one of the above, this format is right for you.

Primary Resume Components

- Career Summary
- Detailed presentation of professional experience (the cornerstone of Resume Format #3)
- Education

Steven Meyers, CFA

21 Harrison Boulevard
Waltham, MA 02454

smeyers@xyz.com

(617) 498–5551 (home)
(978) 397–2630 (cell)

PROFILE

Hard-working and versatile Investment Analyst experienced in performing economic analyses and evaluating market expectations. Proven ability to develop accurate and efficient procedures and to meet tight deadlines. Team player, able to work well independently. B.A. in Economics, with strong knowledge of business and mathematics. Background includes:

- Competitive Analysis
- Marketing Presentations
- Risk Management
- Asset Allocation
- Portfolio Recommendations
- Forecasting

WORK EXPERIENCE

Investment / Financial Analyst – Internet Investments Corp., Boston, MA   2000–2002
(Paris-based company that has designed financial-planning software for the B2B market.)

- Constructed, calculated, and maintained capital-market expectations and portfolio recommendations for a family of global asset-allocation portfolios of varying levels of risk.
- Collaborated with Vice President to determine methodology for the design of a questionnaire to determine investors' risk tolerance / risk aversion.
- Managed competitive analysis process as part of strategic planning effort and company valuation process.
- Led the creation of marketing and business development strategies and presentations.

Institutional Marketing Manager – Freedom Funds, Boston, MA   1998–2000

- Managed product-comparison process of separate accounts and mutual funds for presentation to institutional clients.
- Conducted performance attribution, style, and portfolio-composition analyses for various product types and audiences.
- Designed, prepared, and compiled presentation material for full line of institutional-investment products.
- Coordinated and managed responses to consultant databases and maintained internal records.
- Managed the new-business proposal-production process.

EDUCATION AND TRAINING

B.A., Economics, The University of Rochester, Rochester, NY   1998

- Minor in Entrepreneurship and Management.
- Received Henry D. Porter Scholarship for Academic Performance junior and senior years.
- Accepted as a junior in high school, completed high school requirements during freshman year.

Association for Investment Management and Research

- Chartered Financial Analyst – 2001

COMPUTER EXPERIENCE / SKILLS

Eviews, Zephr StyleADVISOR, Ibbotson, Nelson's Institutional Marketplace, Eager Tracker, Morningstar Principia, Lotus 1-2-3, Excel, PowerPoint, Word, extensive Internet research and database development.

An example of Resume Format #3 (resume written by Wendy Gelberg).

WHY FORMAT IS SO IMPORTANT

To see how important choosing the right format is to the success of your resume and job search, carefully review the following two resumes. They are prime examples of why Resume Format #1 (described previously) is the ideal format for a returning-to-work parent.

Both resumes are for the same job seeker but use a different format. When you read the first resume, which follows the traditional chronological format, you're instantly drawn to the fact that Brenda has been a homemaker since January 1992. This fact is positioned obviously near the top of the page. Ten years is a long time to be unemployed, and this fact alone may leave a not-so-positive impression with the hiring manager or recruiter. Her skills might be considered outdated, and she's in a tough position.

Now, look at Brenda's second resume. What you see is an individual with an excellent range of professional qualifications, key words integrated throughout, and a strong presentation of her skills. The focus is on what she knows and not her chronological work history. In fact, it's not until you flip to the second page that you even see that she's been a homemaker for the past 10 years. Hopefully, by that point, the interviewer will already be impressed with her qualifications and the 10 years won't eliminate her from consideration.

Brenda Bonner
4310-1 McClellan Loop
Fort Riley, KS 66442
Home: 785-784-4114
Email: brenda_bonner@hotmail.com

Objective

Interested in a full-time Office Administration position where my past experience, education, and interpersonal skills can be valued.

Summary of Qualifications

Possess knowledge and skills in the administrative field as well as in customer service. Duties also extended to postal regulations and procedures to include maintaining security of personnel and sensitive equipment within a 24/7 shop. Currently hold an Associate's Degree in Computer Science / Networking Systems Administration. Experience with supervising and teaching techniques to personnel in a classroom environment as well as training in the field.

Experience

Homemaker   January 1992–Present
Colorado Springs, CO, and Fort Riley, KS

Coordinated spouse's career movements by being flexible and supportive. Maintained family finances in an efficient and successful manner. Managed children's education, school activities, and extracurricular activities by volunteering within the community. Supported the family's interests by preparing and distributing reports for multiple associations of which we were members.

Tools Team Member   January 1991–December 1991
The Print Specialists, Colorado Springs, CO

Provided first-level print support for the company's global print servers and systems. Used a variety of troubleshooting procedures to resolve customers' complaints involving print issues, location of files, and MPE/UNIX print-server management. Used various electronic tools such as Batchnet, Maestro, Spool, and Spyvision to investigate and quickly solve customer complaints to the satisfaction of team members as well as management officials. Developed and wrote processes and procedures for team members to use as a reference to identify and resolve problems and improve customer service.

Computer Lab Technician   December 1989–December 1990
Colorado State Technical College, Colorado Springs, CO

Assisted the Network System Administrator in the installation, maintenance, troubleshooting, and repair of personal computers and workstations on an NT network environment. Configured network cards, printers, and other hardware peripherals for use in a technical-training environment. Software installation included but was not limited to disk imaging and ghosting methods as well as loading various software programs onto several different operating systems. Assembled a new computer lab to include CAT5 cabling.

Brenda's resume in chronological format (resume written by Jim Walker).

Brenda Bonner Page 2

Experience, continued

Nuclear, Biological, Chemical (NBC) Specialist   October 1987–December 1989
U.S. Army, Mannheim, Germany

Supervised, trained, and advised the operators on the maintenance and use of NBC detection and decontamination equipment. Provided supervision and training on the proper use and maintenance of personal protective gear and equipment. Established and administered the training and application of NBC defense measures in an aviation organization. Maintained accountability and security of all NBC equipment assigned to approximately 150 personnel.

Nuclear, Biological, Chemical (NBC) Specialist   August 1986–October 1987
U.S. Army, Fort Polk, LA

Established the highest standards for personal equipment, training, and maintenance. Supervised and managed the individual and team training programs while adhering to and enforcing all safety requirements. Accounted for and managed the utilization of all equipment assigned to the company.

Lance Missile Crewmember   August 1982–March 1986
U.S. Army, Fulda, Germany

Maintained, operated, and trained on a variety of vehicles and equipment used to launch the Lance missiles. Team participated in and won a competition regarding the live firing of missiles into the Mediterranean Sea. Handled additional duties as an Administrative Specialist as well as Mail Clerk. Prepared personnel action requests and provided customer service in a professional and timely manner. Collected, distributed, and re-addressed misdirected mail. Maintained the physical security of the mailroom and all individual/unit mail, stamps, equipment, and the cash drawer.

Education

- Associate of Computer Science—Networking Systems Administration, Colorado Springs Community College, Colorado Springs, CO, 1998

- Graduate, Basic Leadership and Management Course, 4 weeks, U.S. Army, Fort Sill, OK, 1987

- Graduate, Intermediate Chemical Supervisory Management Course, 11 weeks, U.S. Army, Fort McClellan, AL, 1986

- Certificate, Lance Missile Training Course, 4 weeks, U.S. Army, Fort Sill, OK, 1982

BRENDA BONNER

4310-1 McClellan Loop, Fort Riley, KS 66442

785-784-4114   brenda_bonner@hotmail.com

OBJECTIVE

Interested in a full-time Office Administration position where my past experience, education, and interpersonal skills can be valued.

SUMMARY OF QUALIFICATIONS

Possess knowledge and skills in the administrative field as well as in customer service. Duties also extended to postal regulations and procedures to include maintaining security of personnel and sensitive equipment within a 24/7 shop. Currently hold an Associate's Degree in Computer Science/Networking Systems Administration. Experience with supervising and teaching techniques to personnel in a classroom environment as well as training in the field.

ADMINISTRATION

Prepared professional documents upon request as directed by guidelines set by the company. Operated various automated devices within an office and workstation environment. Maintained various security levels of personnel information, correspondence, and personal mail. Proficiently handled collection, distribution, and redirection of company mail as well as maintained the security of such items.

CUSTOMER SERVICE

Listened and responded to customers' complaints, requests, and questions with professionalism and respect while on the phone as well as in person. Provided routine customers with solutions that were within my level of expertise and handled priority requests and complaints appropriately and in a timely manner.

NETWORKING

Managed print servers for a large company using various operating environments such as MPE and UNIX. Used the utmost respect and care in handling time-sensitive print issues for clients. Assisted the Network Systems Administrator with the installation, operation, maintenance, and repair of more than 200 networking systems to include detection and resolution of network transmission problems. Handled upgrading procedures, as specified by management officials, by applying personal knowledge, training, and professionalism.

COMPUTER MAINTENANCE

Installed, maintained, and repaired computer-hardware components and peripherals for more than 175 communication devices and systems. Assembled a new computer lab to include hardware and peripherals, software packages, and physical setup of workstations. Experience with various hardware peripherals and components such as 486 and Pentium processors, network interface cards, modems, memory, floppy/hard/jazz drives, mouse, keyboards, motherboards, and power supplies.

Brenda's new resume, which emphasizes her skills and downplays her absence from the workforce (resume written by Jim Walker).

Brenda Bonner   Page 2

TRAINING Planned, coordinated, and taught various subjects and tasks for use in training subordinates on nuclear, biological, and chemical operations. Subject matter included detection, use, and decontamination of personnel and team chemical equipment. Applied teaching and management techniques in both the classroom and training environments.

EDUCATION
- Associate of Computer Science—Networking Systems Administration, Colorado Springs Community College, Colorado Springs, CO, 1998
- Graduate, Basic Leadership and Management Course, 4 weeks, U.S. Army, Fort Sill, OK, 1987
- Graduate, Intermediate Chemical Supervisory Management Course, 11 weeks, U.S. Army, Fort McClellan, AL, 1986
- Certificate, Lance Missile Training Course, 4 weeks, U.S. Army, Fort Sill, OK, 1982

EXPERIENCE
- Homemaker, Colorado Springs, CO, and Fort Riley, KS, 1992–Present
- Tools Team Member, The Print Specialists, Colorado Springs, CO, 1991
- Computer Lab Technician, Colorado State Technical College, Colorado Springs, CO, 1989–1990
- Nuclear, Biological, Chemical (NBC) Specialist, U.S. Army, Mannheim, Germany, 1987–1989
- Nuclear, Biological, Chemical (NBC) Specialist, U.S. Army, Fort Polk, LA, 1986–1987
- Lance Missile Crewmember, U.S. Army, Fulda, Germany, 1982–1986

Step-by-Step: Writing the Perfect Resume

This section is a detailed discussion of the various sections that you might include in your resume (for example, Career Summary, Professional Experience, Education, Technical Qualifications, Professional Memberships, and Volunteer Experience) and what each section should include.

CONTACT INFORMATION

Before we get into the major sections of the resume, let's briefly address the very top section: your name and contact information.

Name

You'd think writing your name would be the easiest part of writing your resume! But there are several factors you might want to consider:

- Although most people choose to use their full, formal name at the top of a resume, it has become increasingly more acceptable to use the name by which you prefer to be called.

- Bear in mind that it's to your advantage when readers feel comfortable calling you for an interview. Their comfort level may decrease if your name is gender-neutral, difficult to pronounce, or very unusual; they don't know who they're calling (a man or a woman) or how to ask for you. You can make it easier for them by following these examples:

  Lynn T. Cowles (Mr.)

  (Ms.) Michael Murray

  Tzirina (Irene) Kahn

  Ndege "Nick" Vernon

Address

You should always include your home address on your resume. If you use a post-office box for mail, include both your mailing address and your physical residence address if possible.

Telephone Number(s)

Your home telephone number must be included so that people can pick up the phone and call you immediately. In addition, you can also include a mobile phone number (refer to it as "mobile" rather than "cellular," to keep up with current terminology) or a pager number (however, this is less desirable because you must call back to speak to the person who called you). You can include a private home fax number, if it can be accessed automatically.

E-mail Address

Without question, if you have an e-mail address, include it on your resume. E-mail is now often the preferred method of communication in job search, particularly in the early stages of each contact. If you do not have an e-mail account, you can obtain a free, accessible-anywhere address from a provider such as www.yahoo.com, www.hotmail.com, or www.netzero.com.

As you look through the samples in this book, you'll see how resume writers have arranged the many bits of contact information at the top of a resume. You can use these as models for presenting your own information. The point is to make it as easy as possible for employers to contact you!

Page Two

We strongly recommend that you include your name, phone number, and e-mail address at the top of the second page of your resume and any additional pages. If, by chance, the pages get separated, you want to be sure that people can still contact you, even if they have only page two of your resume.

Now, let's get into the nitty-gritty of the core content sections of your resume.

CAREER SUMMARY

The Career Summary is the section at the top of your resume that summarizes and highlights your knowledge and expertise. You might be thinking, "But shouldn't my resume start with an Objective?" Although many job seekers still use Objective statements, we believe that a Career Summary is a much more powerful introduction. The problem with Objectives is that they are either too specific (limiting you to an "Electrical Engineering position") or too vague (doesn't everyone want "a challenging opportunity with a progressive organization offering the opportunity for growth and advancement"?). In addition, objective statements can be read as self-serving because they describe what *you* want rather than suggesting what you have to offer an employer.

In contrast, an effective Career Summary allows you to position yourself as you want to be perceived and immediately "paint a picture" of yourself in relation to your career goal. It is critical that this section focus on the specific skills, qualifications, and achievements of your career that are related to your current objectives. Your summary is *not* an historical overview of your career. Rather, it is a concise, well-written, and sharp presentation of information designed to *sell* you into your next position.

This section can have various titles, such as:

> Career Summary
>
> Career Achievements
>
> Career Highlights
>
> Career Synopsis
>
> Skills Summary
>
> Executive Profile
>
> Expertise
>
> Highlights of Experience
>
> Management Profile
>
> Professional Qualifications
>
> Professional Summary
>
> Profile

Summary

Summary of Achievements

Summary of Qualifications

Or, as you will see in the Headline Format example shown later, your summary does not have to have any title at all.

The Career Summary section of the resume is often vitally important for job seekers returning to work because it allows you to present all your key skills, qualifications, achievements, technology proficiencies, project highlights, and more. Your goal is to capture your reader's attention and immediately communicate the value you bring to their organization. As such, when they arrive at your listing of employment experience, they're already impressed with you. The fact that you are currently unemployed will be of lesser consequence.

Here are five sample Career Summaries. Consider using one of these as the template for developing your Career Summary, or use them as the foundation to create your own presentation. You will also find some type of Career Summary in just about every resume included in chapters 4 through 15.

Most importantly, if your goal is to follow Resume Format #1 as your preferred style, the Career Summary is the focal point of your resume. Be sure to package and sell all of your qualifications as they relate to your current career goals. Don't be concerned if your Career Summary is longer than normal. This section is the foundation for your entire resume, so be thorough and sell yourself into your next job.

Detailed Career Summary

──HIGHLIGHTS──

- Fifteen years of government experience at various administrative levels.
- Numerous college-level business courses.
- Outstanding follow-up skills; goal-driven; always seek to bring projects to completion on time and within budget.
- Self-starter who sees what has to be done, then does it.
- Recipient of many Outstanding Service Awards.

──RELEVANT SKILLS & EXPERIENCE──

Office Technology

- Keyboarding skills of 50 wpm.
- Mastery of MS Office Suite (Word, Excel, Access) and Windows 98 environment.
- Expertise in other software packages (SAS, WordPerfect, CODAP, SPSS, PROFS, Harvard Graphics, Lotus 1-2-3).

Administration

- Developed organization and command budgets.
- Scheduled and taught training classes.
- Served on personnel screening and selection panels.
- Organized nationwide management conferences.

Leadership

- Supervised 7 to 9 employees as Team Leader for the Configuration Management Task Force.
- Served as Lead Officer in development, implementation, and operation of CAPRMIS, an advanced information systems application supporting the Personnel Information System Command.
- Honored with the Division's Outstanding Leadership Award— Administrative Division.

Writing

- Wrote policy statements, procedures manuals, and programs of instruction.
- Wrote user manuals for 6 new system implementations.
- Wrote comprehensive analysis reports for the Army, Navy, Air Force, and Marine Corps.

Headline Format

INTERNATIONAL SALES & MARKETING PROFESSIONAL

Telecommunications Products, Solutions & Technologies

MBA, Executive Management, Harvard University

Cornell University Executive Sales Leadership

Paragraph Format

CAREER SUMMARY

ENGINEERING TEAM LEADER with extensive experience in lifecycle project management—from design, development, and testing through final product delivery, commercialization, and market launch. BSCE Degree. Recipient of numerous awards for engineering and project-management excellence.

Core Competencies Summary Format

QUALIFICATIONS SUMMARY

CUSTOMER SERVICE
Staff Training / Employee Supervision / Sales Support

▸ Customer Relationship Management	▸ Sales & Marketing
▸ Customer Satisfaction & Retention	▸ Purchasing & Auditing
▸ Quality & Cost Control	▸ Employee Relations & Leadership
▸ Employee Relations & Leadership	▸ Quality & Cost Control
▸ Problem Solving & Resolution	▸ Sales & Service Training
▸ Staffing & Scheduling	▸ Efficiency Improvement

Bullet List Format

PROFESSIONAL QUALIFICATIONS:

Sales Professional/Account Executive with a Chicago-based Fortune 500 company.

- ❑ Consistent record of over-quota sales with an average **22% sales increase** for the past six years.
- ❑ Effective relationship-builder who is personable and caring; aggressive in **pursuing and capturing new accounts.**
- ❑ Outgoing personality with strong commitment to developing and maintaining a **profitable customer base.**
- ❑ **Goal-oriented team player** who is ethical, is versatile, and has what it takes to do the job well.
- ❑ Outstanding **presentation, negotiation,** and **sales closing** skills.
- ❑ Excellent **communication, organizational,** and **project-management** abilities.

EDUCATION, CREDENTIALS, AND CERTIFICATIONS

Your Education section should include college, certifications, credentials, licenses, registrations, and continuing education. This section will be particularly important to you if Resume Format #2 is the most appropriate for your situation. In this instance, as mentioned previously in this chapter, your education is your primary selling point. Be sure to display it prominently, when appropriate, to ensure that prospective employers immediately see your educational qualifications.

Here are five sample Education sections that illustrate a variety of ways to organize and format this information.

Academic Credentials Format

EDUCATION AND CREDENTIALS

▶ **M.S., Counseling Psychology,** University of Akron, 1996
▶ **B.S., Psychology,** University of Miami, 1994

▶ **Highlights of Continuing Professional Education:**
— Organizational Management & Leadership, Ohio Leadership Association, 2001
— Industrial Relations, Purdue University, 2000
— Conflict Resolution & Violence Management in the Workplace, Institute for Workplace Safety, 1998

▶ **Licensed Clinical Psychologist,** State of Ohio, 1996 to Present
▶ **Licensed Recreational Therapist,** National Recreation Association, 1998 to Present

Executive Education Format

EDUCATION

Executive Leadership Program	STANFORD UNIVERSITY
Executive Development Program	NORTHWESTERN UNIVERSITY
Master of Business Administration (MBA) Degree	HARVARD UNIVERSITY GRADUATE SCHOOL
Bachelor of Science Degree	UNIVERSITY OF PENNSYLVANIA

Certifications Format

TECHNICAL CERTIFICATIONS & DEGREES

Registered Nurse, University of Maryland, 1988

Certified Nursing Assistant, University of Maryland, 1986

Certified Nursing Aide, State of Maryland, 1982

Bachelor of Science in Nursing (BSN), University of Maryland, 1988

Associate of Arts in General Studies, Byerstown Community College, Byerstown, Delaware, 1986

Specialized Training Format

TECHNICAL LICENSES & CERTIFICATIONS:

- Rhode Island Journeyman License #67382
- Vermont Journeyman License #LK3223839
- Licensed Electrician #8737262
- Construction Supervisor #99089
- Impact Training, Motor Control Seminar, 2001
- CAT-5 Certification, 2000
- Variable Speed Drive Certification, 1999
- Soars Grounding of Electrical Systems For Safety Certification, 1998
- Graduate, Jefferson Forest High School, Lynchburg, VA, 1995

Non-Degree Formats

TRAINING & EDUCATION

UNIVERSITY OF FLORIDA, Tampa, Florida

    BS Candidate—Business Administration (Senior class status)

UNIVERSITY OF OREGON, Portland, Oregon

    Dual Majors in Business Administration & Computer Science (2 years)

Professional Development   Completed 100+ hours of continuing professional education through the University of Miami, University of Georgia, and University of Phoenix. Topics included business administration, finance, strategic planning, organizational development, team building, and communications.

PROFESSIONAL EXPERIENCE

If the best style for you is Resume Format #3, then Professional Experience is the real meat of your resume. It's what gives your resume substance, meaning, and depth. It is also the section that will take you the longest to write. If you had the same position for 10 years (and that was 5 years ago), how can you consolidate all that you have done into one short section? If, on the opposite end of the spectrum, you had several short-term jobs before your current period of unemployment, how can you make your experience seem substantial and noteworthy? And, for all of you whose experience is in between, what do you include, how, where, and why?

These are not easy questions to answer. In fact, the most truthful response to each question is, "it depends." It depends on you, your experience, your achievements and successes, your current career objectives, and the reason for your recent period of unemployment.

Here are five samples of Professional Experience sections. Review how each individual's unique background is organized and emphasized, and consider your own background when using one of these as the template or foundation for developing your Professional Experience section.

Achievement Format

Emphasizes each position, the overall scope of responsibility, and the resulting achievements.

PROFESSIONAL EXPERIENCE

ALBANY COUNTY FIRE DEPARTMENT, Colonie, NY   1990 to 2001

▶ **DIRECTOR OF EMERGENCY MEDICAL SERVICES** (1998 to 2001)
▶ **SHIFT COMMANDER—CAPTAIN** (1994 to 1998)
▶ **ENGINE COMPANY OFFICER—LIEUTENANT** (1992 to 1994)
▶ **EMERGENCY MEDICAL TECHNICIAN—ENGINEER** (1990 to 1992)

Supervised Emergency Medical Services comprising 45 EMTs and paramedics at three fire stations. Participated in the direction of all aspects of personnel relations including hiring, disciplinary action, training, development, and evaluations. Served as Incident Commander at medical emergencies and structure fires. Coordinated all phases of EMS and served as Chairman of EMS Operations Committee. Wrote and implemented EMS protocols.

Achievements

- Planned, organized, and executed EMS training, testing, and recertification for 63 EMTs. Served as Emergency Medical Services Training Officer.

- Catalyst in the conceptualization of paramedic program for Albany County Fire Department, creating model for state licensure for other fire departments.

- Instrumental in developing a medical director contract that became the model for other EMS agencies.

- Established and launched Fire Cadet Program (paid internship) to allow 17- to 21-year-olds to participate in fire service through a comprehensive training and mentoring opportunity.

- Streamlined process to provide medical oxygen to EMS through small cylinders, eliminating rental fees and saving 50% on oxygen cost.

Challenge, Action, and Results (CAR) Format

Emphasizes the challenge of each position, the action you took, and the results you delivered.

PROFESSIONAL EXPERIENCE

Corporate Sales Manager, 1998 to 2000   DOLINVEST CORPORATION, Chicago, Illinois

Challenge——— To plan and execute a complete turnaround, revitalization, and return to profitability of the non-performing Chicago metro sales region for this $20 million specialty gift products manufacturer.

Action——— Revitalized relationships with over 300 accounts throughout the region, launched a massive image-building campaign, and recruited/trained three top-notch sales associates.

Results———
- Achieved/surpassed all turnaround objectives and returned the operation to profitability in first year. Delivered strong and sustainable gains:
  — 128% increase in sales revenues over 12 months.
  — 8.5% increase in bottom-line profitability.
  — $1.8 million in sales from new products.
  — 100% on-time customer delivery.
- Developed and taught the corporation's flagship Sales Training and Account Management program.
- Restored credibility with the largest customer in the region and closed a new contract for $2.6 million.
- Won the company's 2001 Leadership Achievement Award.
- Quoted in the National Sales Association's annual publication as one of 1999's "Turnaround Specialists."

Functional Format

Emphasizes the functional areas of responsibility within the job and associated achievements.

Employment Experience

Corporate Trainer	WILLIAMS-OWENS COMPANY, Duluth, MN	1995 to 1999

Member of 6-person corporate training and development organization supporting 2,000-person workforce at one of the world's largest gumball manufacturing facilities. Scope of training responsibility was extensive and included:

Curriculum/Instruction

✓ Supervised development of training plans, programs, goals and objectives; develop new course offerings in PC and SAP technology, process improvement techniques, and team-building.

✓ Created multimedia instructional tools and programs to supplement classroom education; created self-paced programs to encourage the development of supervisory staff for both production and production-support areas.

✓ Recruited, interviewed, hired, and directed work performance of training support staff and administrators.

Staff Training & Development

✓ Orchestrated professional development opportunities for training staff across all training, technology, business, and operational areas.

✓ Introduced PC-based instructional tools and programs to enhance the development of the company's professional training staff.

✓ Supervised and coordinated work of team leaders responsible for training of craftspersons, laborers, and other production-floor personnel.

Outreach & Communications

✓ Revitalized fledgling employee newspaper, recruited a talented team of volunteer writers and production personnel, and expanded distribution to include all employees.

✓ Wrote and published press releases, flyers, and other promotional materials to encourage employee participation in work-sponsored training programs.

✓ Led public-speaking engagements at area vocational schools and technical colleges to recruit qualified personnel.

Project Highlights Format

Describes the activities and results of specific roles, assignments, or projects.

Manager–Special Events, Fundraising & Public Relations   1996 to 2002
REISER EVENTS, INCORPORATED, Kalamazoo, Michigan

Planned and coordinated conferences, meetings, and special events for companies, professional associations, and arts/cultural and other organizations nationwide. Developed program content and administered budgets. Arranged all on-site logistics including transportation, accommodations, meals, guest speakers and entertainers, and audiovisual support. Project highlights included:

- ▸ **Toledo Arts Council.** Created cultural events that boosted membership enrollment by better than 60%.

- ▸ **National Speakers Association.** Organized 5 well-attended conferences, each with an average increase in annual attendance of more than 18%. Net revenues from events increased by 26%.

- ▸ **Oxford, Ohio, Community Revitalization Campaign.** Managed volunteer staff of 12 during the design and execution of 6 community-based safety training and awareness programs.

- ▸ **New Covenant Hospital Corporation.** Co-chaired capital fund campaign that raised $3.5 million for construction of new medical facility.

- ▸ **Purdue University.** Coordinated 3 auctions raising over $200,000 to fund library expansion at Purdue.

- ▸ **BSX Bank, N.A.** Authored marketing portfolio to launch $25,000 in community financing programs, attract investors, and encourage applicants.

Experience Summary Format

Briefly emphasizes specific highlights of each position. Best used in conjunction with a detailed Career Summary.

EXPERIENCE SUMMARY_____

Site Superintendent, ABX REMEDIATION SERVICES CORPORATION, Cincinnati, OH – 1999 to 2001

Investigated, analyzed, and identified objectives for remedial actions/cleanups throughout the Midwest.

Coordinated remediation of 50,000 tons of lead-contaminated soil from 150 residential sites two weeks ahead of schedule and $56,000 under budget.

Managed outside liaison affairs with contractors, consultants, and regulatory agency personnel.

Senior Electrician, ABX ELECTRICAL SERVICES, Cincinnati, OH – 1994 to 1999

Installed electrical, plumbing, and gas systems in decontamination, office, lab trailers, and project sites.

Trained and supervised newly hired electricians and apprentices.

Maintained electrical and plumbing systems, equipment, controls, and pumps.

Electrician, MYERS ELECTRIC, Coswell, KY – 1992 to 1994

Installed, maintained, and repaired residential electric systems and service.

THE "EXTRAS"

The primary focus of your resume is on information (most likely, your professional experience and academic credentials) that is directly related to your career goals. However, you should also include things that will distinguish you from other candidates and clearly demonstrate your value to a prospective employer. And, not too surprisingly, it is often the "extras" that get the interviews.

Following is a list of the other categories you might or might not include in your resume depending on your particular experience and your current career objectives. Review the information. If it's pertinent to you, use the samples for formatting your own data.

Remember, however, that if something is truly impressive, you might want to include it in your Career Summary at the beginning of your resume in order to draw even more attention to it. If this is the case, it's not necessary to repeat the information at the end of your resume.

Technology Skills and Qualifications

Many technology professionals have a separate section on their resumes for technology skills and qualifications. It is here that you will summarize all the hardware, software, operating systems, applications, networks, and more that you know and that are relevant to your current career objectives.

You'll also have to consider placement of this section in your resume. If the jobs for which you are applying require strong technical skills, we recommend that you insert this section immediately after your Career Summary (or as a part of it). If, on the other hand, your technical skills are more of a plus than a specific requirement, the preferred placement is further down in your resume.

Either way, these skills are vital in virtually any technology-related position. As such, this is extremely important information to a prospective employer, so be sure to display it prominently.

Here are two different ways to format and present your technical qualifications.

technology profile--

Operating Systems:	Windows 98/95/3.x; Novell 3.x/4.x; NT 4.0 Workstation; MS-DOS 6.22
Protocols/ Networks:	TCP/IP, NetBEUI, IPX/SPX, Ethernet 10/100Base-T
Hardware:	Hard drives, printers, scanners, fax/modems, CD-ROMs, Zip drives, Cat5 cables, hubs, NIC cards
Software:	Microsoft Office Modules, FileMaker Pro, PC Anywhere, MS Exchange, ARCserve, Project Manager

TECHNOLOGY SKILLS SUMMARY		
Windows 98/95/3.x	SAP	TCP/IP
Novell 3.x/4.x	MRP	Ethernet 10
NT 4.0 Workstation	DRP	IPX/SPX
Microsoft Office	MS Exchange	ARCserve
Project Manager	PC Anywhere	FileMaker Pro

If your goal is to simply mention the fact that you are proficient with specific PC software, a quick line at the end of your Career Summary or at the bottom of your resume should cover this information. For example:

PC Proficient with Word, Excel, Access, PageMaker, and WordPerfect.

Equipment Skills and Qualifications

Many people employed in the manufacturing, construction, engineering, and related industries will have a unique portfolio of equipment skills and knowledge. It is critical that you communicate this information in your resume, highlighting all the equipment with which you are proficient or familiar to demonstrate that you have the knowledge and skills for a particular position. Consider this format for an individual with extensive experience in pharmaceutical product packaging.

Trained in and worked on a diversity of packaging equipment and technology, including R.A. Jones, Hoppmann, Syntron, Lakso, Scandia, Westbrook, Wexxar, and Edson:

Leaflet Inserters	Cappers	Bottle Cleaners & Elevators
Fillers	Desiccants	Neckbanders
Heat Tunnels	Labelers	Cartoners
Case Packers & Sealers	Hoppers	Bundlers
Sorters	Carousels	Cottoners

Honors and Awards

If you have won honors and awards, you can either include them in a separate section near the end of your resume or integrate them into the Education or Professional Experience section if they are particularly noteworthy or related to your current career objectives. If you choose to include them in a separate section, consider this format.

- ☑ Winner, 2001 **"Sales Performance"** award from the Bechtel Mortgage Company, Inc.
- ☑ Winner, 1998 **"Customer Service"** award for outstanding contributions to customer service and retention from Kraft Foods, Inc.
- ☑ Named **"Employee of the Year,"** Kraft Foods, Inc., 1997
- ☑ **Cum Laude Graduate,** Southern Illinois University, 1989

Public Speaking

Experts are the ones who are invited to give public presentations at conferences, seminars, workshops, training programs, symposia, and other events. So if you have public-speaking experience, others must consider you an expert. Be sure to include this very complimentary information in your resume. Here's one way to present it.

- **Keynote Speaker,** "Architectural Engineering & Design," AAI National Conference, New York City, 2000
- **Panel Presenter,** "Maximizing Space Design & Utilization," AAI National Conference, Dallas, 1998
- **Session Leader,** "Ergonomic Design," Ohio Society of Architects, Cleveland, 1997

Publications

If you're published, you must be an expert (or at least most people will think so). Just as with your public-speaking engagements, be sure to include your publications. They validate your knowledge, qualifications, and credibility. Publications can include books, articles, online Web site content, manuals, and other written documents. Here's an example.

Co-Author, *Computer-Aided Design of Hybrid Microcircuits*, National Electronic Packaging Conference, 2001.

Author, *Subtle Aspects of Micro-Packaging*, Product Assurance Conference, 1998.

Author, *Micro-Packaging Practices, Policies, and Processes*, IBM Training Manual, 1996.

Teaching and Training Experience

Many professionals, regardless of their industry or profession, also teach or train at colleges, universities, technical schools, and other organizations, in addition to training that they may offer "on the job." If this is applicable to you, you will want to include that experience on your resume. If someone hires you (paid or unpaid) to speak to an audience, it communicates a strong message about your skills, qualifications, knowledge, and expertise. Here's a format you might use to present that information.

Adjunct Faculty, Department of Chemical Engineering, Texas A&M University, 1997 to 2001. Taught Introductory and Advanced Chemical Engineering.

Guest Lecturer, Department of Statistics, Reynolds Community College, 1996 to 1999. Provided semi-annual, day-long lecture series of the applications of statistics and statistical theory in the workplace.

Trainer, Macmillan School of Engineering, 1992 to 1996. Taught "Chemical Engineering 101" and "Chemical Lab Analysis" to first-year students.

Committees and Task Forces

Many professionals serve on committees, task forces, and other special project teams either as part of, or in addition to, their full-time responsibilities. Again, this type of information further strengthens your credibility, qualifications, and perceived value to a prospective employer. Consider a format such as the following.

> ▸ Member, 2000–01 Corporate Planning & Reorganization Task Force
>
> ▸ Member, 1999 Study Team on "Redesigning Corporate Training Systems to Maximize Employee Productivity"
>
> ▸ Chairperson, 1997–98 Committee on "Safety & Regulatory Compliance in the Workplace"

Professional Affiliations

If you are a member of any educational, professional, or leadership associations, be sure to include that information on your resume. It communicates a message of professionalism, a desire to stay current with the industry, and a strong professional network. What's more, if you have held leadership positions within these organizations, be sure to include them. Here's an example.

> **NATIONAL EDUCATION ASSOCIATION (NEA)**
> Professional Member (1992 to Present)
> Fundraising Committee Member (1994 to 1996)
> Curriculum Committee Member (1996 to 1998)
>
> **NATIONAL TEACHERS ASSOCIATION (NTA)**
> Professional Member (1993 to Present)
> Instructional Materials Design Committee Member (1998 to 2002)
> Technology Task Force Member (1996 to 1998)
>
> **LAFAYETTE TEACHERS ASSOCIATION (LTA)**
> President (2000 to 2002)
> Vice President (1998 to 2000)
> Member (1988 to Present)

Civic Affiliations

Civic affiliations are fine to include if they

- are with a notable organization;

- demonstrate leadership experience; or

- may be of interest to a prospective employer.

However, things such as treasurer of your local condo association and singer with your church choir are not generally of value in marketing your qualifications unless, of course, that experience is directly relevant to your current career objectives. Here's an example of what to include and how.

> ▴**Volunteer Chairperson,** United Way of America—Detroit Chapter, 1998 to Present
>
> ▴**President,** Greenwood Environmental District, 1997 to Present
>
> ▴**Treasurer,** Habitat for Humanity—Memphis Chapter, 1996 to 1997

Personal Information

We do not recommend that you include such personal information as birth date, marital status, number of children, and related data. However, in some cases, personal information might be appropriate. If this information will give you a competitive advantage or answer unspoken questions about your background, then by all means include it. Here's an example.

> ✓ Born in Belgium. U.S. Permanent Residency Status since 1997.
>
> ✓ Fluent in English, French, German, Flemish, and Dutch.
>
> ✓ Competitive Triathlete. Top-5 finish, 1987 Midwest Triathlon and 1992 Des Moines Triathlon.

Note in the preceding example that the job seeker is multilingual. This is a particularly critical selling point and, although it could be listed under Personal Information (as in this example), we think that it is more appropriately highlighted in your Career Summary.

Consolidating the Extras

Sometimes you have so many extra categories at the end of your resume, each with only a handful of lines, that spacing becomes a problem. You certainly don't want to have to make your resume a page longer to accommodate five lines, nor do you want the "extras" to overwhelm the primary sections of your resume. Yet you believe the information is important and should be included. Or perhaps you have a few small bits of information that you think are important but don't merit an entire section. In these situations, consider consolidating the information using one of the following formats. You'll save space, avoid over-emphasizing individual items, and present a professional, distinguished appearance. Here are two examples of how to consolidate and format your "extras."

PROFESSIONAL PROFILE

Technology Qualifications	IBM & HP Platforms Microsoft Office Suite, SAP R/3, ProjectPlanner, MRP, DRP, LAN, WAN, KPM, Lotus 1-2-3, Lotus Notes, Novell Networks
Affiliations	Association of Quality Control Institute of Electrical & Electronic Engineers American Electrical Association
Public Speaking	Speaker, IEEE Conference, Chicago, 2001 Presenter, AEA National Conference, Miami, 1998 Panelist, IEEE Conference, Detroit, 1996
Languages	Fluent in English, Spanish, and German

ADDITIONAL INFORMATION
- Co-Chair, Education Committee, Detroit Technology Association.
- PC literate with MRP, DRP, SAP, and Kaizen technologies.
- Available for relocation worldwide.
- Eagle Scout ... Boy Scout Troop Leader.

Writing Tips, Techniques, and Important Lessons

At this point, you've done a lot of reading, probably taken some notes, highlighted samples that appeal to you, and are ready to plunge into writing your resume. To make this task as easy as possible, we've compiled some "insider" techniques that we've used in our professional resume-writing practices. These techniques were learned the hard way through years of experience! We know they work; they will make the writing process easier, faster, and more enjoyable for you.

GET IT DOWN—THEN POLISH AND PERFECT IT

Don't be too concerned with making your resume "perfect" the first time around. It's far better to move fairly swiftly through the process, getting the basic information organized and on paper (or on screen), rather than agonizing about the perfect phrase or ideal formatting. When you've completed a draft, we think you'll be surprised at how close to "final" it is, and you'll be able to edit, tighten, and improve formatting fairly quickly.

WRITE YOUR RESUME FROM THE BOTTOM UP

Here's the system:

1. **Start with the easy things**—Education, Technology, Professional Affiliations, Public Speaking, Publications, and any other extras you want to include. These items require little thought and can be completed in just a few minutes.

2. **Write short job descriptions for your older positions, the ones you held years ago.** Be very brief and focus on highlights such as rapid promotion, achievements, innovations, professional honors, or employment with well-respected, well-known companies.

> **NOTE:** Even if you plan to create a functional resume that combines job achievements in one "front-and-center" location, we recommend that you first draft these descriptions in a chronological format. It will be easier to remember what you did if you take each of your jobs in turn. Later you can regroup your statements to emphasize related skills and abilities, and leave your employment history as a simple list or brief description.

Once you've completed this, look at how much you've written in a short period of time! Then move on to the next step.

3. **Write the job descriptions for your most recent positions.** This will take a bit longer than the other sections you have written. Remember to focus on the overall scope of your responsibility, major projects and initiatives, and significant achievements. Tell your reader what you did and how well you did it. You can use any of the formats recommended earlier in this chapter, or you can create something that is unique to you and your career.

   Now, see how far along you are? Your resume is 90 percent complete with only one small section left to do.

4. **Write your career summary.** Before you start writing, remember your objective for this section. The summary should not simply rehash your previous experience. Rather, it is designed to highlight the skills and qualifications you have that are most closely related to your current career objective(s). The summary is intended to capture the reader's attention and "sell" your expertise.

That's it. You're done. We guarantee that the process of writing your resume will be much, much easier if you follow the "bottom-up" strategy. Now, on to the next tip.

INCLUDE NOTABLE OR PROMINENT "EXTRA" STUFF IN YOUR CAREER SUMMARY

Remember the "extra-credit sections" that are normally at the bottom of your resume? If this information is particularly significant or prominent—you won a notable award, spoke at an international conference, developed a new teaching methodology, designed a new product that generated tens of millions of dollars in new revenues, or slashed 60% from operating costs—you might want to include it at the top in your Career Summary. Remember, the summary section is written to distinguish you from the crowd of other qualified candidates. As such, if you've accomplished anything that clearly demonstrates your knowledge, expertise, and credibility, consider moving it to your Career Summary for added attention. Refer to the sample career summaries earlier in the chapter for examples.

USE RESUME SAMPLES TO GET IDEAS FOR CONTENT, FORMAT, AND ORGANIZATION

This book is just one of many resources where you can review sample resumes to help you in formulating your strategy, writing the text, and formatting your resume. What's more, these books are published precisely for that reason. You don't have to struggle alone. Rather, use all the available resources at your disposal.

Be forewarned, however, that it's unlikely you will find a resume that fits your life and career to a "t." It's more likely that you will use "some of this sample" and "some of that sample" to create a resume that is uniquely "you."

INCLUDE DATES OR NOT?

Unless you are over age 50, we recommend that you date your work experience and your education. Without dates, your resume becomes vague and difficult for the typical hiring manager or recruiter to interpret. What's more, it often communicates the message that you are trying to hide something. By including the dates of your education and your experience, you create a clean and concise picture that one can easily follow to track your career progression.

Because you are a "returning to work" candidate, however, it makes sense to deemphasize dates rather than immediately show the reader that you haven't worked in a year or longer. Instead of setting them prominently at the right margin or using bold type to highlight them, consider placing your employment dates in small, non-bold type immediately after the name of your company or title of your position—or even at the end of the descriptive paragraph for each position. Or you might want to leave them off altogether.

An Individual Decision

If you are over age 50, dating your early positions must be an individual decision. On the one hand, you do not want to "date" yourself out of consideration by including dates from the 1960s and early 1970s. On the other hand, those positions might be worth including for any one of a number of reasons. Further, if you omit those early dates, you might feel as though you are misrepresenting yourself (or lying) to a prospective employer.

Here is a strategy to overcome those concerns while still including your early experience: Create a separate category titled "Previous Professional Experience" in which you summarize your earliest employment. You can tailor this statement to emphasize just what is most important about that experience.

If you want to capitalize on the good reputation of your past employers, include a statement such as this:

> • Previous experience includes supervisory positions with IBM, Dell, and Xerox.

If you want to focus on the rapid progression of your career, consider this example:

> • Promoted rapidly through a series of increasingly responsible sales and marketing management positions with Hilton Hotels.

If you want to focus on your early career achievements, include a statement such as this:

> • Member of 6-person task force credited with the design and rollout of Davidson's first-generation videoconferencing technology.

By including any one of the preceding paragraphs, under the heading "Previous Professional Experience," you are clearly communicating to your reader that your employment history dates further back than the dates you have indicated on your resume. In turn, you are being 100 percent aboveboard and not misrepresenting yourself or your career. What's more, you're focusing on the success, achievement, and prominence of your earliest assignments.

Include Dates in the Education Section?

If you are over age 50, we generally do not recommend that you date your education or college degrees. Simply include the degree and the university with no date. Why exclude yourself from consideration by immediately presenting the fact that you earned your college degree in 1958, 1962, or 1966—about the time the hiring manager was probably being born? Remember, the goal of your resume is to share the highlights of your career and open doors for interviews. It is *not* to give your entire life story. As such, it is not mandatory to date your college degree.

However, if you use this strategy, be aware that the reader is likely to assume there is *some* gap between when your education ended and your work experience started. Therefore, if you choose to begin your chronological work history with your first job out of college, omitting your graduation date could actually backfire, because the reader might assume that you have experience that predates your first job. In this case, it's best either to *include your graduation date* or *omit dates of earliest experience,* using the summary strategy discussed earlier.

ALWAYS SEND A COVER LETTER WHEN YOU FORWARD YOUR RESUME

Sending a cover letter every time you send a resume is expected and is appropriate job search etiquette. What's more, for all of you reading this book and for all return-to-work job seekers, your cover letter is *vital* to the success of your job search campaign.

Consider the following: When you write a resume, you are writing a document that you can use for each and every position you apply for, assuming that the requirements for all of those positions will be similar. You invest a great deal of time and effort in crafting just the "right" resume for you, but once it's done, it's done.

Your cover letter, however, is a document that is constantly changing to meet the needs of each individual situation for which you apply. In essence, it is the tool that allows you to customize your presentation to each company or recruiter, addressing their specific hiring requirements. Use your cover letter to highlight the most important qualifications, experiences, and achievements you bring to that specific company so that a prospective employer doesn't have to search through your resume to find what is most important. It is also the appropriate place to include any specific information that has been requested, such as salary history or salary requirements (see the following section for more on including salaries).

What's more, your cover letter will allow you to briefly explain why you're not currently working. Although you do not want to go into substantial detail in your letter (you can tell them more at the interview), you do want to mention the reason for your unemployment. Some examples might include the following.

> After two years of caring for my elderly parents, who have subsequently passed away, I am now ready to return to the workforce and resume my career in the financial planning industry.

> After a one-year sabbatical researching coastal erosion in Crete, I have now returned to the U.S., completed my M.S. degree, and am ready to launch my professional career.

> For the past 10 years, I've been a stay-at-home parent, volunteer, community activist, and part-time sales associate, all great experiences that have equipped me with a vast array of skills. Now I am anxious to re-enter the workforce and am looking at administrative and executive support positions.

> My 14-year career with ExPeTe International was an extraordinary experience, highlighted by rapid promotions and numerous corporate commendations. However, the company fell on hard times in the late 1990s and my position was eliminated in April 2002. As such, I am currently pursuing new challenges and professional opportunities in the same industry where I can apply my years of experience, training, and success.

Our policy is that it's always best to be honest and upfront right from the beginning so that you can never be accused of hiding information. However, temper your enthusiasm for honesty with a practical approach to sharing only what is necessary to appropriately and quickly explain periods of unemployment.

NEVER INCLUDE SALARY HISTORY OR SALARY REQUIREMENTS ON YOUR RESUME

Your resume is *not* the correct forum for a salary discussion. First of all, you should never provide salary information unless a company has requested that information and you choose to comply. (Studies show that employers will look at your resume anyway, so you might choose not to respond to this request, thereby avoiding pricing yourself out of the job or locking yourself into a lower salary than the job is worth.)

When contacting recruiters, however, we recommend that you do provide salary information, but again, only in your cover letter. With recruiters you want to "put all of your cards on the table" and help them make an appropriate placement by providing information about your current salary and salary objectives. For example, "Be advised that my most recent compensation was $55,000 annually and that I am interested in a position starting at a minimum of $65,000 per year." Or, if you would prefer to be a little less specific, you might write, "My annual compensation over the past three years has averaged $50,000+."

ALWAYS REMEMBER THAT YOU ARE SELLING

As we have discussed over and over throughout this book, resume writing is sales. Understand and appreciate the value you bring to a prospective employer, and then communicate that value by focusing on your achievements. Companies don't want to hire just anyone; they want to hire "the" someone who will make a difference. Show them that you are that candidate.

CHAPTER 3

Printed, Scannable, Electronic, and Web Resumes

After you've worked so tirelessly to write a winning resume, your next challenge is the resume's design, layout, and presentation. It's not enough for it to read well; your resume must also have just the right look for the right audience. And, just as with everything else in a job search, no specific answers exist. You must make a few decisions about what your final resume presentation will look like.

The Four Types of Resumes

In today's employment market, job seekers use four types of resume presentations:

- Printed
- Scannable
- Electronic (e-mail attachments and ASCII text files)
- Web

The following sections give details on when you would need each type, as well as how to prepare these types of resumes.

THE PRINTED RESUME

We know the printed resume as the "traditional resume," the one that you mail to a recruiter, take to an interview, and forward by mail or fax in response to an advertisement. When preparing a printed resume, you want to create a sharp, professional, and visually attractive presentation. Remember, that piece of paper conveys the very first impression of you to a potential employer, and that first impression goes a long, long way. Never be fooled into thinking that just because you have the best qualifications in your industry, the visual presentation of your resume does not matter. It does, a great deal.

THE SCANNABLE RESUME

The scannable resume can be referred to as the "plain-Jane" or "plain-vanilla" resume. All of the things that you would normally do to make your printed resume look attractive—bold print, italics, multiple columns, sharp-looking type-style, and more—are stripped away in a scannable resume. You want to present a document that can be easily read and interpreted by scanning technology.

Although the technology continues to improve, and many scanning systems in fact can read a wide variety of type enhancements, it's sensible to appeal to the "lowest common denominator" when creating your scannable resume. Follow these formatting guidelines:

- Choose a commonly used, easily read font such as Arial or Times New Roman.

- Don't use bold, italic, or underlined type.

- Use a minimum of 11-point type size.

- Position your name, and nothing else, on the top line of the resume.

- Keep text left-justified, with a "ragged" right margin.

- It's okay to use common abbreviations (for instance, scanning software will recognize "B.S." as a Bachelor of Science degree). But, when in doubt, spell it out.

- Eliminate graphics, borders, and horizontal lines.

- Use plain, round bullets or asterisks.

- Avoid columns and tables, although a simple two-column listing can be read without difficulty.

- Spell out symbols such as % and &.

- If you divide words with slashes, add a space before and after the slash to be certain the scanner doesn't misread the letters.

- Print using a laser printer on smooth white paper.

- If your resume is longer than one page, be sure to print on only one side of the paper; put your name, telephone number, and e-mail address on the top of page two; and don't staple the pages together.

- For best possible results, mail your resume (don't fax it), and send it flat in a 9 × 12 envelope so that you won't have to fold it.

Of course, you can avoid scannability issues completely by sending your resume electronically, so that it will not have to pass through a scanner to enter the company's databank. Read the next section for electronic resume guidelines.

THE ELECTRONIC RESUME

Your electronic resume can take two forms: e-mail attachments and ASCII text files.

E-mail Attachments

When including your resume with an e-mail, simply attach the word-processing file of your printed resume. Because a vast majority of businesses use Microsoft Word, it is the most acceptable format and will present the fewest difficulties when attached.

However, given the tremendous variety in versions of software and operating systems, not to mention printer drivers, it's quite possible that your beautifully formatted resume will look quite different when viewed and printed at the other end. To minimize these glitches, use generous margins (at least 0.75 inch all around). Don't use unusual typefaces, and minimize fancy formatting effects.

Test your resume by e-mailing it to several friends or colleagues, and then having them view and print it on their systems. If you use WordPerfect, Microsoft Works, or another word-processing program, consider saving your resume in a more universally accepted format such as RTF or PDF. Again, try it out on friends before sending it to a potential employer.

ASCII Text Files

You'll find many uses for an ASCII text version of your resume:

- To avoid formatting problems, you can paste the text into the body of an e-mail message rather than send an attachment. Many employers actually prefer this method. Pasting text into an e-mail message lets you send your resume without the possibility of also sending a virus.

- You can readily copy and paste the text version into online job application and resume bank forms, with no worries that formatting glitches will cause confusion.

- Although it's unattractive, the text version is 100 percent scannable.

To create a text version of your resume, follow these simple steps:

1. Create a new version of your resume using the Save As feature of your word-processing program. Select "text only" or "ASCII" in the Save As option box.

2. Close the new file.

3. Reopen the file, and you'll find that your word processor has automatically reformatted your resume into Courier font, removed all formatting, and left-justified the text.

4. To promote maximum readability when sending your resume electronically, reset the margins to 2 inches left and right, so that you have a narrow column of text rather than a full-page width. (This margin setting will not be retained when you close the file, but in the meantime you can adjust the text formatting for best screen appearance. For instance, if you choose to include a horizontal line [perhaps something like this: +++++++++++++++++++++++++] to separate sections of the resume, by working with the narrow margins you won't make the mistake of creating a line that extends past the normal screen width. Plus, you won't add hard line breaks that create odd-length lines when seen at normal screen width.)

5. Review the resume and fix any "glitches" such as odd characters that may have been inserted to take the place of "curly" quotes, dashes, accents, or other nonstandard symbols.

6. If necessary, add extra blank lines to improve readability.

7. Consider adding horizontal dividers to break the resume into sections for improved skimmability. You can use any standard typewriter symbols such as *, -, (,), =, +, ^, or #.

To illustrate what you can expect when creating these versions of your resume, on the following pages are some examples of the same resume in traditional printed format, scannable version, and electronic (text) format.

THE WEB RESUME

This newest evolution in resumes combines the visually pleasing quality of the printed resume with the technological ease of the electronic resume. You host your Web resume on your own Web site (with your own URL), to which you refer prospective employers and recruiters. Now, instead of seeing just a "plain-Jane" version of your e-mailed resume, with just one click a viewer can access, download, and print your Web resume—an attractive, nicely formatted presentation of your qualifications.

What's more, because the Web resume is such an efficient and easy-to-manage tool, you can choose to include more information than you would in a printed, scannable, or electronic resume. Consider separate pages for achievements, technology qualifications, equipment skills, honors and awards, management skills, and more, if you believe they would improve your market position. Remember, you're working to sell yourself into your next job!

For those of you in technologically related professions, you can take it one step further and create a virtual multimedia presentation that not only tells someone how talented you are, but also visually and technologically demonstrates it. Web resumes are an outstanding tool for people seeking jobs in technology-based industries.

To see a sample of a Web resume, visit this site: www.newleafcareer.com/samples/index.html. You can see the print version of this resume on pages 210–211.

A simplified version of the Web resume is an online version of your Microsoft Word resume. Instead of attaching a file to an e-mail to an employer, you can include a link to the online version. This format is not as graphically dynamic as a full-fledged Web resume, but it can be a very useful tool for your job search. For instance, you can offer the simplicity of text in your e-mail, plus the instant availability of a printable, formatted word-processing document for the interested recruiter or hiring manager. For a demonstration of this format, go to www.e-resume-central.com and click on "SEE A SAMPLE."

SAMUEL FEINMAN

489 Smithfield Road
Salem, OR 97301
503.491.3033
samfine@earthlink.net

SALES PROFESSIONAL

Dynamic, motivated, award-winning sales professional with extensive experience. Troubleshooter and problem-solver. Team player who can motivate self and others. Excellent management and training skills.

RELATED EXPERIENCE

WetWater Pool Products, Salem, OR
Sales/Customer Service   1995–2000
- Advised customers to purchase products that best met their needs, while focusing attention on products more profitable to company.
- Troubleshot and solved customer problems, identifying rapid solutions and emphasizing customer satisfaction and retention.
- Oversaw shipping and receiving staff.

Afford-A-Ford, Albany, NY
General Manager   1990–1995
- Consistently in top five for sales in district; met or exceeded sales objectives.
- Supervised, hired, and trained staff of 90.
- Converted a consistently money-losing store into a profitable operation by end of first year.
- Focused on customer satisfaction through employee satisfaction and training.
- Built strong parts and service business, managing excellent interaction among parts, service, and sales.
- Instituted fleet-sales department, becoming top fleet-sales dealer three years running.
- Built lease portfolio from virtually none to 31% of retail.

Jack's Chevrolet, Springfield, MA
General Manager   1988–1990
- Reached top-ten volume dealer three years straight in New England.
- Managed all dealership operations including sales, parts, service, and administration.
- Profitably operated dealership through difficult economic times.
- Raised customer satisfaction to zone average.
- Met or exceeded parts, sales, and service objectives.
- Maintained high-profile used car operation.

ADDITIONAL EXPERIENCE

State of Oregon, Salem, OR
Computer Technician   2000–2002
- Built customized computers for state offices.

EDUCATION

AS, Hudson Valley Community College, Troy, NY   Major: Business Studies

The print version of the resume.

SAMUEL FEINMAN
489 Smithfield Road
Salem, OR 97301
503.491.3033
samfine@earthlink.net

SALES PROFESSIONAL

Dynamic, motivated, award-winning sales professional with extensive experience. Troubleshooter and problem-solver. Team player who can motivate self and others. Excellent management and training skills.

RELATED EXPERIENCE

WetWater Pool Products, Salem, OR
SALES/CUSTOMER SERVICE, 1995–2000
- Advised customers to purchase products that best met their needs, while focusing attention on products more profitable to company.
- Troubleshot and solved customer problems, identifying rapid solutions and emphasizing customer satisfaction and retention.
- Oversaw shipping and receiving staff.

Afford-A-Ford, Albany, NY
GENERAL MANAGER, 1990–1995
- Consistently in top five for sales in district; met or exceeded sales objectives.
- Supervised, hired, and trained staff of 90.
- Converted a consistently money-losing store into a profitable operation by end of first year.
- Focused on customer satisfaction through employee satisfaction and training.
- Built strong parts and service business, managing excellent interaction among parts, service, and sales.
- Instituted fleet-sales department and became top fleet-sales dealer three years running.
- Built lease portfolio from virtually none to 31% of retail.

Jack's Chevrolet, Springfield, MA
GENERAL MANAGER, 1988–1990
- Reached top-ten volume dealer three years straight in New England.
- Managed all dealership operations including sales, parts, service, and administration.
- Profitably operated dealership through difficult economic times.
- Raised customer satisfaction to zone average.
- Met or exceeded parts, sales, and service objectives.
- Maintained high-profile used car operation.

ADDITIONAL EXPERIENCE

State of Oregon, Salem, OR
COMPUTER TECHNICIAN, 2000–2002
- Built customized computers for state offices.

EDUCATION

AS, Hudson Valley Community College, Troy, NY
Major: Business Studies

The scannable version of the resume.

```
SAMUEL FEINMAN
489 Smithfield Road
Salem, OR 97301
503.491.3033
samfine@earthlink.net


==============================================
SALES PROFESSIONAL

Dynamic, motivated, award-winning sales professional with
extensive experience. Troubleshooter and problem-solver. Team
player who can motivate self and others. Excellent management and
training skills.


==============================================
RELATED EXPERIENCE

WetWater Pool Products, Salem, OR
SALES/CUSTOMER SERVICE, 1995-2000
* Advised customers to purchase products that best met their
needs, while focusing attention on products more profitable to
company.
* Troubleshot and solved customer problems, identifying rapid
solutions and emphasizing customer satisfaction and retention.
* Oversaw shipping and receiving staff.


Afford-A-Ford, Albany, NY
GENERAL MANAGER, 1990-1995
* Consistently in top five for sales in district; met or exceeded
sales objectives.
* Supervised, hired, and trained staff of 90.
* Converted a consistently money-losing store into a profitable
operation by end of first year.
* Focused on customer satisfaction through employee satisfaction
and training.
* Built strong parts and service business, managing excellent
interaction among parts, service, and sales.
* Instituted fleet-sales department and became top fleet-sales
dealer three years running.
* Built lease portfolio from virtually none to 31% of retail.

Jack's Chevrolet, Springfield, MA
GENERAL MANAGER, 1988-1990
* Reached top-ten volume dealer three years straight in New
England.
* Managed all dealership operations including sales, parts,
service, and administration.
* Profitably operated dealership through difficult economic
times.
* Raised customer satisfaction to zone average.
* Met or exceeded parts, sales, and service objectives.
* Maintained high-profile used car operation.


==============================================
ADDITIONAL EXPERIENCE

State of Oregon, Salem, OR
COMPUTER TECHNICIAN, 2000-2002
* Built customized computers for state offices.


==============================================
EDUCATION

AS, Hudson Valley Community College, Troy, NY
Major: Business Studies
```

The electronic/text version of the resume.

The Four Resume Types Compared

This chart quickly compares the similarities and differences between the four types of resumes we've discussed in this chapter.

	PRINTED RESUMES	**SCANNABLE RESUMES**
TYPESTYLE/ FONT	Sharp, conservative, and distinctive (see our recommendations in chapter 1).	Clean, concise, and machine-readable: Times New Roman, Arial, Helvetica.
TYPESTYLE ENHANCEMENTS	**Bold,** *italics,* and underlining for emphasis.	CAPITALIZATION is the only type enhancement you can be certain will transmit.
TYPE SIZE	10-, 11-, or 12-point preferred... larger type sizes (14, 18, 20, 22, and even larger, depending on typestyle) will effectively enhance your name and section headers.	11- or 12-point, or larger.
TEXT FORMAT	Use centering and indentations to optimize the visual presentation.	Type all information flush left.
PREFERRED LENGTH	1 to 2 pages; 3 if essential.	1 to 2 pages preferred, although length is not as much of a concern as with printed resumes.
PREFERRED PAPER COLOR	White, Ivory, Light Gray, Light Blue, or other conservative background.	White or very light with no prints, flecks, or other shading that might affect scannability.
WHITE SPACE	Use appropriately for best readability.	Use generously to maximize scannability.

ELECTRONIC RESUMES	**WEB RESUMES**
Courier.	Sharp, conservative, and distinctive... attractive onscreen and when printed from an online document.
CAPITALIZATION is the only enhancement available to you.	**Bold,** *italics,* and underlining, and color for emphasis.
12-point.	10-, 11-, or 12-point preferred... larger type sizes (14, 18, 20, 22, and even larger, depending on typestyle) will effectively enhance your name and section headers.
Type all information flush left.	Use centering and indentations to optimize the visual presentation.
Length is immaterial; almost definitely, converting your resume to text will make it longer.	Length is immaterial; just be sure your site is well organized so viewers can quickly find the material of greatest interest to them.
N/A.	Paper is not used, but do select your background carefully to maximize readability.
Use white space to break up dense text sections.	Use appropriately for best readability both onscreen and when printed.

Are You Ready to Write Your Resume?

To be sure that you're ready to write your resume, go through the following checklist. Each item is a critical step that you must take in the process of writing and designing your own winning resume.

- ❑ Clearly define "who you are" and how you want to be perceived.

- ❑ Document your key skills, qualifications, and knowledge.

- ❑ Document your notable career achievements and successes.

- ❑ Identify one or more specific job targets or positions.

- ❑ Identify one or more industries that you are targeting.

- ❑ Research and compile key words for your profession, industry, and specific job targets.

- ❑ Determine which resume format suits you and your career best.

- ❑ Select an attractive font.

- ❑ Determine whether you need a print resume, a scannable resume, an electronic resume, a Web resume, or all four.

- ❑ Secure a private e-mail address.

- ❑ Review resume samples for up-to-date ideas on resume styles, formats, organization, and language.

PART II

Sample Resumes for People Returning to Work

CHAPTER 4: Resumes for People Returning to Work After Raising Children

CHAPTER 5: Resumes for People Returning to Work After Divorce, Death of Spouse, or Financial Reversal

CHAPTER 6: Resumes for People Returning to Work with Extensive Volunteer Experience

CHAPTER 7: Resumes for People Returning to Work After Serving as a Caregiver

CHAPTER 8: Resumes for People Returning to Work After Illness

CHAPTER 9: Resumes for People Returning to Work After Incarceration

CHAPTER 10: Resumes for People Returning to Work After a Sabbatical

CHAPTER 11: Resumes for People Returning to Work After Relocating

CHAPTER 12: Resumes for People Returning to Work After Retirement

CHAPTER 13: Resumes for People Laid Off, Downsized, or Otherwise Out of Work for More Than Six Months

CHAPTER 14: Resumes for People Returning to Work After Additional Education

CHAPTER 15: Resumes for People Returning to Work After an Entrepreneurial Venture

CHAPTER 4

Resumes for People Returning to Work After Raising Children

Out of the workforce for two, five, ten, or more years raising children, most of these back-to-work candidates used a functional format so that their lengthy absence is not the highlight of the resume. In some cases, recent part-time or volunteer work provides credentials and achievements related to the current job target; in other cases, prior professional experience provides the strongest qualifications.

Judith A. Blackman
464 Vickers Lane ◆ Morristown, NJ 07960
973-455-1689 rick@targetinterviews.com

RHIT / Medical Records / Medical Office Management

Skills:
- RHIT Certified
- Customer Service
- Insurance Company Relations
- Billing / Claims Handling
- Organizational Skills
- New Program Set-up

Qualifications: Seven years' experience in **medical office management:**
- Managed insurance claims coding, claims filing, payment-data entry, and follow-up communications with insurance companies in a 7-person medical office.
- Created record-keeping system for new mammography service.
- Maintained quality assurance for mammography records.
- Established new Medicare and insurance payment database for a new women's health clinic.
- Processed medical-record requests while ensuring confidentiality of patients.
- Delivered quality customer services for scheduling, medical records filing, and patient check-in and check-out.

Employment History:

Columbus Women's Health Partners	Columbus, OH	
Medical Data Entry	1997	

Female Contemporary Health Care — Columbus, OH
Medical Secretary — 1995–1997
Hired by medical director based on work performed during internship from Columbus State College. **Collected $50,000 of previously unpaid insurance claims.**

Milford, Parker & Haines, PC — Royal Oak, MI
Medical Office Front Desk Personnel — 1978–1981

Burton Hills Retirement Center — East Lansing, MI
Nursing Secretary — 1977–1978

Certification: Registered Health Information Technician (RHIT) Through 12/31/03

Strategy: *Minimize focus on dates of work history through a functional format that presents skills and qualifications up front. Certification, education, and previous work experience emphasize this candidate's knowledge of medical records and office management.*

Judith A. Blackman   **Page 2 of 2**

Education:	Columbus State College Columbus, OH

Associate's Degree — Health Information Management   1995
- Participated in 4-month internship with Female Contemporary Health Care.
- With High Honor — 3.95

Michigan State University   East Lansing, MI
Bachelor of Science — Medical Technology   1977
- With High Honor — 3.65

Community Involvement: St Michael's Catholic Church — Market Day   Westerville, OH
Coordinator 1993–1997
Coordinated monthly fund-raiser that netted the church $35,000 annually:
- Promoted the fund-raiser in the church and the community.
- Ordered all customer requests through the designated vendor.
- Coordinated volunteers for monthly distribution of sales.

St Michael's Catholic Church — PAC   Westerville, OH
Treasurer 1994–1995
Administered the Parents' Association Committee treasury with annual budget of $100,000.

References: Available upon request

SAMANTHA HARDY

1434 Haven Terrace • Cincinnati, OH • 45249
Telephone: (513) 852-7528

Profile

Human Resources / Team Leadership:

- Expertise, qualifications, and experience encompassing all facets of HR-generalist functions.
- Plan, develop, and execute strategic HR recruitment, selection, induction, and training methodologies.
- Full accountabilities for staff payroll, work-care claims, and OH&S compliance.
- Team leader, trainer, and mentor; optimize staff performance and productivity.
- Communicate vision and facilitate team collaboration to surpass company objectives.

Interpersonal / Communication:

- Outstanding interpersonal and communication skills; interfacing with staff, clients, and vendors from diverse backgrounds.
- Exceptional negotiator, evaluating, implementing, and resolving union and staff disputes.

Office Management / Administration / Bookkeeping:

- Proven expertise in all facets of office management and bookkeeping, including financial and executive reporting utilizing MYOB and QuickBooks software.
- Excellent organizational, administrative, and time- and resource-management skills. Ability to set and achieve priorities and manage multiple projects in tandem without compromise in quality. Perform well in busy work environments.

Education & Training

Diploma of Business (Human Resource Practice)	2002
Cert IV in Human Resource Practice/Operations	2001
Cert III, IV, and Diploma of Management	2001
Cert IV in Assessment & Workplace Training	1999

Professional Experience

GUARDEM ENGINEERING, INC., Hamilton, OH   8 years
Office Manager
Diverse hands-on management role, performing HR, bookkeeping, secretarial, administrative, and clerical functions. Recruited and trained administration staff with ongoing direction, motivation, and supervision.

- **Payroll and personnel management:** Calculated hourly rates/overtime, pay reviews, work-cover claims, superannuation, and personnel file management.
- **Extensive liaison with clients:** Assisted with sales, queries, and problem resolution, utilizing diplomacy and assertiveness to achieve mutually beneficial outcomes.
- **Accounting and administration:** Set up and trained on QuickBooks accounting software. Completed financial reporting; interfaced with accountant as required. Authored correspondence, quotations, sales/promotional material, and management reports.

Continued...

Strategy: *Display broad skills and diverse experience through a lengthy Profile section, followed by recently earned educational credentials that relate to her job target. Eliminate dates of employment and simply show job tenure.*

SAMANTHA HARDY

Page 2

- **Evaluated, developed, and implemented office procedures.** Problem-solved computerized financial records requiring investigation and rectification of incorrectly recorded information. Organized managers' international travel and accommodation. Planned and prepared international Trade Show events, including promotional material, display products, and subsequent sales staff traveling arrangements and accommodation.
    - Spearheaded set-up of computerized financial information onto QuickBooks.
    - Effectively coordinated the entire office, maintaining operational efficiency.
    - Streamlined quotation department through development, preparation, and implementation of job-costing procedures.
    - Successfully mediated internal and external conflicts between staff, clients, and unions, demonstrating exceptional negotiation and communication skills.
    - Facilitated an encouraging work environment, which improved internal staff communication and cooperation.
    - Researched, planned, and authored job descriptions for each role within the organization.

BUSYBOOKS SERVICES, Cincinnati, OH   3 years

Bookkeeper / Office Manager

On- and off-site bookkeeping, payroll, secretarial, and administrative support. Utilized QuickBooks accounting software.

- Combined sound computer literacy with implementation of strategic operational initiatives to enhance quality, client service, technology, and overall bottom-line performance.

Volunteer Experience

Treasurer / President   2 years

Casey Kindergarten

Chaired monthly meetings; led, interfaced with, and provided direction for other committee members. Collected and banked fees; chased overdue accounts; organized and paid various vendor invoices. Reconciled and prepared monthly budget versus actual expenditure reports and presented at monthly meetings. Represented Kindergarten at various promotional events. Calculated and paid teacher and assistant wages and benefits.

- Collaborated with committee members in the recruitment and selection of a Kindergarten Teacher Assistant.

Technology

- MS Word • MS Excel • MS PowerPoint • MYOB • QuickBooks

Professional references available upon request

Sheryl A. Porter

18 Carriage Way
Boston, MA 02053

Phone: 508/555-1212
sherylAporter@msn.com

DATA ENTRY • RECEPTION • CUSTOMER SERVICE • OFFICE SUPPORT

Conscientious professional exploring opportunities in a business environment where expertise in customer service and office administration will contribute to company goals and objectives.

SKILLS

Data Entry	Reception	Microsoft Office
Office support	Multi-line console	Windows 95/98
Customer Service	Scheduling	Lotus 123

EXPERIENCE

- Prioritized and responded to high volume of inbound calls for professional businesses.
- Identified urgency of calls and proceeded efficiently and effectively in a time-sensitive environment.
- Furnished detailed messages, scheduled appointments, and communicated effectively with professional colleagues and clients.
- Recognized for providing excellent customer service, resulting in advancement to Lead Sales Associate with specialty retailer.
- Researched and entered competitive marketing analysis data for retail advertisers.

WORK HISTORY

Midtown Discount, Boston, MA   1993–1994
State-wide discount retailer

Pet Super Discount, Boston, MA   1991–1993
Retailer specializing in supplies and services for domestic animals

Ace Marketing, Clinton, MA   1989–1991
Providers of competitive analysis for retail advertisers

EDUCATION

Newbury College, Boston, MA   Associate's degree, 1988

References available

Strategy: *Use a functional format to emphasize relevant skills that support her goal of a mid-level office-support position in a smaller environment with reasonable flexibility regarding hours.*

RESUME 4: LINDA WUNNER, CPRW, CEIP, JCTC; DULUTH, MN

Cindy Castiglione, C.T.M.

5555 Taft Street ✦ Cincinnati, OH 45212 ✦ (513) 891-5554 ✦ ccastiglione@yahoo.com

Tour Manager ✦ Special Events Coordinator ✦ Airport Hospitality

TRAVEL EXPERIENCE

- Traveled in 7 European countries—Switzerland, Italy, Germany, Sweden, Finland, Norway, and extensively in France. Traveled throughout U.S. (Great Lakes states, New England, Colorado, Texas, and California).
- Completed independent study projects in Switzerland and Quebec.

LANGUAGES

Bilingual English/French; Taught Spanish I

TRAVEL MANAGEMENT

- Co-leader for high-school student tour of France.
- Coordinator for annual student trips to Festival of Nations.
- Facilitated arrivals and departures for international exchange programs.

EDUCATION

- International Guide Academy, Denver, CO   **Certified Professional Tour Manager**
- University of Cincinnati, Cincinnati, OH   **Bachelor of Arts in French Education,** *Summa Cum Laude*
  Bachelor of Arts in Sociology/Social Service, *Cum Laude*

COMMUNITY

- **Area representative** for international student-exchange program.
- **Advisor,** World Language Club.
- **Host** for international guests from France, Russia, and Scandinavia.
- **Organized cultural programs** for university and community.
- **Performed administrative duties** for volunteer organizations—youth soccer club, church groups, and community theater.

COMMUNICATION SKILLS

- Degree in social services.
- Certified in crisis-intervention counseling.
- Public speaking experience with large groups.
- Open, personable demeanor, with genuine respect for individuals.

SPECIAL INTERESTS

- **Member,** Le Club Francais
- **Actress,** long-time member Taftville Playhouse Community Theater
- **Member,** Taftville Symphony Chorus

WORK EXPERIENCE

Social Services, 7 years; Teaching, 9 years

Strategy: *Bring volunteer and community work to the fore because it supports her job target. Eliminate all specifics of early, unrelated work experience.*

DAVID M. WALTERS

1066 West Riverside Avenue
Spokane, Washington 99201
(509) 886-5294
dmwalt@aol.com

CLASSROOM / TEACHER AIDE

Professional Profile:

Mature and caring individual with a commitment to working with children with special needs. Over 7 years' experience as a full-time, stay-at-home parent, caring for disabled children. Provide a nurturing, compassionate, and supportive environment while encouraging academic, physical, and personal growth.

Summary:
- Assist children with fitness, recreational, and academic activities.
- Ensure the health and safety of children.
- Evaluate children's performance and keep track of progress.
- Utilize special skills in working with children with various disabilities, including autism and learning disabilities.
- Initiate and supervise activities to encourage learning and healthy, structured play.
- Provide exceptional care, assessing children's needs and resolving their problems.
- Encourage appropriate socialization and interaction.
- Create and carry out arts and crafts projects.
- Instruct children in math, language, and reading lessons.
- Demonstrate superior skills in making students feel comfortable and at ease, resulting in a trusting relationship.
- Convey a friendly, gentle, and positive attitude to children of all ages.

Experience:

Stay-at-Home Dad, Spokane, Washington (1995–2002)

Manager/Owner, Spokane Antique World, Spokane, Washington (1987–1994)

Manager, East Valley Antiques, East Valley, Washington (1982–1986)

Corporate Services Representative, Chase Manhattan Bank, Spokane, Washington (1977–1981)

Education:

Spokane Community College, Spokane, Washington
Liberal Arts courses with a concentration in Art and Photography.

Volunteer:

Chaperone and Parent Aide for numerous school field trips and activities.

References:

Furnished upon request.

Situation: *This dad remained at home full time for seven years raising two disabled children. This experience motivated him to pursue a career working with children, so his resume emphasizes his nurturing personality as well as his experience. His early, unrelated employment is listed without detail.*

RESUME 6: LINDA MATIAS, JCTC, CEIP; SMITHTOWN,

Samantha Rodriguez

475 Red Bridge Road
Melville, NY 11747
sam@email.com
(631) 382-2425

Customer Service Representative

Experienced in providing direct customer support by answering inbound calls and providing in-person customer service. Solid customer-satisfaction and account-management skills that contribute to increased revenue and long-standing customer relationships.

Qualifications include:

- Timely assessment and understanding of customer expectations. Take a hands-on approach in clarifying customer expectations and resolving issues efficiently.
- Answer and follow up on customer inquiries, generate sales, and handle complex discrepancies related to transaction processing.
- Maintain existing client accounts and process inbound paperwork after receipt, including system update and customer notification.
- Described as courteous, patient, and respectful of client concerns.
- Portray a professional image and properly handle confidential information.
- Strong verbal, written, interpersonal communication, and data-entry skills. Focus on detail and accuracy.
- Solid computer skills including MS Word, Excel, Access, and Outlook.

PROFESSIONAL EXPERIENCE

CUSTOMER SERVICE REPRESENTATIVE, Advantage Banking Services, 1993–1996, Dix Hills, New York

Serviced customers including processing and disbursing loans; opening, closing, and reconciling accounts; processing payroll deductions and direct-deposit requests; processing modifications to existing accounts; and marketing additional banking services and products to customers.

CUSTOMER SERVICE ASSOCIATE, Bank of Long Island, 1991–1993, Huntington, New York

Provided information to customers on issues such as account balances and CD and loan rates. Recommended services such as stop-payment orders, check cards, and fund transfers; processed on-line applications. Verified deposits and answered questions regarding products and services.

SUPPORT SERVICE REPRESENTATIVE, Mortgage Homes and Loans, 1990–1991, Huntington, New York

Input member information in main system for easy, up-to-date access of data. Maintained files and documentation regarding member accounts. Performed various clerical duties including answering phones, distributing mail, and filing. Offered support to other members of Service Center team.

EDUCATION

Liberal Arts, Suffolk County Community College, Brentwood, New York, 1995

Strategy: *Deemphasize dates of employment through effective formatting; highlight qualifications in a lengthy summary. Note effective listing for education without a degree.*

RESUME 7: GAYLE HOWARD, CPRW, CRW, CCM; MELBOURNE, AUSTRALIA

Lynda Britton

2 Jackson Street, Melbourne, 3116
Telephone: 8429 0049
Email: brittonl@bigpool.com

> Receptionist
> Customer Service
> Customer Relations

SUMMARY

Outgoing, energetic individual liberated from the full-time demands of family and poised to enter the next round of professional and life opportunities. Excel in influential communications—listening to the customer, resolving problems, and recommending products and courses of action. Expertly restore order from chaos, manage multiple tasks simultaneously, and rise to the challenge of deadlines and pressure.

Never shirking from less-than-glamorous tasks, have demonstrated capacity to "roll up the sleeves and pitch in" to ensure a task is completed on time, to high professional standards. Cited by past employers for good-natured, cooperative outlook, willingness to work hard, and team contributions.

Professional strengths include:

- Diplomatic & Expeditious Problem Solving
- Staff Supervision
- Dispute Mediation/Negotiation/Resolution
- New Product Development
- Continuous Improvement
- Quality Control
- Workplace Health & Safety
- Staff Rosters
- Stock Ordering/Inventory Control
- Staff Training & Development
- Customer Relationship Management
- Procedure & Process Streamlining
- Special Sales/Retail Promotions
- Telephone Communications
- Cost Containment Initiatives
- Cash Balancing

Software knowledge: Microsoft Word, Excel, Access, PowerPoint; Internet and email.

EXPERIENCE SUMMARY

Organizational & Workflow Management

- Successfully settled staff unrest over rigid work roster system at a retail bakery. Revamped staff scheduling to achieve a more equitable mix of skills that allowed for personal flexibility, while meeting the demands of peak customer periods.
- Commended by management and team members alike for ability to meet the challenges of high-pressure, fast-paced environments.
- Revamped storage areas to maximize space and provide easier and safer selection of frequently used supplies.

Sales & Communications

- Assumed role of staff mentor and trainer to enhance the knowledge base of subordinates. As Factory Outlet Manager overseeing the retail arm of a small manufacturing firm, translated and communicated retail-sales policies, conflict-resolution techniques, and important occupational health and safety issues to staff.
- Developed outstanding relationships by individualizing and nurturing loyal/regular clients, remembering pertinent facts from previous sales and/or communications.
- Spearheaded several small-scale promotional competitions that invited proactive customer involvement, encouraged repeat business, and built business goodwill.
- As a senior sales assistant and team member, identified underlying tensions negatively impacting the work environment. Steadily and quietly mediated conflicts between disgruntled staff and management that, when resolved, infinitely improved staff demeanor and productivity.
- Won back wholesale buyer, returning up to $800 a week to business revenues.

TRAINING

Receptionist/Front Desk Training Course (March 2002)
Introduction to Computers, Allwood House (2001)

Lynda Britton | Page 1 | Confidential

Strategy: *To help this returning-to-work mom transition to a new field (all her experience was in retail), clearly convey her related expertise on page 1; then on page 2 include stories that support these skills.*

PROFESSIONAL EXPERIENCE

FLOURY FINGERS BAKEHOUSE, Hurstbridge   1988–1998
Popular pastry and bread bake-house; family-owned with staff of 10.

Senior Sales Assistant

As the longest-serving staff member, recognized for senior-level knowledge of bake-house operations. Headed a small, tight-knit customer-service team. Multifaceted role touched several core business disciplines from sales and marketing through customer service, team leadership and training, inventory control, and new product development. Frequently acted as "fire-fighter," mediating conflicts between staff and management to maintain workplace harmony.

Selected accomplishments

- Restored confidence of VIP client—a wholesaler buyer previously contributing up to $800 a week to the bottom line. Citing irreconcilable differences with the owner, the buyer was resistant to reversing decision yet responded positively to subtle maneuvering intended to re-open lines of communication. Mediated steadily between both parties to resolve areas of contention. The buyer returned to bake-house and preferred product.
- Reversed employee turnover and strengthened retention rates by encouraging business owner to adopt a "worker-friendly" approach. Successfully and diplomatically demonstrated the positive effects of a non-confrontational management style, assuring improved staff motivation and productivity.
- Completely revamped staff roster system, winning across-the-board approval for initiatives in achieving more equitable time and skills mixes.
- Conducted formal and informal training to new recruits to ensure optimum customer service and promote workplace safety.
- Initiated several ideas for new products that served to stimulate customers' interest and prompt repeat business. Reduced food wastage by suggesting several new derivative products that could successfully utilize unsold items; turned a loss into a revenue raiser.
- Refurbished stock area, restoring order to chaos, improving worker safety, and providing at-a-glance information on existing supply holdings.
- Instrumental in staging special store promotions including customer competitions.

HOOPERS SUPERMARKET, Croydon   1994–1998
Local supermarket with busy lottery outlet.

Sales Assistant

For small country supermarket providing personalized customer service, performed counter sales, processed stock orders, checked deliveries against order tickets for accuracy, and relieved staff in the adjacent Tattlslotto area, selling lottery tickets, renewing memberships, and paying prizes.

NUTS 'R US, Preston   1984–1988
Wholesale nut and confectionary processor and distributor with small retail "factory outlet" store.

Factory Outlet Manager

Managed factory outlet shop. Stocked shelves, balanced takings, filled customer orders, answered telephones, collected mail, administered daily banking, initiated customer order deliveries, and trained factory staff.

PERSONAL

Leisure interests include reading, crosswords, jigsaw puzzles, computers, walking, and craft work.
Served as Committee Member and Youth Club Leader for local primary school, netball/youth clubs.

RESUME 8: LAURA DECARLO, CCM, CPRW, JCTC, CECC, CCMC, CRW; MELBOURNE, FL

Donald P. Dotson

55 S.W. 15th Avenue
Greensboro, NC 27402

(336) 334-5551

dpdotson@attbi.com

ENVIRONMENTAL PROTECTION

*Lifelong interest in and study of plants, wildlife, and environmental protection
enhanced by educationally focused studies and experience at nature centers*

- Skilled in collection, identification, cataloguing, and study of data from various biological and ecological sources; experienced in plant taxonomy, ethnobotany, and botany.
- Proven ability in analysis, scientific theories, and procedures; strong laboratory and field-analysis skills.
- Detail-oriented, with ability to create scientific drawings.
- Confident communicator; comfortable providing tours.
- Member, Nature Conservancy and Save the Birds.
- Computer application skills using Microsoft Office and Windows.

EDUCATION

B.S. in Biology, Minor in Zoology, Florida State University, Tallahassee, FL
A.A. in General Education, Valencia Community Collage, Orlando, FL

Relevant Curricula

• Entomology	• Local Flora	• Zoology
• Botany/Ethnobotany	• Ecology	• Animal Physiology
• Plant Taxonomy	• Molecular Cell Biology	• Herpetology
• Plant Kingdom	• Organic Chemistry	• Oceanography

RELEVANT EXPERIENCE

Biological Sciences
- Worked in the arboretum and herbarium at Greensboro Butterfly Haven and Garden for summer independent study credit.
  - Assisted in relocation and replacement of herbarium — entire library of specimens.
  - Maintained arboretum hothouse and grounds, handling transplanting, building of arbors, weeding, and identification and labeling of tree species.
- Performed wild-bird rescue, capturing, transporting, and splinting injured birds for Save the Birds.
- Researched and created scientific drawings of cellular organisms utilizing a microscope for class.
- Collected, preserved, identified, and catalogued different plant species; developed extensive knowledge of vascular plants with emphasis on the flora of peninsular Florida for class.

Public Relations, Administration & Coordination
- Performed extensive event coordination as a PTO volunteer and volunteer teacher at Spectrum.
  - Handled program planning of student graduation and field trips to include selecting location, recruiting and coordinating volunteers, negotiating prices, securing donations, and setting up.
  - Assisted students in the classroom and on field trips; designed and taught curriculum.
- Managed the diverse aspects of running a business to include management of inventory, development of customer relations, administrative control, human resources, and budgeting at Don's Hoagies.

WORK / VOLUNTEER EXPERIENCE

Biology Independent Study, Greensboro Butterfly Haven & Gardens, Greensboro, NC, 2002
Rescue Volunteer, Save the Birds, Greensboro, NC, 1996–Present
Volunteer, PTO & Volunteer Teacher, Spectrum Elementary School, Orlando, FL, 1994–1997
Manager, Don's Hoagies, Orlando, FL, 1989–1996

Strategy: *Demonstrate skills and knowledge gained through experiences and schooling completed while a stay-at-home dad, using a functional style that presents strong credentials for his current job target.*

REGINA HUCKLEBERRY, R.N.

531 Elm Road • Rosemont, PA 19012 • ReginaRN@msn.com • 610-507-2242

PROFESSIONAL OBJECTIVE & PROFILE

Dedicated health-care professional looking to utilize experience and education within an established organization. Skilled in medical, surgical, coronary, and critical-care environments.

√ Demonstrated ability to remain calm and focused in high-stress/fast-paced environment while providing quality care and meeting patients' needs.
√ Self-motivated, dependable, flexible, loyal, and a quality team leader.
√ Instrumental in building positive relationships with administration, physicians, peers, patients, and families; genuine concern and sensitivity for others.
√ Exceptional communication, organizational, time-management, and problem-solving skills.
√ Proficient in all paperwork, documentation, and records management, with careful attention to patient confidentiality.
√ Computer skilled in Microsoft Word and Internet applications.

SUMMARY OF PROFESSIONAL EXPERIENCE

➢ Served as Head Nurse, Charge Nurse, and Staff Nurse in various health-care settings.
➢ Skilled in MED, CCU, ICU, OR, Ortho, telemetry, and step-down care.
➢ Evaluated performance of Registered Nurses, Licensed Practical Nurses, and Certified Nurses' Aides.
➢ Developed, coordinated, and implemented comprehensive nursing assessments and care plans.
➢ Administered appropriate medication as ordered by attending physician.
➢ Monitored, assessed, and communicated patient progress to attending physician on a periodic basis.
➢ Participated in care-planning meetings with departmental advisors, clients, and family members.
➢ Prepared and educated patient/family members on required care and instruction following discharge.
➢ Taught and mentored fellow nurses, delivered orientation courses, and conducted in-service programs.
➢ Selected to serve on numerous health-care committees.

PROFESSIONAL EXPERIENCE

Medical-Surgical RN (Per Diem)	Medical College of Pennsylvania, Philadelphia, PA	1985–1990
Coronary Care RN	Holy Cross Hospital, Silver Spring, MD	1979–1983
Telemetry/Step-Down Unit Head RN	Queens Medical Center, Honolulu, HI	1974–1976
Coronary Care Head RN		
Instructor RN		
Medical-Surgical-Ortho-ICU RN		
Internal Med-Cardiac Rehab Office RN	Windward Medical Center, Kailua, HI	1974

EDUCATION & LICENSE

Master's Degree: Counseling Psychology, University of Maryland at College Park
Bachelor of Science: Dual Major: Psychology/Zoology, University of Maryland at College Park
Summa Cum Laude Graduate
Associate of Science: Nursing, University of Hawaii

State of Pennsylvania License

CERTIFICATIONS

Basic Cardiac Life Support • American Heart Association CPR Certified • Intravenous Certified Nurse

Strategy: *Highlight her strong professional experience, downplaying the fact that it occurred more than a decade ago. She is seeking to return to the same field.*

RESUME 10: LAURA WEST, CCMC, CJST, JCTC; CORVALLIS, MT

WENDI JACKMAN
5921 SW Hillcrest Drive ▪ Lakeside, Oregon 97886
Residence: (503) 825-1468 ▪ E-mail: wendycj5921@home.com ▪ Mobile: (503) 825-1469

MARKETING ▪ ADVERTISING ▪ STRATEGIC COMMUNICATIONS

Creative, self-motivated, and solutions-driven business professional offering 10 years' expertise in marketing and business management. Expert communicator with ability to simplify complex issues, cultivate key relationships, and build cohesion across all corporate levels. Motivational leader, inspiring staff to new levels of performance. Resourceful problem-solver with natural business savvy and proven ability to coordinate projects from inception to completion. Strength in planning, multi-tasking, organizing, and time management.

AREAS OF EXPERTISE

Tactical Marketing & Advertising Campaigns
Public & Media Relations
New Product Development
Corporate Branding
Agency / Contractor Relationships
Training & Development

Strategic Planning & Communications
Media Production
Direct Mail / Promotions / Special Events
Team Building & Leadership
Budget Administration / Fundraising
Market Research

CAREER HIGHLIGHTS

MARKETING COORDINATOR / ADVERTISING DEPARTMENT MANGER / BANK OFFICER
Western Bancorp, Inc. — Los Angeles, California (7 years)

Fast-track progression from Marketing Coordinator to Bank Officer for $4 billion, statewide holding company with 22 bank locations. Controlled $2.5 million annual advertising budget. Directed 5-member advertising department. Selected primary advertising agency partnership. Identified and targeted new niche markets.

Piloted strategic and promotional plans for each division and member bank. Coordinated product development, internal and external communications, direct mail campaigns, public relations, research, training, collateral materials, and special events. Supervised production of television and radio ads.

- Built advertising department from ground up as company's first Advertising Department Manager.
- Reorganized and centralized marketing and advertising functions of 22 separate banks during merger, increasing budget efficiencies by as much as 30%.
- Created and maintained graphics standards for new organization.
- Designed new corporate sales materials and brand image, achieving 60% increase in institutional recognition and 10% rise in tagline recognition.
- Developed, directed, and appeared in series of corporate training videos used to train employees in member banks on marketing objectives and strategies. Resulted in 10% decrease in training expenses.
- Nearly doubled market share in 5 years.
- Garnered statewide press coverage in *The Los Angeles Times* for highly successful TV/radio/print corporate-image campaign.
- Orchestrated several advertising and direct mail campaigns recognized with local and national Advertising Federation awards.

Strategy: *To hide more than 15 years out of the workforce, eliminate dates and focus on experience and achievements, all of which relate to her goal of returning to the field of marketing and advertising. More recent volunteer experience is included because it also links to her job target.*

RESUME 10, CONTINUED

WENDI JACKMAN
Résumé ▪ Page 2

CAREER HIGHLIGHTS CONTINUED...

MEDIA PLANNER & BUYER
News Media & Barnsdale Advertising — Denver, Colorado (3 years)

Recommended, coordinated, and executed media options for financial service, telecommunication, public-utility, and airline clients in sync with corporate marketing and sales objectives. Optimized diverse marketing venues including television, radio, newspaper, magazine, direct mail, and outdoor media.

Interfaced with market research to determine return on investment for media costs. Tracked sales increases to prove positive, bottom-line results for wide range of client companies.

ADDITIONAL EXPERIENCE

Event Coordinator & Fundraising Sales Chair — Oregon Episcopal School

Fully managed highly demanding and time-sensitive sales project equivalent to a small business. Led PR, product distribution, database management, sales training, coordination of 60 volunteers, presentations, complex reporting, vendor and product expense control, and incentives.

- Catalyst for fundraiser's most successful years in its 20-year history, generating $75,000 in funds over two-year span.

Registrar & Database Manager for 500 members — Vista Soccer Club
Auction Chair & Fundraising Committee — Lakeside Transitional School for the Homeless
Budget Committee — The Junior League of Lakeside
Advisory Board & Big Sister — Big Sisters of America
Funds Allocation Committee — United Way of Denver

EDUCATION & TRAINING

B.S. in Business Administration / Marketing — University of Denver, Colorado

Professional Development
Microsoft Office Training — Portland Community College
International School of Bank Marketing Graduate — Boulder, Colorado (2-yr. program)

Technical Skills
MS Office Suite (Word, Excel, and Power Point), Quick Books Pro

CHAPTER 5

Resumes for People Returning to Work After Divorce, Death of Spouse, or Financial Reversal

A sudden change in circumstances can dictate the need to find work—fast. The resumes in this chapter show gaps in employment from less than a year to more than a decade, but in each case there is an urgent need for employment. Both functional and chronological formats are used.

ALLY JACKSON

P.O. Box 266
Grandview, Washington 98930
Phone: 509-882-5281
Email: allyj@yahoo.com

SUMMARY OF QUALIFICATIONS

- ☑ Outside Sales
- ☑ Customer Service
- ☑ Account Management

- ☑ Staff Supervision
- ☑ Cashier Operations
- ☑ Conflict Resolution

PROFESSIONAL HIGHLIGHTS

01/02 to INDUSTRIAL SUPPLY – Yakima, Washington
03/02 **Outside Sales**
Accepted the challenge of straight commission sales, marketing industrial lubricants to residential and commercial property-management companies, municipalities, and businesses in Central Washington and the valley.
- ➢ Produced over $9,000 in new business, including $3,000 during training, in the first 7 weeks of employment. Added 15 new customers in the first 4 weeks after training.
- ➢ Gained expertise in account identification and qualification, cold-calling, needs assessment, presentations, and closing. Cold-called, on average, 15 businesses daily.
- ➢ Oversaw account management: re-orders, customer service, and issue resolution.

2000 to MOM'S BEST FRIEND – Yakima, Washington
2001 **Nanny**
Provided childcare and parenting services in a variety of environments. Assisted with homecare, nutrition, and transportation. Experienced in grief management, conflict resolution, and emotional stress.

1980 to SAFEWAY – Grandview, Washington
1985 **Service Manager (1982 to 1985)**
Oversaw the efficient operations of the "front of the house," guiding the efforts of 10 cashiers and sackers. Prepared cash drawers, ensured check-out supplies, monitored work schedules, approved personal checks, and assisted customers with issues.
- ➢ Established a five-year record of excellent dependability and consistent merit raises and promotions.

Cashier (1980 to 1982)

CIVIC CONTRIBUTIONS

GRANDVIEW SOFTBALL LEAGUE – 1997 to 2001
Coach
Municipal league for 7- to 8-year-olds.

CYSTIC FIBROSIS – 1997 to 2001
Referee
Assisted with athletic events for the physically challenged.

Strategy: *A chronological format is used to show recent work history as this candidate seeks a sales position with a good base salary and benefits. Fortunately she had some success in her recent short-term, straight-commission job; for sales resumes, numbers are all-important.*

RESUME 12: ALICE P. BRAXTON, CPRW, CEIP; BURLINGTON, NC

Davida M. Meiner

(919) 549-9033   313 Milton Place, Durham, NC 27701   davame421@hotmail.com

Customer Service Representative

Relevant Skills & Strengths
- ✓ Dependable, flexible, resourceful and adaptable.
- ✓ Even tempered — able to calm the troubled client or dissatisfied customer.
- ✓ Organized and quick to prioritize.
- ✓ Communications, oral and written — one-on-one and in groups.
- ✓ Computer skills: Windows, MS Word, Excel, and WordPerfect 6.1.

Experience
Durham County Housing Authority, Durham, North Carolina   04/01–02/02
Office Assistant (VISTA Volunteer — stipend compensation through AmeriCorps)
- ✓ Typed letters and memos, ordered supplies, sent faxes, made copies, and answered phones.
- ✓ Assisted housing residents with community resource referrals.
- ✓ Planned and secured door prizes for Career Fair and Community Day and sent thank-you letters to all participating resources and donors.
- ✓ Facilitated after-school homework tutoring program.

Commercial Cleaning Service, Philadelphia, Pennsylvania, Part-time   04/99–08/00
Cleaning Technician
- ✓ Cleaned, dusted and vacuumed a large chemical company.
- ✓ Recognized by owner and given a merit raise for dedication to quality.
- ✓ Kept only master set of keys held by an employee.

MRG Corporation (Contractor for Municipal Utilities Department), Philadelphia, Pennsylvania   01/98–06/98
Customer Service Representative
- ✓ Calmly handled complaints and answered questions for disgruntled customers.
- ✓ Scheduled appointments for owner-supervised installation of utility meters.

Programs in Counseling, Reading, Pennsylvania   09/97–12/97
Office Manager/Client Services (Completed as part of training in Office Assistant program)
- ✓ Scheduled appointments and maintained office supplies.
- ✓ Transcribed doctors' notes and recommendations.
- ✓ Dealt at reception desk with sometimes-difficult "criminally mentally disturbed" clients.
- ✓ Commended for calm handling of difficult clients.

Community Service
Parent-Teacher Association Volunteer — Homeroom Mother
President of Head Start parent group
Church secretary and Sunday School teacher
Organized Community Services Christmas parties for children with mental and physical disabilities — 3 years

Education
Paramount Associates Institute, Reading, Pennsylvania   Diploma, Office Assistant — 2 year program, 1997
Central Pennsylvania College, Summerdale, Pennsylvania   Completed 1 year

Military
U.S. Army Reserves, 6 years — E-4, Honorable Discharge, 1990

Will continue education or training to optimize performance! Willing to commute.

Strategy: *Use a bold headline to immediately focus the resume on her job target, even though her experience in this field is limited. Do not mention the part-time nature of all of her prior positions; instead, focus on what she did and how well she did it.*

RESUME 13: DEBRA O'REILLY, CPRW, JCTC, CEIP; BRISTOL, CT

Sandra Mann

291 Dawson Avenue
Madisonville, KY 42431

Home: 270-555-5555
E-mail: Mannsan@aol.com

◆◆◆
MEDICAL TRANSCRIPTIONIST
◆◆◆

Over ten years of medical transcription and secretarial experience in private medical, clinical research, and corporate office environments. Familiarity with medical terminology; skilled in dictaphone use.

◆
HIGHLIGHTS OF MEDICAL TRANSCRIPTION EXPERIENCE
◆

Orthopedic Associates, Los Angeles, CA   1988–1993
Medical Transcriptionist

Recorded physician observations / findings during patient evaluations for this orthopedic surgeon who specialized in Workers' Compensation cases. Subsequently transcribed the information (compiling data from doctor's tapes and evaluation notes) for claim reports.

• Consistently earned annual merit bonuses based on volume and quality of work.

California College Research Center, Los Angeles, CA   1981–1982
Medical Transcriptionist / Word Processing Secretary, Oncology Department

Typed patient protocol reports, working closely with residents, interns, and physicians in an intensive, fast-paced office.

• Selected to assist the Grant Administrator in the preparation of annual NIH grant applications.

◆
HIGHLIGHTS OF SECRETARIAL / ADMINISTRATIVE EXPERIENCE
◆

Home-Based Business, Madisonville, KY   1994–Present
Administrator

Conduct all office administration and sales for a home-based business, using excellent organizational and time management skills and adhering to a high standard for quality work. Skilled in use of computer word-processing, desktop-publishing, accounting, and spreadsheet applications on Macintosh and Virtual PC.

Professional Engineers, Evanston, IL   1984–1988
Secretary

Served four engineers and supported a 20-engineer department. Produced documents ranging from correspondence to technical reports. During automation of office, mastered the new software and trained the engineers in its use.

Executive Offices, Cicero, IL   1983–1984
Head Secretary

At this innovative executive office suite, was selected to direct the workflow of three secretaries supporting office administration for ten tenant companies in a new facility. Typed, edited, and proofread correspondence. Coordinated conference calls, managed mass mailings, and maintained extensive customer databases.

◆
EDUCATION
◆

B.A., California College, Los Angeles, CA   M.A., Northwestern University, Evanston, IL

Strategy: *Choose her most "marketable" skills (medical transcription) and isolate/highlight those by breaking her experience into two discrete sections.*

RESUME 14: LINDA MATIAS, JCTC, CEIP; SMITHTOWN, NY

Howard Hirsch

46 Brook Hollow Road
Selden, New York 11700

(631) 382-2425
hirsch@online.com

Qualifications

➢ **Fifteen years** of progressive experience handling multiple lines of insurance claims.
➢ Experience in handling property claims, Commercial Auto Liability, Bodily Injury, and General Liability lines.
➢ Knowledge of applicable insurance contracts (commercial P&C), laws, and DOI regulations.
➢ Interfaced effectively with policy holders, claimants, physicians, medical providers, attorneys, and repair shops.

Work History & Summary of Key Skills

Claims Department Manager/Supervisor (15 years), ProCar Insurance, Garden City, New York
Initially hired as a Claims Representative Trainee, quickly promoted to Senior Claims Representative, and ultimately selected as Claims Department Manager/Supervisor. **Prevented losses, contained costs, exercised initiative, and demonstrated independent good judgment.**

Effective Negotiation Abilities	Negotiated property damage and personal injury claims on both first- and third-party claims. Authority to **negotiate up to $500,000** per claim.
	Evaluated settlement strategies and alternatives. Determined settlement value and analyzed the potential costs, benefits, and risk of litigation.
	Attended mediation conferences and claim committee meetings to **achieve fair and equitable settlements.**
Keen Investigative Skills	Investigated commercial auto property damage claims. Acquired information and maintained accurate records regarding accidents from policy holders and claimants.
	Conducted investigations of accidents, screened vehicles, researched missing information on claim forms, and processed claims from first to last step.
	Arranged independent medical exams, reviewed reports, and followed up on inconsistencies and/or coverage issues.
Strong Leadership Qualities	Managed a staff of 6 claims representatives, 2 claims processors, and 2 appraisers.
	Assigned incoming claims and **monitored process** to ensure accurate and timely handling of all claims. Held biweekly claim-committee meetings to evaluate and delegate authority to settle third-party claims.
	Interviewed and trained staff in technical software, company procedures, and claims regulations/statutes.

Education

Bachelor of Arts, Finance, State University of New York at Stony Brook, Stony Brook, New York

Strong references available upon request.

Strategy: *To hide employment experience that occurred more than 15 years ago, eliminate dates and show only length of employment. Emphasize skills and key achievements with bold type.*

RESUME 15: ALICE BRAXTON, CPRW, CEIP; BURLINGTON, NC

CYNTHIA B. LAMB

4100 FERNWAY DRIVE
GREENSBORO, NC 27403

(336) 299-2588
CLAMB2000@AOL.COM

OBJECTIVE

FLIGHT ATTENDANT

EDUCATION

Wake Forest University, Winston-Salem, NC
Bachelor of Arts degree in Communications
Emphasis — Radio, TV, and Journalism

SKILLS SUMMARY

Organizer/Planner/Leader
- Planned activities for spouses/guests during international accounting conferences — traveled extensively in U.S., Canada, England, Scotland, Turkey, Mexico, Germany, France, Italy, Holland, Austria, and Switzerland.
- Sat 2 years on gated community Architectural Review Committee with 3 builders, the project developer, and 3 homeowners.
- Chaired and coordinated volunteers for successful Spring Gala including selection of wines and cheeses for wine-tasting event and procuring items for a silent auction.

Sales/Marketing/Customer Service
- Contracted by furniture manufacturers to represent product lines during Furniture Market in High Point, NC.
- Marketed and leased personal home to executive groups for Furniture Market including lease preparation, negotiation, and daily restocking of linens and supplies.
- Assisted upscale caterer with serving of elegant sit-down dinners for 200-400 guests during Furniture Market for manufacturer show rooms and *House Beautiful* and *Architectural Digest* groups.

Public Presentation
- Modeled and emceed in fashion shows in the community to raise funds for charities.
- Studied and interned in radio and television journalism in college.
- Entertained and hosted social events on behalf of largest CPA firm in North Carolina.

Personal Strengths
- Articulate and persuasive
- Energetic, flexible, and adaptable
- Exceptional interpersonal skills

Computer Experience
- MS Word, Internet, and E-mail

COMMUNITY INVOLVEMENT

Board member, committee member, volunteer for children's liturgy group, children's choir, Bible schools, and nursery department for local church.

Strategy: *Mine extensive volunteer and community experience to hide the fact that she had no professional employment whatsoever. Highlight key skills areas that relate to her flight-attendant goal.*

RESUME 16: MICHELE J. HAFFNER, CPRW, JCTC; GLENDALE, WI

BETTY JONES

1129 North Prospect Avenue #211
Milwaukee, Wisconsin 53202

Residence: 414-272-9191
bjones@hotmail.com

EXPERTISE

SALES MANAGEMENT AND MERCHANDISING: A goal-oriented, dedicated, and sincere sales professional who is highly organized and analytical. New York markets buying experience. Familiar with Microsoft products including Word and Excel. Demonstrated expertise in the following areas:

- Client Relationship Management
- Target Market Development
- Consultative & Influential Selling

- Quality Product Assurance
- Personal Goal Setting & Sales Results
- Strategic Business Planning

Excellent communicator capable of working effectively with individuals from all backgrounds and levels of education.

MERCHANDISING EXPERIENCE

Educational Buyer—Worthington Hobby House, Worthington, Ohio
Jewelry & Women's Apparel Buyer—Jewelry Now, Worthington, Ohio

Highlights: Accountable for product selection and purchasing of educational materials and trend items for a craft and hobby retail establishment. Identified trends and developed production assortment to meet needs of consumers within an affluent suburban community. Traveled to New York City markets to make product selections. Managed point-of-purchase and merchandising activities to drive sales. Developed marketing and public-relations campaigns to increase traffic and revenue.

- Achieved success with several product assortments that created tremendous interest and generated high sales volume.

MANAGEMENT EXPERIENCE

Medical Office Manager — Dr. P. Stein and Dr. F. Rothman Medical Offices, Toledo, Ohio
Legal Office Manager — Williams, Johnson, and Smith Legal Offices, Toledo, Ohio

Highlights: As medical office manager, accountable for ordering medical/dental supplies, managing patient scheduling, and providing patient assistance within medical practices offering OB/GYN and cardiac care. Met with suppliers and vendor representatives, organized product choices, and negotiated pricing. As legal office manager, conducted medical/legal research for malpractice cases. Assisted with human-resources activities. Attended legal conferences and other public-relations/marketing events to promote business.

EDUCATION

- Bachelor of Education
  Ohio State University, Columbus, Ohio

- Bachelor of Health/Science
  University of Toledo, Toledo, Ohio

AFFILIATIONS

- Alpha Psi—Ohio State University Alumni Association
- University of Toledo Alumni Association

- Eta Sigma Gamma Sorority
- St. Vincent Hospital Auxiliary

Strategy: *Pull together relevant work history to show that she's qualified for a sales or merchandising position. Completely eliminate dates—essential because she was in her late 50s and had not worked for most of her lengthy marriage.*

MARIA CLARKE
879 North Street • Teaneck, NJ 07666

(201) 530-9089

mariaclarke789@aol.com

SUMMARY

Ten years of experience in insurance underwriting, customer service, and management combine with a background in community relations, event planning/coordination, fundraising, and administration. Recognized as a well-organized, efficient professional with a strong work ethic and leadership qualities. Proven ability to meet deadlines, reach goals, and deliver results. Excellent public/customer-relations skills. Computer literate.

Earned Charter Property Casualty Underwriter designation.

INSURANCE EXPERIENCE

NEW JERSEY INSURANCE COMPANY, Teaneck, NJ

Assistant Manager (1984–1990)
Senior Account Analyst / Account Analyst (1980–1984)

Promoted to supervisory role with increasing responsibilities in Commercial Lines Unit for marketing, profitability, customer service, agency relations, and underwriting. Assisted District Manager in new program-development and decision-making activities in the unit. Supervised, trained, motivated, and evaluated team of 7 underwriters. Recruited, appointed, and maintained positive relationships with up to 30 agents. Implemented new product programs and trained agents.

Accomplishments:

- Assumed supervisor's role during leave of absence and ensured smoothly running unit operations.
- Consistently achieved/exceeded goals for production, new business development, and profitability.
- Assisted in implementing District Assistant Program and trained new staff in essential job functions.
- Reorganized District Assistant Program, resulting in earlier renewal processing and issuance.
- Supervisor's evaluation: *"Maria continually distinguishes herself with hard work and dedicated effort. She is an extremely important part of the operation."*

COMMUNITY RELATIONS EXPERIENCE

TEANECK HIGH SCHOOL, Teaneck, NJ (1990–Present)

Board of Directors Member/Fundraising — Sports Club (3 years)
- Contributed to event-planning, organizational, and administrative activities to benefit school programs. Created display posters to promote events; coordinated raffles and direct mail campaigns. Established sponsorships and led fundraising efforts that generated over $100,000.

Teaneck Parent Teacher Association (10 years)
Various leadership roles in the organization:

- **Co-chair/Committee Member — Cultural Enrichment** (4 years) — Researched, planned, and coordinated cultural/educational programs presented to audiences of 600 students at the elementary and middle schools. Managed program budget. Earned "Person of Character" Award in 1996 by Governor Whitman.

- **Chair — Membership** (2 years) — Coordinated efforts that increased new membership by 10-15%.

- **Chair — Safe Homes** (2 years) — Compiled and distributed directories to parents.

- **Fundraising Chair — Cub Scouts Award** (3 years) — Honored for service and dedication.

EDUCATION

Bachelor of Arts (English), Fairfield University, Fairfield, CT

Strategy: *Create a split-chronological resume, highlighting insurance experience up front to support her current career goal. Explain her absence from the workforce through extensive Community Relations section. Overall, provide substantial information to give the reader a strong sense of her capabilities.*

RESUME 18: JANE ROQUEPLOT, CBC; SHARON, PA

ROBERTA H. PETERSON

91955 Jefferson Avenue
Shippingport, PA 15077   990.455.5512   rpeterson@hotmail.com

CAREER OBJECTIVE

Customer Service / Inside Sales position utilizing my extensive professional experience

EMPLOYMENT BACKGROUND
(20⁺ years)

RELEVANT QUALIFICATIONS

Management / Customer Service
- Quickly attain responsible track record / diligently earn management status.
- Entrusted by senior executives to complete all administrative responsibilities.
- Assist client in accurate assessment of needs.
- Perform comprehensive interviewing, training and supervision of staff.
- Coordinate complex schedules for training programs.
- Regularly compile monthly corporate reports for international headquarters.
- Competently manage advertising, accounts, inventory / purchasing requirements.
- Handle product orders with attention to detail.

OTHER QUALIFICATIONS

Museum Research / Historical Film Production / Processing
- Expert photographic and textual researcher for museum exhibits, publications, films.
- Compile artifact collection / construct exhibit with regard to space requirements.
- Descriptively compose labels for artifacts on display.
- Practice safe storage and transport of exhibit items.
- Maintain precise edit logs for film-to-video transfer.
- Complete fund-raising proposals, grant and film festival applications.
- Professionally operate color processor / printer for refined photographic development.

EDUCATION

UNIVERSITY OF PENNSYLVANIA
Bachelor of Arts Degree, Film Studies / History Minor
Earned **Summa Cum Laude**

Awards and Scholarships
- Scholarship (Upper Class)
- Alumni Merit Award (Outstanding Academic Achievement)
- Levy Scholar (1991–1992) / Golden Key National Honor Society
- Dean's List (1988–1992)

Courses and Seminars
- Carnegie Course in Effective Speaking and Human Relations
- Carnegie Management Seminar

PERSONAL HIGHLIGHTS

Creative / Team Player / Quality Oriented / Strong Detail Emphasis

PINEHURST REALTY COMPANY
Beaver, PA
Secretary

Strategy: *A strong functional format allows "up-front" presentation of her qualifications, earned through both volunteer and employment experience over many years. Omit dates from employment.*

CHAPTER 6

Resumes for People Returning to Work with Extensive Volunteer Experience

For some back-to-work candidates, volunteer experience provides essential qualifications. In these resumes, that volunteer experience is highlighted appropriately because it supports the candidates' current goals. Even if the experience is not paid, it is verifiable and recent, and so it makes up the bulk of the resume.

RESUME 19: ROLANDE LaPOINTE, CPC, CIPC, CPRW, IJCTC, CCM; LEWISTON, ME

Eileen U. Doughty

3 Danforth Street, Norway, Maine 04268
Telephone: (207) 333-8945
edough22@netscape.com

Career Profile

Multi-faceted individual with many years of experience in varied areas of business ranging from business ownership and operation to academic and banking positions. Growth within the banking industry started with responsibilities as a bank teller and loan closer, later promoted to loan officer. Additional interpersonal skills developed though working and volunteering in Singapore for five years.

Skills Summary

- Excellent Customer Service
- Business Management
- Typing / Data Entry / Word Processing
- Real Estate
- Sales (Service & Retail)
- Telephone & Switchboard Handling

- Diversified Office Support & Secretarial
- Bookkeeping (Full-Charge) & Collections
- PC & Mainframe Operation
- Staff Supervision
- Cash Handling & Balancing
- Banking Operations

Experience

Fundraiser (American Women's Association, Singapore) (Volunteer)   1995–2002
- Leveraged international military relationships, tapping network to raise funds for local charities.

Banking Positions (Bank of America, Tucson, AZ)   1989–1995
- Started as a <u>bank teller part-time</u> in operations; transferred to sales in 1991 as a <u>loan officer</u>. Opened checking, savings, and CD accounts; processed car loans and small consumer loans. Resolved problems with customer accounts and various reports.

Owner/Operator (Dee's Florals, Tucson, AZ)   1987–1989
- Managed all areas of business (including all accounting functions).

Secretary/Registrar (Horizon Elementary School, Tucson School District, Tucson, AZ)   1985–1987
- Handled all student enrollment; performed general secretarial and switchboard operation duties.

Bank Loan Closer (Security Savings, Scottsdale, AZ)   1980–1985
- Processed documents for mortgage loans and worked with clients to ensure all were completed properly; entered necessary data on computer and distributed funds for loan.

Education

Associate Degree in Business   Tucson Community College, Glendale, AZ
American Institute of Banking (A.I.B.)   Varied Locations in Arizona
Norway High School, Norway, ME   Diploma

References Available Upon Request

Strategy: *Just a brief description of each position (paid or volunteer) allows ample room on the page for a concise profile and detailed skills summary.*

MIA F. BAZETH

562 Greengrass Road • Deaucape, Missouri 63703
(573) 556-8322   mia_bazeth@yahoo.com

STATEMENT OF QUALIFICATIONS

Multi-dimensional and highly competent administrative and creative professional with 15+ years experience in all aspects of successful event/program and fundraising management. Demonstrated ability to recruit, motivate, and build cohesive teams that achieve results. Sourced vendors, negotiated contracts, and managed budgets. Strong organizational, interpersonal, and communication skills. Possess professionalism, poise, and diplomacy.

❖ **Special Event Management:** Conceptualization, coordination, and implementation of special events, providing strategic and tactical actions to meet objectives. Developed and administered budgets.

❖ **Fundraising and Public Relations:** Created, planned, and managed all aspects of several major fundraising campaigns resulting in significant contributions. Recruited volunteers and developed sponsorships. Generated media coverage through effective promotional and public relations strategies.

❖ **Administration:** Consistently effective in providing administrative leadership, enhancing work processes, and improving productivity. Experience in organizational, implementation, and team building/leadership.

❖ **Sales/Customer Service:** Demonstrated record of outstanding sales achievements. Introduced and promoted new products. Developed strategies to win customer loyalty. Effectively managed accounts and resolved questions and problems.

RELATED EXPERIENCE

Rainbow Art Institute — Paletteers   1985–2000
- President (2 years); Board of Directors (8 years); Chair — Publicity Coordinator (2 years)
- Projects: Wassail Feast Co-Chair/Founder (4 years)
  Renaissance Festival Chair — Prop/Costume Design Committee
  Spring Garden Sale Chair

Pace Medical Center Wives Group   1983–1998
- President (2 years)
- Annual Flower Sale (5 years)
- Classic Auction/Gala Co-Chair (10 years)

Western Royal   1990–1998
- Children's Art Committee

Northwest High School   1990–1997
- PTA — Fundraising
- Swim Team Booster Club — President (2 years); Chair Fundraising (4 years)

EMPLOYMENT HISTORY

PAW LAND, Brown, KS   1997–1999
CUSTOMER SERVICE: Provided customer service for a designer pet boutique specializing in customized dog beds, placements, and accessories. Presented community awareness programs.

QSP, Pittsburg, KS   1993–1997
SALES TECHNICIAN, School Coordinator: Recruited to coordinate magazine displays and sales in Shawnee Mission, Leavenworth, and Blue Valley school districts. Recruited, trained, and supervised volunteers in operations, finance, and promotional incentives.

EDUCATION

BS, Vocational Home Economics, SOUTHEAST MISSOURI STATE UNIVERSITY   Cape Girardeau, MO

Strategy: *More than ten years of active volunteerism have developed strong skills that can be exploited for a paid position. An expansive summary takes up nearly half of the page.*

Samantha K. Barnett

9 Plymouth Court
West Kingston, RI 02892

(401) 495-5054
sbarnett@snet.com

PROFESSIONAL PROFILE

High-energy individual offering the value of an advanced degree in Education with a solid background in counseling, therapeutic approaches, and training—combined with extensive experience in finance, database systems, and program management. Offer a strong commitment to the delivery of high-quality educational programs with a personal and professional interest in the area of autism. Skilled lecturer, presenter, and writer. Published in *The Newport Journal* and *Spirit of Counseling Magazine*.

Successful in developing and presenting case studies, capturing students' interest, and creating an innovative, progressive learning environment that prompts critical thought and class participation. Detail-oriented and perceptive; determined spirit and character. High professional ethics and personal integrity.

EDUCATION

M.Ed., 1997—*Cum Laude*—**PROVIDENCE COLLEGE**, Rhode Island

Coursework Highlights:

Principles Of Guidance
Measurement & Group Tests
Group Counseling
Fundamentals of Research

Counseling & Guidance
Theories of Counseling
Counseling Practicum
Families in Crisis

B.S., 1982—*Cum Laude*—**FINANCE**—**UNIVERSITY OF CONNECTICUT**, Storrs

TEACHING EXPERIENCE

Gained practical teaching experience through special assignments in fulfillment of the requirements of the graduate program in Education. Provided instruction to other graduate degree candidates in a formal classroom setting using teaching models, formats, and platforms pertinent to the topic. Developed lesson plans, defined learning objectives, developed materials and teaching tools, led classroom presentations, oversaw discussions, and assessed the effectiveness of the programs. Highlights:

- **Case Studies**—Instructed students in client-centered and therapeutic approaches to resolve issues governing "at risk" children, alcoholism, and divorce. Presented situation, knowledge, and foundation theories and outlined techniques of counseling.

- **Professional Development**—Led several presentations on contemporary counseling methodologies and techniques. Demonstrated and effectively communicated an understanding of the role/function of counseling, best professional practices (including legal and ethical considerations), and individual/group approaches to effective assessment and evaluation.

- **Internship, Linkhorne Middle School**—Counseled adolescents in the areas of substance abuse, attention deficit disorder, family relationships, depression, peers, and school. Assisted troubled youths with building self-esteem, formulating realistic goals, and understanding the importance of positive peer models. Encouraged family members to take an active role in their children's development and progress. Demonstrated ability to incorporate effective counseling skills in a school setting.

Strategy: *This resume combines diverse volunteer, educational, and work experience to paint a picture of a highly qualified teaching professional.*

SAMANTHA K. BARNETT

Page Two   sbarnett@snet.com

COMMUNITY/VOLUNTEER EXPERIENCE:

Volunteer/RI Representative—Autism Network For Dietary Intervention 1997 to Present

Assist parents with the implementation of *Beat Autism Now!*, a biomedical protocol and gluten/casein-free dietary program for the disorder's underlying metabolic and immune dysfunction. Concurrently, conduct ongoing research and serve as Rhode Island Representative for the sponsoring national organization.

Union Steward—National Association of Government Employees, Newport, RI 1996 to 1997

Member of a community-based human-services organization specializing in employment-related services for personnel with the Naval Undersea War Center. Provided one-on-one counseling to employees with varying backgrounds in grievances, employee rights, and other work issues.

- Served as a direct intermediary between union and management officials. Credited with facilitating negotiations, forging positive relationships, and promoting conflict resolution.

Volunteer Counselor—Child & Family Agency, Warren RI   1996 to 1997

Provided volunteer counseling services specializing in marriage, relationships, depression, stress, abuse, trauma, chronic illness, and grief. Designed individualized treatment plans and objectives, maintained/updated client documentation, and built a strong working rapport with clients.

- Evaluated needs, identified appropriate coping mechanisms, and designed/implemented individualized counseling programs.
- Effectively conducted counseling sessions with particular emphasis on promoting self-actualization and healthy integration of difficult life experiences. Resulted in a high number of successful completions.
- Documented benefits of treatment and discussed future interventions.

Mentor Program Coordinator—Naval Underwater Defense Center, Newport, RI 1995 to 1997

Led the development and implementation of a mentor program between the Naval Underwater Defense Center and Linkhorne Middle School. Focused on partnering engineering professionals (serving as volunteers) with student candidates. Charted the program's vision, established objectives, and coordinated schedules.

- Orchestrated training/orientation programs and served as liaison between volunteers and students. Successfully developed opportunities for participants.
- Contributed ongoing motivation and support and served as a mentor to several students.

Editor—Creative Rehab, Newport, RI   1990 to 1992

Edited a quarterly newsletter dedicated to the rehabilitation of spinal cord injury patients. Full responsibility for interviews, story assignments, articles, and editorial content.

BUSINESS EXPERIENCE:

Naval Underwater Defense Center, Newport, RI   1983 to 1997
Data Management Specialist (1990 to 1997)
Configuration Management Specialist (1985 to 1990)
Program Analyst (1983 to 1995)

Earned a series of performance-based promotions with this government affiliate in the defense industry. Scope of responsibility during tenure encompassed database systems management, high-level project planning and management, policy and procedure development, analysis, auditing, configuration management, financial and statistical analysis, quality assurance, training, and team leadership.

RESUME 22: VIVIAN VAN LIER/PHOENIX CAREER GROUP; VALLEY GLEN, CA

PAULA E. LANDER

459 Sherman Oaks Drive
Van Nuys, California 91400

(818) 555-5555
pelander@hotmail.com

MANAGEMENT / ADMINISTRATIVE PROFESSIONAL
Strengths in Project Coordination & Management

Highly motivated, well-organized, and hard-working professional with track record of streamlining systems and procedures to maximize productivity, minimize costs, and directly contribute to organizational goals. Resourceful in meeting challenges and solving problems. Work well under pressure to meet critical deadlines. Possess outstanding written and oral communication skills including correspondence, public speaking, and presentations.

Work well independently as well as collaboratively in a team setting. Get along well with diverse clients and co-workers at all levels. Computer expertise on Macintosh and PC.

Strengths include:
Project Management / Office Administration / Client & Vendor Relations / Hiring, Training & Supervision
Oral & Written Communications / Consensus Building / Conflict Resolution / Research & Analysis
Budget Management / Team Building & Leadership / Meeting & Event Coordination

Program Director — 1996 to 2002
HENDERSONVILLE ROAD PRESBYTERIAN CHURCH, Van Nuys, CA (*1998–2002*)
SOUTHSIDE CHRISTIAN CHURCH, Fresno, CA (*1996–1997, concurrent with full-time studies*)
As a volunteer, coordinated and directed programs and business functions for small congregations.
- Instituted sound business and administrative practices, including introduction of computer technology, to ensure smooth functioning of operations with minimum staffing and budgets.
- Coordinated promotional efforts, including cable TV and radio spots, to increase public awareness of community events. Drew attendance of 1400 over five evenings for special event in small community.
- Established and nurtured partnerships with business community.
- Grew youth-group participation fivefold.
- Produced youth concert that drew record attendance.
- Completed community demographic studies and implemented computerized database to facilitate communications and community outreach efforts.

Partner / General Manager — 1984 to 1994
LANDER & COMPANY, San Francisco, CA
Oversaw day-to-day operations, marketing efforts, and project management for civil engineering firm specializing in "overnight" corporate identity changes for major banking and franchise operations. Supervised cross-functional team of 15 project managers, engineers, and clerical staff.
- Represented company at trade shows throughout the U.S. to generate new business. Developed and delivered comprehensive slide and PowerPoint presentations.
- Generated and analyzed competitive bids from prospective vendors; awarded contracts.
- Surveyed facilities, developed specifications, and planned and managed field work. Multimillion-dollar projects included coordination and implementation of multi-site "overnight" identity changes for 8,000+ BP gasoline stations and 400+ Cracker Barrel restaurants. Other corporate accounts included Bank One, Signet Bank, and Wendy's restaurants.
- Established internal administrative and operating procedures to streamline productivity, minimize costs, and maximize productivity.
- Implemented cutting-edge computer applications.
- Designed and delivered training classes.
- Coordinated meetings and travel arrangements.

Strategy: *Sex-change surgery required time out of the workforce for this candidate. Now that she's ready to return to work, she has refocused her career goal, and her recent volunteer experience becomes all-important.*

PAULA E. LANDER
RÉSUMÉ PAGE TWO

EDUCATION

Master's Degree — SOUTHERN BAPTIST THEOLOGICAL SEMINARY, Fresno, CA
Bachelor of Science (*Civil Engineering*) — UNIVERSITY OF SOUTHERN CALIFORNIA, Los Angeles, CA

Professional Development
Completed Management Course, Owens Graduate School of Management, Vanderbilt University, San Diego, CA
Delivered public presentations and published numerous articles

COMPUTER SKILLS

Proficient on Macintosh and PC Platforms

Hardware
PC, Scanner, Digitizer, Plotter, Digital Camera, PC Presentation, and Projection Equipment

Operating Systems
MS DOS, Windows 9x / 2000

Software Applications
Microsoft Office (Word, Excel, PowerPoint), Corel Office Suite (WordPerfect, Presentations), AutoCAD,
QuickBooks, Lotus 1-2-3; timekeeping, group organization, and mapping software.
Hebrew and Greek language software. Email, Internet.

Other
BASIC Programming, Web Page Design

--- Excellent personal and professional referrals available on request ---

RESUME 23: SUSAN GUARNERI, NCCC, LPC, CCMC, CPRW, CEIP; LAWRENCEVILLE, NJ

Judy Devon Nabors
234 Applegate Court, Basking Ridge, NJ 07920
609-683-5555 Home ▪ jnabors@ixpcom.net

Profile

- ☑ 15 years of administrative, volunteer and team experience in the coordination and implementation of educational, non-profit and community service projects.
- ☑ Quick and eager learner. Proven ability to adapt quickly to a challenge.
- ☑ Demonstrated ability to manage multiple projects simultaneously within deadlines.
- ☑ Outstanding team player with proven record of accomplishments.

Key Skills

Administrative Management
- Increased the visibility of a resale clothing shop, which benefits local charities, while serving as volunteer Store Manager. Raised $80K in 2001–2002, the best year in the history of the shop. On target to surpass sales record in 2002.

Project Management
- Coordinated and solicited 375 auction items (products and services) from northern New Jersey businesses and individuals for the 2000 New Jersey Watershed Fundraising Auction. Managed the acquisition of and arrangements for guest speakers involved in a fundraising six-part lecture series (1999 and 2000).

Leadership
- Spearheaded successful annual fund-solicitation programs as class agent for The Woodbridge Country School from 1997 to 2000, achieving 80% parent participation rate. Chaired fundraising events for The Woodbridge Art Museum and the New Jersey Watershed Association's 2000 Garden Tour.

Interpersonal Skills
- Proven persuasive communication skills. Adept at building and maintaining effective professional relationships. Easily able to win the trust and confidence of diverse individuals. Resolve a wide array of problems, applying diplomacy and assertiveness, while implementing organizational policies and procedures.

Writing & Editing
- For The Woodbridge Country School, wrote successful fundraising solicitation letters that were instrumental in raising $30K–$50K. Wrote weekly community-action newsletters that provided information about zoning, water quality, traffic and business-expansion issues to 300 community residents.

Work History

2000–present	Store Manager / Volunteer, Clothing Resale Shop, Basking Ridge, NJ
1998–2002	Volunteer, Woodbridge Art Museum, Woodbridge, NJ
1996–2000	Volunteer, New Jersey Watershed Association, Woodbridge, NJ
1990–2000	Volunteer, Woodbridge Country School, South Woodbridge, NJ
1998–1999	Chairperson, Applegate Neighborhood Assoc., Basking Ridge, NJ

Education

Bachelor of Arts — History, cum laude, University of Iowa, Waterloo, IA
Master's Degree Program — History (28 credits), Southern University, Atlanta, GA
2001 Introduction to Computing, Rutgers University, New Brunswick, NJ

Strategy: *An "empty nester," this job seeker used functional headings in the Key Skills section to prove her diverse skills.*

RESUME 24: LOUISE GARVER, CPRW, JCTC, CMP, CEIP; ENFIELD, CT

MARILYN NOLAN
22 Meadow Lane, Chicago, IL 89900
(555) 222-1111
MNolan@media.net

■ **PROFILE**

Conferences · Fund-Raising · Trade Shows · Meeting Planning · Cultural Programs

Creative professional with expertise in all aspects of successful event/program planning, development and management. Excel in managing multiple projects concurrently with strong detail, problem solving and follow-through. Demonstrated ability to recruit, motivate and build cohesive teams. Sourced vendors, negotiated contracts and managed project budgets. Superb written communications, interpersonal and presentation skills.

■ **SELECTED ACCOMPLISHMENTS**

Special Events Management:

Planned and coordinated conferences, meetings and events for companies, professional associations, arts/cultural, and other organizations. Developed program content and administered budgets. Arranged all on-site logistics, including transportation, accommodations, meals, guest speakers and entertainers, and audiovisual support. Coordinated participation and represented companies at industry trade shows. Recognized for creating and planning some of the most successful events ever held statewide.

♦ **Created cultural events for an arts organization that boosted membership enrollment.**
♦ **Organized 5 well-attended conferences for 2 national professional associations.**
♦ **Designed successful community educational campaigns promoting safety awareness.**

Fund-raising & Public Relations:

Created, planned and managed all aspects of several major fund-raising campaigns resulting in a significant increase in contributions raised for each function over prior years. Recruited volunteers and developed corporate sponsorships. Generated extensive media coverage through effective promotional and public relations strategies. Created newsletters distributed to employees, customers and others.

♦ **Co-chaired capital fund campaign raising $3.5 million for new facility.**
♦ **Coordinated 3 auctions raising over $140,000 for an educational institution.**
♦ **Initiated successful publication generating $25,000 to finance community programs.**

Sales & Marketing:

Selected by management to spearhead opening of regional office, including all logistics, staff relocation and business development efforts. Designed and implemented creative sales and marketing strategies to capitalize on consumer trends and penetrate new market. Coordinated and conducted sales training.

♦ **Developed and managed 17 key accounts generating $10 million annually.**
♦ **Recognized for managing top revenue-generating program company-wide.**
♦ **Consistently exceeded sales forecast and led region to rank #1 out of 6 in profitability nationwide.**

■ **EXPERIENCE**

Event/Program Coordinator (Volunteer), ARTS COUNCIL, BOTANICAL GARDENS & CULTURE EXCHANGE, Chicago, IL (1998--present).

Promoted from **Regional Manager, Account Executive** and **Financial Underwriter**, MARCON FINANCIAL SERVICES COMPANY, Chicago, IL (1988–2000).

■ **EDUCATION**

B.A. in Business Administration, Springfield College, Springfield, MA

Strategy: *When a layoff called a halt to this candidate's career, she focused on volunteer activities that became the basis for her new career.*

DAVID E. BRUCE

SALES MANAGEMENT / RETAIL OPERATIONS

Manager with high integrity always eager to produce high-quality work.

PROFESSIONAL PROFILE

- Excellent leadership skills combined with an ability to motivate others while delivering projects on time.
- Highly effective communication and interpersonal skills; ability to work with diverse personalities both internal and external.
- Outstanding abilities in problem identification, resolution, and follow-through. Talent for troubleshooting and making maximum use of available resources.

QUALIFICATIONS

- Two years' management experience with focus in the entertainment industry.
- Managed and directed all phases of daily business operations including hiring, training, staff supervision, scheduling, payroll, and maintenance.
- Coordinated company events from fruition to completion.
- Skilled in all areas of personnel management.
- Extensive background in customer service.
- Proficient operation of basic computer programs.

KEY MANAGEMENT SKILLS

• Customer Service	• Office Management	• Budget Analysis
• Sales	• Document Management	• Project Management
• Merchandising	• Staff Development	• Presentations
• Bookkeeping	• Training	• Public Speaking

PROFESSIONAL EXPERIENCE

Lazer Zone, Inc., Balboa, CA   1996–1998
GENERAL MANAGER / PARTNER

Balboa Fun Zone, Inc., Balboa, CA   1995–1998
RIDE OPERATOR

Equitable Insurance Company (Cindy Coumjian, C.F.P.)   1995–1996
PERSONAL ASSISTANT

OTHER EXPERIENCE

The Church of Jesus Christ of Latter Day Saints, Salt Lake City, UT   1998–2000
MISSIONARY, ASSISTANT TO THE MISSIONARY PRESIDENT
- Earned the Master Teacher award.

1864 Stratford Avenue, Salt Lake City, UT 84103 • Mobile Phone: 801-505-5697

Strategy: *A functional format highlights qualifications that relate to this candidate's recent experience as a volunteer missionary.*

RESUME 26: JOHN O'CONNOR, CRW, CPRW, MFA; RALEIGH, NC

LUCY WONG

IT TESTING / TECHNOLOGY MANAGEMENT / TECHNICAL SUPPORT

IT Management

Quality Control

Electronics Testing

Maintenance

Troubleshooting

End-User Support

Sybase

Oracle

Enterprise

Customer Service

Desktop Support

Installations

Conversions

MS Visual Basic

C, C++

SQL

Enterprise

MS Office

Fortran

Pascal

Assembler

Foreign Languages:
Chinese, French

PROFILE OF TRANSFERABLE SKILLS

- *Strong training and transferable skills; returning to the workforce after missions trips to China, Taiwan and Cambodia; during this time continued some self-study in technology and software.*
- *Professional skills include strong educational training in mechanical maintenance with professional experience in the technology field.*
- *Able to conceive and develop new methods that expedite troubleshooting processes and reduce costs.*
- *Have demonstrated ability to accept diverse responsibility; understand the need to communicate and promote communications with those associated with competitive developmental technology/ electronics environment.*
- *Able to troubleshoot electrical and complex mechanical systems in addition to utilizing mechanical engineering training/skills.*
- *Continuous working experiences with all levels of decision-makers, from the worker in the field to the functional department head to the upper- management level.*

PROFESSIONAL WORK HISTORY

RMX TELECOM, Sanford, NC
IT & Database Support Technician (1991 to 1997)
- Provided extensive coaching and development of the testing system to support maintenance, sales and other administrative areas of the company. Experience base in this area totals nearly three years of dedicated network/software support management from 1994 to 1997.
- Provided environment for testing of new software and hardware installations as well as network troubleshooting and security testing.
- Helped oversee design and implementation of enterprise-wide business workstation builds.
- Planned and deployed build of various programs.
- Assisted in inventory management and tracking functions for the company.
- Controlled inventory through critical data analysis, accurate data entry, procedural tracking, and development of enterprise-wide inventory system.
- Consulted with customers on purchase and investment decisions regarding network choices and new systems.
- Resolved security problems during migrations and changes as well as unexpected shutdowns.

SYLEX, INC., Cary, NC
Computer Support Specialist II (1988 – 1990)
Computer Technician — Co-op (1986 – 1988)
- Assisted in inventory management and tracking functions.
- Consulted with customers regarding network choices and new systems from the ground up.
- Resolved security problems.

EDUCATION

NORTH CAROLINA STATE UNIVERSITY, Raleigh, NC; *Master of Science in Computer Engineering (January 1985)*
BOSTON COLLEGE, Boston, MA; *Bachelor of Science in Computer Technology (May 1982)*

| 6789 BrightLeaf Court Apex, North Carolina 27601 | lwwong@intercon.net | Home: (919) 786-4467 Mobile: (919) 276-8257 |

Strategy: *A brief explanation of mission work is included in the Profile to explain a five-year absence from the workforce, but overall the resume focuses on professional skills from her prior experience.*

CHAPTER 7

Resumes for People Returning to Work After Serving as a Caregiver

Tending to aging parents, disabled children, or others who need full-time care requires an absence from the workforce for many. When returning to work, the challenge is to not get "derailed" by focusing on the period of absence; instead, your resume should emphasize relevant skills and experience related to the job target.

RESUME 27: ROLANDE LaPOINTE, CPC, CIPC, CPRW, IJCTC, CCM; LEWISTON, ME

CONNIE A. YOUNG

79 Court Street
Turner, Maine 04282

Telephone: (207) 999-3862   Email: Younger@aol.com

CAREER PROFILE

Exceptional Customer Service Representative with extensive experience in retail and real-estate sales, service, and related support functions. Skilled at managing multiple departments and staff. Experienced buyer having worked with extensive clothing lines and accessories for men, women, and children. Successful real-estate sales individual with the ability to follow through while applying a keen attention to detail. Willing to put to use transferable skills in most any interesting and challenging position and business environment.

TRANSFERABLE SKILLS

- Proven skills in sales and customer service; strong attention to detail.
- Effective business manager and staff trainer/supervisor.
- Thorough knowledge of retail clothing buying, marketing, and sales.
- Earned credentials for real estate sales in the State of Maine.
- Knowledgeable in varied clerical functions and office procedures.

WORK ETHICS

- Dependable, loyal, and punctual.
- Ability to accept responsibility while consistently meeting deadlines.
- Experienced in handling and working with large amounts of cash.
- Unblemished personal and professional work history.
- Previously screened, cleared, and employed by the Federal Government.

WORK EXPERIENCE

Century 21 Realty & Peterson Realty (Portland, Maine)   **1987–1999**
Licensed Sales Agent

Cortell's (Brunswick, Maine)   **1975–1986**
Buyer/Department Manager
  <u>Hired as a Salesperson</u> in the Children and Infants Department. After four months, was promoted to Buyer/Department Manager with varied responsibilities including personnel management, accurate record-keeping of merchandise ordered and received, and department display setup. Made frequent buying trips to the New York and Boston markets. Demonstrated efficient merchandise management, inventory control, and merchandise history-keeping skills.

(Continued on Page 2)

Strategy: *To support multiple job targets for this "flexible" job seeker, transferable skills and personal attributes are highlighted.*

CONNIE A. YOUNG   Résumé (Page 2 of 2)

WORK EXPERIENCE (continued)

Senter's (Brunswick, ME)   1975–1986
Buyer/Department Manager

Promoted to Buyer/Department Manager Sportswear and Accessory Departments
(1977), then the management of the Petite Sportswear Department was also added
(1980).

Functioned as Fashion Coordinator (simultaneously), with responsibility for the
organization of fashion shows including selection of models and merchandise, writing
commentary, preparing advertising, and coordinating all aspects of the show.

Organized special events such as the annual Town Hall Tent Sale, the Store
Anniversary Sale, and other special promotions as needed.

Promoted to Floor Manager (1985) responsible for overseeing the entire store with
regard to employee job performance and other general management issues and
problems. Involved in management policy decisions.

Personal Services (Brunswick, ME)   1973–1975
Naval Air Station

Worked as a Personal Services Coordinator. Started out as a Volunteer beginning with
a few hours per week; eventually became the Personal Services Coordinator working
forty hours per week. Position involved complex and varied duties including answering
the telephone, keeping cash records, operating and managing a rental service (household
items), and making babysitting arrangements. Also involved in varied crisis and
emergency situations.

Federal Bureau of Investigation (Washington, DC)   1971–1973
Identification Division

Classified and researched fingerprints sent to the Bureau for identification.

EDUCATION

- Completed requirements for Real Estate Sales & Licensing — State of Maine.
  (Served as Chair for the Portland, Maine, Real Estate Board.)
- Completed extensive training in Retail Sales, Service, Management & Merchandising.
- Attended American Airline Institute (Minneapolis, Minnesota) — Completed one year.
- Freeport Area High School (Freeport, Maine) — Diploma, Cum Laude.

References Available Upon Request

Tony Romero

87 Maple Street   (617) 555–5555
Watertown, MA 02492   tromero@abc.com

Qualifications

♦ Successful record working with children/adolescents with severe special needs.
♦ Strong behavioral management background.
♦ Positive and encouraging attitude, combined with consistent, patient manner.
♦ Experience managing complex cases.
♦ Effective working independently and as a member of a team.
♦ Ability to coordinate services with multiple care providers and agencies.

Relevant Experience

BOSTON CHILDREN'S CENTER, Boston, MA, 1983–1988

Teacher II (1984–1988)
Teacher I (1983–1984)

• Provided case management for special-needs children ages 11-19; assigned two of the more complicated cases, requiring coordination with multiple agencies and professionals.
• Coached and instructed children and adolescents in activities of daily living, behavior management, and academic and vocational skills, according to needs of each child.
• Wrote individualized educational plans and student behavior plans that resulted in measurable behavioral improvements.
• Consulted with other professionals to develop and implement effective strategies.
• Collaborated with speech/language specialist to develop communication books designed for non-communicating children.
• Trained new staff in standard procedures for the care of autistic children.
• Communicated with parents on a regular basis to inform them of their children's progress, and instructed parents on effective techniques for working with their children.
• Offered management position but elected to continue in a case management and direct teaching role.

Other Experience

MARIO'S RESTAURANT, Boston, MA, 1988–1997

Manager

• Trained, supervised, and scheduled employees, ensuring high employee morale.
• Greeted guests and maintained friendly atmosphere, which generated repeat business.

Education

Boston University — Enrolled in Bachelor's Program in Psychology, 1980–1984

Strategy: *Most recent experience is placed last because it does not support the current job target for this individual. This candidate gained extensive at-home experience caring for sick children to supplement his prior professional teaching experience.*

RESUME 29: FREDDIE CHEEK, M.S.ED., CPRW, CWDP, CRW; AMHERST, NY

WILLIAM F. GROSSMAN

19 Conway Avenue
Spokane, Washington 99217
(509) 732-9238

CUSTOMER SERVICE
Staff Training / Employee Supervision / Sales Support

Professional Profile

Mature worker with a solid work history that shows reliability, responsibility, and high-quality performance. Team member with an interest in learning and applying new skills. Strengths include customer support and staff training with demonstrated attention to detail, efficiency, and productivity. Recent computer training.

Core Skills:
Customer Interface ... Sales / Marketing ... Communication ... Employee Relations .... Banking ...
Purchasing ... Auditing ... Supervision ... Customer Satisfaction ... Human Services ... Quality / Cost Control

Summary:
- Assisted individuals with accessing medical, insurance, and legal services, including Medicaid.
- Performed a wide range of human resource functions, including recruiting, interviewing, hiring, training, motivating, and evaluating employees.
- Supervised sales, customer service, cashier, maintenance, food service, stock, and office personnel.
- Handled purchasing, security, marketing, and merchandising, and secured licenses and permits.
- Conveyed a friendly, helpful, and positive attitude to customers and co-workers.
- Developed reliable and profitable relationships with vendors.
- Interacted effectively with people of all ages and backgrounds.

Experience

Family Caregiver Spokane, Washington (1985–2002)

Manager York Steak House, Atlanta, Georgia, and Orlando, Florida (1975–1985)

Area Supervisor Quickie Food Marts, Atlanta, Georgia (1974–1975)

Insurance Adjuster Seligman & Co., Lynbrook, New York (1974)

Field Representative Southland Corp., Valley Stream and Westchester, New York (1970–1974)

Education

Adelphi University, Garden City, New York
B.S. in Business, 1970
Major: Industrial Relations

Computer Training:
Spokane Employment and Training Center, Spokane, Washington
    Microsoft Office, 2002
West Valley Continuing Education, West Valley, Washington
    Introduction to Computers, 2001

References

Furnished upon request.

Strategy: *Returning to work after 16 years caring for three elderly relatives, this individual wanted a low-stress, regular-hours job that would allow him to effectively manage his diabetes. Early career success is downplayed so that he will not appear overqualified for the jobs he's seeking now.*

RESUME 30: SUSAN GUARNERI; NCCC, LPC, CCMC, CPRW, CEIP; LAWRENCEVILLE, NJ

Sarah Maxwell Turner, RN
7333 Sugarhill Lane, Princeton, NJ 08540
(609) 683-5555 Home ▪ smturn@netcom.com

PROFILE

Registered Nurse ▪ **Case Manager** ▪ **Medical Auditor** with clinical / auditing experience, including medical treatment documentation reviews, DRGs, CPT coding, and ICD-9-CM coding. Knowledgeable of the disease process, findings, course of treatment, quality assurance, and risk management. Demonstrated track record in:

✓ Medical Records Auditing	✓ Practice Compliance Auditing	✓ Medical Bill Auditing
✓ Practice Site Reviews	✓ Managed Care Case Management	✓ HEDIS Assessment
✓ Medicaid Auditing	✓ Field Utilization Review	✓ Electronic Chart Review

Background in managed care protocol and case management for catastrophic trauma, soft tissue damage, and orthopedic injuries. Recent case management professional development. Skilled in M&R guidelines, as well as new hire orientations. Proven ability to interact effectively with healthcare and office staff professionals.

PROFESSIONAL EXPERIENCE

HEALTHCARE SOLUTIONS, INC. (healthcare accreditation firm), Ewing, NJ   1997–2000

Nurse Reviewer
Field position with multiple long- and short-term assignments. Audited, examined, and verified medical records and monitored practice sites to ensure documentation accuracy and compliance with standard medical practices and criteria. Conducted 15–18 on-site appointments weekly at medical clinics, hospitals, health plans, and physicians' offices. Reviewed 40–70 charts daily. Completed 3–4 practice site reviews daily.

- **Capital Health Plan.** Performed HEDIS effectiveness of care audits, Medicaid audits, and Healthy Start Program and follow-up visit tracking. Practice compliance audits involved medical record reviews for specific disease conditions and/or routine care, including diabetes blood work, asthma management, immunizations, OB-GYN well visits, and OB care.

- **Americaid.** Conducted medical record documentation reviews and practice site reviews for medical standards and credentialing purposes.

- **National Medical Accreditation Program (NMAP)** — Illinois foundation for medical care information system. Managed data collection for the New York Medical Society. Performed medical-record review and site assessment to determine clinical performance based on set standards and criteria.

AMERICAN INSURANCE COMPANY, Trenton, NJ   1987–1997

Out-of-Network Utilization Review Specialist — American Healthcare, Ewing, NJ (1996–1997)

- Identified and implemented appropriate level of care based on health insurance policy provisions and medical need. Scope of authority included pre-authorization, review, and discharge planning.

- Monitored for quality of care based on ethical and medical standards and criteria, as well as timeliness and cost effectiveness. Ensured compliance with federal, state, and industry medical-management regulations. Utilized computer-based records-management procedures for documenting and retrieving clinical data.

Page 1 of 2

Strategy: Lead with a strong profile, laden with key words to show her level of experience and expertise. Mention recent professional development to show recent career-related activity. Because there is only a two-year employment gap, continue with a traditional chronological format.

Sarah Maxwell Turner, RN
(609) 683-5555 Home ▪ smturn@netcom.com   Page 2

PROFESSIONAL EXPERIENCE

Field Concurrent Review Nurse — American Healthcare, New York, NY (1993–1996)

- Performed on-site concurrent chart reviews for in-patient populations at area teaching medical centers, investigating medical status, appropriateness of stay, and quality of care.

- Monitored clinical outcomes and consulted with network physicians and medical director for case management review, ensuring timely delivery of optimum-level patient care.

- Proactively addressed network gaps by researching and recruiting specialty physicians and facilities to provide continuum of care within the network.

- Effectively balanced patients' medical needs with health plan benefits to appropriately implement discharge planning to home or alternate-level setting.

Rehabilitation Coordinator — Property & Casualty Insurance Division, Trenton, NJ (1987–1993)

- Designed and delivered field case management within the Personal Injury Protection (PIP) unit. Caseload consistently averaged 40–55 catastrophic and/or traumatic personal injury cases. Coordinated client benefits between American Insurance and the State of New Jersey.

- Audited medical bills and hospital charts, evaluating coding and reviewing all related medical treatment documentation. Negotiated and resolved discrepancies.

- Monitored cases from initial medical assessment through ultimate disposition, coordinating healthcare at all levels in compliance with the New Jersey No-Fault statute.

- Received American's **Annual Customer Service and Leadership Award** in 1993.

NATIONAL REHABILITATION CONSULTANTS, INC., Princeton, NJ   1983–1987
Insurance Rehabilitation Specialist. Consultant for NJ-based insurance companies. Case managed traumatic injury cases from initial assessment through resolution, addressing all medical, legal, and financial issues.

WEST WINDSOR HOSPITAL, West Windsor, NJ   1981–1983
Staff Nurse – Medical / Surgical and Orthopedic Units.

EDUCATION

Diploma — Nursing, Mid-Atlantic School of Nursing, Newark, NJ
University of Pennsylvania — College of Nursing, Continuing Education Certificates:
The Nurse as Case Manager (65 contact hours), 2002; RN Re-Entry into Practice (180 contact hours), 2001
Professional development (clinical experience and seminars) in healthcare delivery practices.

CERTIFICATIONS

Registered Nurse — New Jersey (License # 12345)
Certified Case Manager — 1993 (Certification # 56789)

RESUME 31: LAURA DECARLO, CCM, CPRW, JCTC, CECC, CCMC, CRW; MELBOURNE, FL

KAREN C. LANEY

555 Casey Key Road
Sarasota Springs, FL 34236
(941) 957-0836
KCL@hotmail.com

ADMINISTRATIVE PROFESSIONAL

Management / Training / Sales & Business Development

- Extensive background in training and education, working with adults, elementary education and developmentally disabled.
- Vibrant and expansive communication style with ability to build rapport with anyone; skilled in public relations, staff development and as a company rep.
- Comfortable with bottom-line responsibilities such as setting goals and directing teams to accomplish those goals. Extremely intuitive problem solver.
- Talented salesperson with awards for outstanding performance.

PROFESSIONAL EXPERIENCE

Home Care to Family Members, Sarasota Springs, FL, 1996–Present
Director of Recruitment, Osler Employment Services, Tampa, FL, 1991–1995
Resident Assistant, Christian Academy of Women, Tampa, FL, 1988–1990
Sales Manager, Amodeo Marketing, West Palm Beach, FL, 1986–1988
Third Grade / Special Ed. Teacher, Garden Elementary, Sarasota, FL, 1982–1985

Management & Business Development
- Hired and trained all recruiters at Osler, setting goals and encouraging high performance levels through team building and motivational techniques.
  – Developed recruitment programs, achieving quotas and winning company sales competitions.
- Performed business development for advertising sales through Amodeo Marketing for a new Florida territory encompassing South Florida.
  – Handled recruitment, hiring and training of staff.
  – Performed administrative detail involving money collection, banking and record keeping.

Troubleshooting & Streamlining
- Troubleshot recruitment problems at Osler locations throughout Florida, increasing enrollments in stagnating locations.
- Designed training manuals and implemented new policies and procedures at Amodeo and Osler.

Communications & Teaching
- Managed a multi-cultural dormitory of young ladies as Resident Assistant, monitoring behavior, accompanying on field trips, providing private counseling and resolving conflicts.
- Taught math, reading comprehension, language arts, writing and other core subjects to third-grade students at Garden Elementary.
- Worked closely to assist children with special-education needs in taking steps toward self-sufficiency and literacy at Garden Elementary.

EDUCATION & AFFILIATIONS

B.S. in Adult Education, University of South Florida, Tampa, FL; GPA: 3.7

Member, Adult Literacy Abroad Program

Strategy: *"Home care to family members" is listed in the Professional Experience section to provide an explanation for the gap in employment. A focused summary and extensive functional skills list communicate key areas of strength.*

CHAPTER **8**

Resumes for People Returning to Work After Illness

Physical and/or emotional problems may cause an extended absence from work and may dictate a change in professions once the individual is ready to return. It's important not to let the recent absence or any disabilities overshadow real qualifications. Any need for accommodation can be discussed in the interview.

ADELE S. NELSON

423 Frost Boulevard, #4	Spokane, Washington 99203
(509) 437-6534	asnelson@hotmail.com

COMPUTER PROFESSIONAL
Database Specialist / Web Site Developer / Software Designer

Professional Profile:

Creative database manager and website administrator with superior microcomputer training and hands-on programming experience. Skilled in training users on new and enhanced technology. Able to interface with customers, identify their business needs, and develop computer systems and applications to fulfill those requirements.

Core Skills:
Database Development ... Computer Graphics ... Electronic Spreadsheets ... Desktop Publishing ... Search Engine Management ... Programming ... Software Development ... Electronic Presentations

Computer Proficiencies:

Advanced Access 2000	FrontPage 2000	Crystal Reports 6.0
Publisher 2000	Visio 2000	Quicken 2000
PowerPoint 2000	Advanced Excel 2000	Internet Explorer
Programming with Access, FORTRAN and Ingres (Embedded SQL)		

Education:

Spokane University, School of Information Technology, Spokane, Washington
Certificate in Access Database Specialist, 2001
Certificate in Advanced Word 2000, 2001
Certificate in Word Processing Specialist, 2001
Certificate in Microcomputer Applications Specialist, 2000

Spokane University, Spokane, Washington
Bachelor of Arts – Mathematics, 1981

Experience:

Hillyard Square Community Center, Spokane, Washington   1998–2000
Part-Time Tutor
Provided remedial tutoring to individuals and groups to reinforce academic skills.
• Assisted students in improving classroom performance.

Schenker Manufacturing Contracting, Inc., Seattle, Washington   1992–1997
Associate Engineer
Assisted senior management and engineers with proposal development and packaging for local and international clients. Performed market research, estimated definitive costs, and prepared chemical process plant contracts. Worked with vendors and engineers in procuring and inspecting equipment and raw materials.
• Made significant contributions to company's being awarded major contracts.
• Negotiated rates and enabled company to benefit from price breaks and discounts.

Strategy: *Support a career shift (from aerospace engineer to database manager/Web-site designer) by highlighting extensive computer knowledge and training and then using employment experience to show technical expertise and business savvy.*

Adele S. Nelson   **Page Two**

Boeing Aircraft Company, Seattle, Washington   1984–1990
Software Engineer
Participated in software design, development, and testing of three major applications: Off-Line Data Reduction (OLDR), Track History (TH), and Radar Control Systems. Designed, documented, coded, tested, and maintained various scientific software applications. Utilized FORTRAN and Ingres on DEC VAX/VMS network.

Martin Marietta Aerospace Company, Sunnyvale, California   1982–1984
Associate Engineer
Designed and documented a software application which performed data analysis from experimental laser weapon system.

References:

Furnished upon request.

Charlotte L. Cast

(712) 835-5585 171 Farm Road, Sioux City, IA 51104 clcast@comcast.com

MANAGEMENT PROFESSIONAL

- 12 years of successful administration, supervision, and management experience.
- Caring, resourceful, flexible, practical, and self-motivated professional. Strive to improve upon processes and tasks.
- Strong interpersonal and communication skills.
- Consistent pattern of realizing profits and surpassing projections.
- Strengths in delegation, organization, long-range strategic planning, and project implementation.

EDUCATION

University of Iowa, Iowa City, IA
POST GRADUATE STUDIES (3.6 GPA)
- Interdisciplinary Studies including Performing Arts.
- Received outstanding commendation for submitted work.
- Self-supporting while attending graduate school.

BACHELOR OF ARTS, BIOLOGY

WORK HISTORY

CONTRACTED TOURISM MANAGER   R. J. HOULE TOURISM INFORMATION CENTER, Sioux City, IA
- Contracted to update, upgrade, and operate the facility.
- Surveyed major tourism businesses to assess needs.
- Addressed Chamber of Commerce with goal of stimulating interest for meeting future tourists' needs.
- Assisted visitors with information regarding sites and accommodations in area. Hired staff.

ON-SITE PROJECT MANAGER   DAKOTA COUNTY FINANCIAL HOUSING CORPORATION, Sioux City, IA
- Rented, set policy, and managed new apartment complex for profit and non-profit ownership. Adhered to strict government guidelines.
- Hired and supervised staff of 5.
- Successfully negotiated terms that led the corporation out of harmful litigation.

WEEKEND MANAGER   SIOUX CITY SCIENCE MUSEUM, Sioux City, IA
- Managed "Trading Post," an educational learning center for children and adults. Accompanied adult field trips.

ASSOCIATE DEAN OF STUDENTS/ HOUSING DIRECTOR   MIDWEST COLLEGE OF ART & DESIGN, St. Paul, MN
- Assisted Dean with student affairs such as Foreign Student advisement, and sex and drug abuse workshops.
- Prepared $130,000 housing operation budget.
- Supervised staff of 16.
- Made room assignments and determined rents.

WRITER/EDITOR   CEDAR RIVERSIDE PROJECT AREA COMMITTEE (PAC), Minneapolis, MN
- Produced and edited newspaper for large community.
- Ensured residents received all information regarding government guidelines and rights in this major housing rehabilitation project.
- Performed marketing survey.

GROUP SALES MANAGER   THE GUTHRIE THEATRE, Minneapolis, MN
- Promoted to this position after one season as sales associate.

COMPUTER KNOWLEDGE

- Microsoft Word and WordPerfect for Macintosh and Windows.

Strategy: *To disguise a sporadic work history followed by ten years of unemployment, dates were omitted entirely.*

CAMERON WOLFGANG, AIA

10747 Longview Cir.
El Paso, TX 79924
Phone: (915) 555-6906
Cellular: (915) 555-4192
architectforyou@aol.com

Home Designed by Cameron Wolfgang

ARCHITECT
Member of The American Institute of Architects

CUSTOM RESIDENTIAL DESIGN
NEW HOMES • REMODELING • SPACE PLANNING

"Committed to Architectural Design Excellence for More than 18 Years"

PROFESSIONAL OVERVIEW

Creative and accomplished Architect with 18+ years experience, an excellent reputation, and a solid and *verifiable record of achievement,* gaining the trust and confidence of many of Dallas' top building contractors. Recognized for the ability to *turn a dream into a reality.* Not only involved with the design stage of a project, but *hands-on* involvement in actual construction through final completion.

Profile of Strengths:

- **Unique, imaginative, and livable/comfortable floor plans** tailored to the needs of each client. Designs provide for the maximum use of space, and create total environments that are functional and exciting places in which to live.
- **Strong management skills,** including strategic planning, project development and scheduling, problem solving, client relations, and quality control. Reduce building costs, improve energy efficiencies, and increase future value through good design.
- **Seasoned sales and marketing skills.** Demonstrated ability to gain trust and confidence of both builders and clients.
- **Expertise in managing major/minor project renovations.**
- **Solid design and construction experience in commercial projects** in addition to residential expertise.

PROFESSIONAL EXPERIENCE

Owner/ Architect
THE CJW DESIGN GROUP, Dallas, Texas

Architectural design company specializing in residential homes ranging in price from $250K to $3 million with up to 5000 sq. ft. Established a **regional reputation** for excellence and developed a loyal following with several of the top builders in North Dallas, to include:

- Monroe Custom Homes
- A. E. Homes
- Montwood Homes

EDUCATION

Bachelor of Environmental Design in Architecture
School of Architecture & Design, Dallas, Texas

Strategy: *After a prolonged illness, this architect wanted to return to work in a staff position rather than as a business owner. Dates are omitted, and the architectural graphic is an appropriate attention-getter.*

Frank J. Dawson

125 E. Willis Road
Bayview, FL 32405
(850) 829-6275 ▪ surfn1@aol.com

> *"Chief Dawson is a talented, tireless dynamo I count on for flawless assistance, advice, and products...he's first class all the way!"* — 1996 Performance Evaluation

Management Profile

High-energy, results-driven professional offering illustrious military career reflecting continuous contribution and achievement backed by diverse leadership roles in the private sector. Dynamic problem-solver able to innovate compelling, win-win solutions to complex situations. Exceptional relationship building skills, fostering unified teams and cohesion across all levels of staff, management, and customers. Core areas of expertise encompass:

- Vision & Mission Planning	- Business Administration	- Strategic Problem Solving
- Training & Development	- Change Management	- Human Resources
- Project Lifecycle Management	- High-Impact Presentations	- Operations Management
- Budget Control	- Sales & Marketing	- Team Building & Leadership

Value Offered

Strategic Administration / Operations Management: Top management authority for all aspects of marketing, sales, delivery, and administration. Oversaw inventory display and control, facility management, supplies and equipment, safety, database maintenance, work schedules, and customer service. Military budget, resources, and quality management advisor.

Results-Focused Project/Program Management: Linchpin in base quality improvement programs. Managed Pacific Air Force's complaint program at all levels on nine bases throughout region. Devised new program to ensure equitable tasking, successfully eliminating assignment complaints. Catalyst in success of intramural program and numerous fundraising projects.

Bridging Gaps Through Communication & Relationship Building: Interviewed custodial parents to gather data for child support cases and coordinated with diverse legal and government factions in support of payment orders. Cultivated relationships with prospective customers; served as point-of-contact for existing accounts. Negotiated contracts to close sales. Strengthened communications between commander and squadron members.

Proactive Human Resources: Supervised operations of 70-person personnel office providing support to more than 6,400 military personnel assigned to 122 organizations in 25 locations. Interviewed, hired, and trained new employees. Oversaw morale, welfare, and discipline of Air Force population. Key participant in formulating policy and direct management of various training and personnel services.

Professional Overview

Dynamic 15+-year career, demonstrating excellence in diverse areas of business, operations, relationship building, and personnel management with broad-based roles including:

Series of **progressive leadership positions in the U.S. Air Force.**

Assistant Operations Manager / Human Resource & Training Manager for Target.

Sales Consultant for DeGeorge Home Alliance and Paradise Homes & Development Corporation.

Business Manager for QuickService Delivery.

Revenue Specialist II for the Texas State Department of Revenue / Child Support Enforcement.

Strategy: *To help this veteran, who had been out of the workforce due to mental illness, emphasize "value offered" and support key qualifications with great quotes and recommendations. Eliminate dates.*

Frank J. Dawson
Page 2

Highlights of Professional Achievements

- Superbly coordinated division's quarterly video teleconference training program.

- Authored 7-page complaint processing checklist to better assist field inspector generals; resulted in new management tool to ensure 100% accountability from complaint intake to final response.

- Flawlessly managed office during 75% turnover in personnel with no service degradation.

- Pumped new life into weak in-house training program; designed forms for work centers to serve as documentation and set up impressive continuity book in critical short-tour environment.

- Orchestrated administrative support of squadron by personally editing and finalizing all reports, studies, and correspondence, leading squadron to "excellent" rating from inspection team.

- Guided personnel programs through difficult period of rollbacks, early outs, and new evaluation programs with zero degradation in missions.

- Directly responsible for achieving 124% of goal for blood drive project, collecting 30% of entire amount from Bay County, Florida.

- Achieved success in managing personnel requirements for 26,000-man joint exercise associated with cleanup of largest oil spill in Alaskan history.

- Selected to breathe new life into Commander's Youth Relations Program, effecting immediate results in such programs as Boy Scouts of America and Civil Air Patrol.

- Applied dynamic leadership to overcome tough budget and personnel shortfall issues.

- Took unsatisfactorily rated unit-retention program and turned around to satisfactory status by resolving discrepancies within 90 days.

- Persuaded Air Force to cancel 15% reduction in command training quotas, accomplishing what no other command was able to do.

Character References

"The best of the best! A hands-on, self-motivated complaints specialist who provides blue-ribbon service...Always willing to pitch in and help get the job done...a team player extraordinaire..."
— 1995 Performance Evaluation

"A superb leader and role model for all...Totally dedicated leadership is his strong suit." — 1994 Performance Evaluation

"Dynamic senior NCO who comes through every time, on time." — 1994 Performance Evaluation

"An exceptional leader...He inspires achievement." – 1992 Performance Evaluation

"He is a standout performer with unlimited potential." — 1991 Performance Evaluation

"He's our Personnel Superintendent of the Year because he's the best there is!" — 1989 Performance Evaluation

"His ability to foresee potential problems and react quickly to short-notice changes in schedules made the entire trip a complete success." — 1985 Performance Evaluation

RESUME 36: LAURA DECARLO, CCM, CECC, CCMC, CRW; MELBOURNE, FL

TERENCE P. MORGAN

356 Portland Road   (877) 675-9330
Sacramento, CA 95814   morgan1@sca.rr.com

QUALITY ASSURANCE ~ QUALITY INSPECTION

Multi-faceted quality professional with over 20 years of expertise in Quality Assurance and Inspection. Experience inspecting hi-reliability mechanical parts with dimensional tolerances as low as five hundred thousandths of an inch.

Developed and implemented quality procedures for improving operations and introducing state-of-the-art inspection equipment.

- MIL-STDs, DoD & ISO 9000 Standards
- Quality Audits
- In-Process Inspection
- Test Management
- Pre-Award Surveys
- First Article Inspection
- Final Inspection
- Team Leadership

PROFESSIONAL EXPERIENCE

Providing expertise in Quality Assurance / Quality Inspection in positions including:

- **Quality Assurance Associate / Senior Quality Inspector,** Artigon Corporation - 10 years
- **Quality Assurance Manager,** Tangent Corporation - 3 years
- **Quality Systems Analyst,** United States Air Force - 14 years

ARTIGON CORPORATION
- **Inspections & Surveys:** Traveled to various vendors to ensure product quality standards were consistently being maintained by identifying defects in product, procedures, standards or design.
  - Performed pre-award surveys, quality audits, first article inspection, in-process and final inspections.

- **Hi-Reliability Inspection:** Worked within the plant, inspecting hi-reliability mechanical parts with dimensional tolerances as low as five hundred thousandths of an inch.

TANGENT CORPORATION
- **Standards:** Ensured that the quality program met Military Standards (MILSTD).

- **Inspections:** Performed inspection of machine and plated parts for quality requirements.

- **Process Improvement:** Updated company inspection equipment to state-of-the-art status.

U.S. AIR FORCE
- **Testing:** Conducted tests for numerous U.S. Air Force launches as a Quality Systems Analyst.

- **Quality Program Development:** Selected as 1 of 10 Air Force personnel to be assigned to the Department of Defense (DoD) to establish a procurement quality program: DCAS.

EDUCATION & TRAINING

- Presently pursuing **ASQ Self-Directed Learning Program** and Self-study of **ISO 9000 & ISO 9002.**
- **Credits toward Bachelor of Science Degree,** University of South California.
- **Technology Engineering Program** and **Quality Systems Analysis,** U.S. Air Force.

EMPLOYMENT TIMELINE

- **Employment Hiatus,** Sacramento, CA — 1998 to Present
- **Quality Assurance Associate / Senior Quality Inspector,** Artigon Corporation — 1988 to 1998
- **Quality Assurance Manager,** Tangent Corporation — 1985 to 1988
- **Electrician and Quality Systems Analyst,** U.S. Air Force — 1971–1985

Strategy: *Summarize key qualifications in a "Professional Experience" section without dates and then document actual employment at the bottom of the resume. Emphasize key words for the Quality Assurance profession up front in the summary.*

Charles Malcolm

5839 Wood Lane
Yorba Linda, CA 92714   Email: cmalcolm@cox.net   Home: 714/849-0907
Cell: 714/604-6485

SECURITY / LOSS PREVENTION

Professional security advisor with proven leadership skills and a comprehensive knowledge of security whose effective management of people and resources minimizes criminal activity and maximizes the safety and protection of the public and employees. Provide optimal productivity and efficiency by training clients' personnel to effectively utilize crime and loss prevention techniques. Excellent communication skills with the ability to teach individually and make presentations to groups. Set the highest standards of excellence for myself and team members. Acquired substantial intuitive wisdom and completed extensive courses related to law enforcement, safety, and security as an Officer during nine years with the Los Angeles County Sheriff's Department.

AREAS OF EXPERTISE	PERSONAL QUALITIES
Personal and Corporate Background Checks	Professional, Dedicated, and Ethical
Counter-Surveillance	Motivated, Energetic, and Enthusiastic
Retail / Industrial Theft	Resourceful, Diligent, Decisive, and Results Oriented
Personal Injury	Work Independently and as a Team Member
Highly Publicized Event Security	Quickly Identify, Assess, and Resolve Problems
Labor-Related Investigations	Work Well under Pressure
Missing Persons	Adaptable and Flexible

PROFESSIONAL EXPERIENCE

Law Enforcement Officer, <u>Los Angeles County Sheriff's Department</u>, Los Angeles, CA   1991–2001

- Made arrests and restored order at the Rodney King riots during my first assignment.
- Subsequently assigned to the men's central jail in downtown Los Angeles. Duties included writing criminal reports and supervising and escorting high-security inmates.
- Assigned to an emergency response team in 1994. Duties included responding to countywide emergencies, county jail riots, and major disturbances.
- Promoted to training officer duties (1996-2000). Trained new deputies in laws of arrest, report writing, officer safety, and all necessary duties to be a qualified law enforcement officer.
- Sustained injuries that required a medical retirement in 2001.

EDUCATION / TRAINING

Suicide Prevention, Legal Update, Advanced Officer, First Aid/CPR Courses   1995
- Rio Hondo College, Los Angeles, CA
Certificate of Completion, Los Angeles County Sheriff's Department, Los Angeles, CA   1992
- Finished in the Top Ten (of 126 Cadets) in Academics and Physical Fitness
Criminal Investigations Course, Irvine Valley College, Irvine, CA   1991
Graduate, Pacifica High School, Garden Grove, CA   1985

COMMENDATIONS

- **Personal courage and ethics** in subduing a volatile inmate that resulted in a colleague being cared for and deploying the absolute minimum amount of force necessary to resolve the situation. These actions personified the L.A. Sheriff Department's core values and brought credit to the law enforcement profession (1996).
- **Willingness to step forward and help with a task,** put forth the effort, and go the extra mile to recover lost property that belonged to an inmate. The teamwork attitude and concern displayed was an example of service-oriented policing (1995).
- **Quick response to a potentially violent situation** of racial tension in the Central Jail that was subdued with minimal altercations. Recognized for professionalism, tactics, cooperation, teamwork, and good solid police work (1995).
- **Involvement in helping to subdue a mini-riot** and reinstating order in the Central Jail. Acknowledged for self-discipline, clear thinking, professionalism and custody expertise (1994).

Strategy: *To help this law-enforcement professional transition to private-sector investigative work following an on-the-job injury, emphasize both areas of expertise and personal qualities in an extensive profile. Bolster experience with a strong section of "Commendations."*

RESUME 38: JOHN O'CONNOR, CRW, CPRW, MFA; RALEIGH, NC

JAMIE S. PROTENZA

21203 Teaston Circle
New York, New York 01123
(212) 232-9088
protenza2@intlnet.com

INTERNATIONAL CONSULTING / PROJECT MANAGEMENT

Proven ability to train, lead teams and manage advanced civil engineering projects with extensive expertise in, but not limited to, the design of reinforced concrete, composite and steel structures. Seeking R&D position based in the U.S. that will require some but not extensive travel.

QUALIFICATIONS

- *Familiar with engineering and team management principles that guide one-of-a-kind, advanced-technologies structural projects.*
- *Project leader, innovative project developer and communicator with outstanding technical development achievements.*
- *Developer of innovative structural solutions utilizing a variety of design, software and integrated material-structural engineering techniques. In all projects utilize strong foundation in mechanics, structural and materials engineering.*
- *Skills in research, writing, engineering and innovations with transferable consulting skills that will guide advanced-technologies structural projects.*
- *Able to act as liaison to clients to understand and define their specific, high-tech needs while delivering those solutions through the management of small, research-and-development focused engineering teams.*
- *Present complex engineering problems in clear technical-writing format to various audiences and customers without high-tech engineering skills or background.*
- *Outstanding overall balance of highly technical skills along with the ability to focus multiple internal entities and external customers on product requirements and product solutions.*
- *Technical reviewer for various engineering organizations including National Science Foundation, American Concrete Institute, American Society of Civil Engineers, English Concrete Institute.*
- *Citizenship: United States.*
- *Fluency: Italian, Croatian, German, Japanese, Italian, Spanish, Portuguese, English.*

SKILLS SUMMARY

* *Damage Assessment/Analysis*	* *New Technology Development/Implementation*
* *Non-Destructive Testing*	* *Product Development*
* *Seismic/Non-Seismic Repair/Retrofit*	* *Technology Transfer*
* *Procedure Design & Analysis*	* *Computer Programming/Modeling*
* *Bridge/Building Design & Analysis*	* *Auto-Adaptive Structures*
* *Structural System Analysis*	* *Project Management*
* *Solid Mechanics, Fracture Mechanics &*	* *Technology Evaluation*
Micro-Mechanics of Cementitious Composites	* *Procedure Development & Optimization*
(steel, glass, kevlar, carbon, concrete, etc.)	

EDUCATION

1987   UNIVERSITY OF MASSACHUSETTS, AMHERST, MA *(DIC)*
1986   UNIVERSITY OF LONDON, LONDON, ENGLAND: *Master of Civil Engineering (Specialization in Steel Design)*

Strategy: This individual faced a dual challenge: transitioning from academia to business, and returning to work after a work-related disability that caused a two-year employment gap. Page 1 presents strong qualifications and key skills, followed by a concise career chronology on page 2.

RESUME 38, CONTINUED

JAMIE S. PROTENZA   *Page 2*

CAREER CHRONOLOGY

1997–99	**Assistant Professor** *of Civil Engineering, University of Connecticut*
1995–97	**Director of Scale Structural Testing Laboratory** *(Constructed Facilities Laboratory — Engineering Graduate Research Center, London Common University)*
1992–95	**Assistant Professor** *of Civil Engineering, University of London, London, England*
1991–92	**Visiting Assistant Professor** *of Civil and Environmental Engineering, English Technology Institute, Manchester, England*
1987–91	**Research Assistant,** *SUNY Albany, Albany, NY (European Campus, Belgrade, Yugoslavia)*
Summer 1988	**Structural Engineer,** *PFZ Consultants, Inc., Manchester, England*
1986–87	**Research Assistant,** *London Institute of Science and Technology, London, England*

DESIGN HONORS, AWARDS AND RECOGNITIONS

- **Bellweather Universities Junior Faculty Enhancement Award** (1997)
- **Edward Muir Memorial Prize** for excellence in Concrete Structures and Technology (1987)
- **U.S. Concrete Production Design Award** – Industry Excellence (1986)
- Featured on numerous national and international television and radio interviews and shows including *CNNfn (financial) network, CNN Headline News, CNN Airport Network, CNN International Network, CNN Science and Technology Week, FOX TV, National Public Radio, Voice of America, Associated Press, CNN Radio, KNX Radio — Los Angeles.*
- Featured in popular press articles in ASCE *News, Concrete Construction.*

DEVELOPMENTAL AWARDS, TRAINING & TEAM MANAGEMENT

- Recruited, developed, trained and managed R&D-focused engineering teams that included a total of 111 Research Engineers, 42 Research Associates, 21 Research Scientists and one Visiting Research Scientist from various academies across the U.S. and Europe. Developed and taught numerous undergraduate and graduate courses on Reinforced Concrete Design, Concrete Design, Statics, Structural Mechanics, Construction Materials, Concrete Materials, and Statistics and Probability.
- Won and managed, as the main investigator, a total of $43 million in federal (International Science and Concrete Studies Institute), national and industrial R&D projects on various aspects of assessment of non-seismically designed reinforced concrete frame buildings, development of improved seismic retrofit techniques and design guidelines for bridges and buildings, and development of multiaxial plasticity models for high-performance fiber composites.

COMMUNICATION SKILLS

Presented and published in numerous national and international journals, conferences and meetings on issues related to development of design guidelines for flexural and shear retrofit of reinforced concrete (R.C.) members, seismic retrofit R.C. buildings, punching shear failure of reinforced concrete slabs, reinforcing bar bond behavior, bridge-deck overlays, auto-adaptive and "smart" structures, non-destructive testing of concrete structures, mechanisms of concrete cracking, and development and behavior of high-performance concretes and fiber composites.

- Published 19 <u>peer-reviewed papers</u> in national and international journals (e.g., American Concrete Institute *International Materials Journal, U.S. and European Structural Journal,* and *Journal of Cement and Concrete Composites*) and two book chapters. Presented 39 invited-lectures *(presentations to select audiences by personal invitation only; these do not include invitations to conference presentations).*
- Published 24 conference and workshop papers. Presented 76 conference and international meeting papers.

PROFESSIONAL AFFILIATIONS

- American Concrete Institute (ACI). Full member of ACI Committees 325—Concrete Pavements, 348—Structural Safety, 446—Fracture Mechanics and 544—Fiber Reinforced Concrete
- Associate Member of ACI Committee 440—FRP Bar and Tendon Reinforcement
- American Society of Civil Engineers (ASCE)
- Earthquake Engineering Research Institute (EERI)
- International Association of Bridge and Structural Engineering (IABSE)
- Materials Research Society (MRS)
- Society for Experimental Mechanics (SEM)

Reference, report, seminar and publication information available upon request.

CHAPTER 9

Resumes for People Returning to Work After Incarceration

Turning one's life around and finding employment after incarceration can be a daunting task. These resumes help by focusing on skills and experience; most do not refer to the period of incarceration in any way. This information must be disclosed when asked on a job application, of course, but details are more appropriately addressed in an interview.

ASA J. PETERS

1514 Campbell, D1   Jefferson City, Missouri 64108
(816) 667-0421   (816) 992-1421

AREAS OF RELEVANT SKILLS

Multi-dimensional individual with experience as **heavy equipment operator, driver,** or **laborer** with technical knowledge in surveying, welding, and general maintenance. Excellent safety record and willingness to do more than what is expected. Communicate and interact effectively with diverse cultures.

- ❖ **Heavy Equipment Operations:** Forklift, Tractor, Loader, Backhoe, Motor Grader, Track Loader, Bulldozer, Bobcat Skid/Steer Loader, Scraper
- ❖ **Driver:** Dump Truck, Over-the-Road
- ❖ **Technical:** Surveying, Welding
- ❖ **Maintenance:** General, Preventive, Carpentry, Painting

EDUCATIONAL BACKGROUND

Linn State Technical College   Linn, MO
   Heavy Equipment Operator Certificate Course
   Welding; Blueprint Interpretation; Surveying; Preventive Maintenance

American Truck Driving School   Waco, TX
   Over-the-Road Truck Driving Certificate Course

Northwest Missouri Community College   Jefferson City, MO
   Introduction to Computer Information Systems; Basic Programming;
   Data Files; Structural Programming; Microcomputer Operating Systems

EMPLOYMENT HISTORY

TEMPORARY ASSIGNMENTS, Jefferson City & Cameron, MO   1992–2000
- ➤ Store Clerk/Stocker
- ➤ Library Clerk/Data Entry Clerk
- ➤ Computer Operator/Data Entry Clerk
- ➤ Chapel Head Clerk
- ➤ AM/PM Baker/Store Clerk

LINN TECHNICAL COLLEGE, Linn, MO   1992
- ➤ Maintenance Technician — General maintenance, cleaning, carpentry, and lawn care.

SPRINGFIELD PARKS AND RECREATION DEPARTMENT, Springfield, MO   1991
- ➤ Laborer, Park Maintenance

MAZZIO'S PIZZA, Springfield, MO   1990–1991
- ➤ Delivery Driver

DRIVEWAY PAVING, Toledo, OH   1988–1990
- ➤ Dump Truck Driver/Laborer

NORTH AMERICAN VAN LINES, Ft. Wayne, IN   1987–1988
- ➤ Over-The-Road Driver

Strategy: *Employment during incarceration is addressed in the "temporary assignments" listing in the Employment History section of the resume. Experience and certifications relative to his job target are stressed.*

ARTHUR F. ECK, JR.

639 Arcadia Street ⚓ Rochester, NY 12239
387-458-3241

OBJECTIVE

BREAKFAST and LUNCH COOK

To assist a restaurant in attracting and retaining a strong customer base,
by applying a *passion for the culinary arts* and a *strong work ethic.*

PERSONAL PROFILE

- Experience working in a kitchen environment, filling orders and developing menu items.
- Ability to get the job done by employing critical thinking and problem resolution skills.
- Work well as a *team player* and independently with *very little supervision.*
- Received commendations for being *dependable* and *hardworking.*
- Bilingual, Spanish and English.

COOKING SKILLS

☑ Prepared a selection of entrees, vegetables, desserts, and refreshments.

☑ Cleaned the grill, food preparation surfaces, counters, and floors.

☑ Met high quality standards for food preparation, service, and safety.

☑ Trained and supervised workers.

☑ Maintained inventory logs and placed orders to replenish stocks of tableware, linens, paper, cleaning supplies, cooking utensils, food, and beverages.

☑ Received and checked the content of deliveries and evaluated the quality of meats, poultry, fish, vegetables, and baked goods.

☑ Oversaw food preparation and cooking.

RESTAURANT EXPERIENCE

Kitchen Worker — State of New York (Coxsackie Correctional Facility); Coxsackie, NY
Short Order Cook — Rockies Breakfast Bar; Rochester, NY
Prep Cook/Laborer — New World Diner; Rochester, NY
Lunch and Dinner Cook — Albany's Italian American Restaurant; Albany, NY

MILITARY SERVICE

U.S. Navy — Machinist Mate E-3 — *Honorable Discharge*
GED obtained

Strategy: *A straight functional-style resume is used to emphasize work-related skills. The period of incarceration referred to under the Restaurant Experience section might be interpreted as paid employment.*

Elaine L. Evans

319 Evergreen Street • Worcester, MA 01601 • Phone: (508) 555-1234

Career Scope

Office Assistant position where acquired skills and experience gained during part-time employment while raising a family may now be applied on a full-time basis to a permanent career position in a professional environment.

Summary of Qualifications

- ❑ Comprehensive knowledge of and experience in office procedures — reception, administrative support, and accounting — across multiple industries, including retail, distribution, manufacturing, and hospitality.
- ❑ Demonstrated record of successfully executing day-to-day tasks in fast-paced, time-sensitive environments.
- ❑ Proficient with Microsoft Office Suite products utilized to process correspondence, develop financial spreadsheets, and create presentations for executive-level personnel.
- ❑ Background processing insurance contracts, purchase orders, and transportation vouchers and preparing reports.
- ❑ Skill in assisting customers with product and service inquiries and addressing and resolving problems.
- ❑ Experience processing payroll, training employees, and scheduling appointments.

Experience   1992–2001

Wholesale Club Distributors, Inc.	Natick, MA	Inventory Control
Days Inn Hotel	Southboro, MA	Accounting Clerk
Rawley International	Boston, MA	Office Assistant
Convenience Mart	Milford, MA	Assistant Manager
Interstate Transit Company	Brookfield, MA	Reservationist
Annual Lawn Associates	Brookfield, MA	Customer Service
Humboldt Distributors, Inc.	Princeton, MA	Secretary

Training & Education

Quinsigamond Community College, Worcester, MA
Business Communication and Administration Certification

Dean Junior College, Franklin, MA
Small Business Management Certification

KEYWORDS: Office Assistant, Administration, Customer Service, Accounting, Training, Data Entry, Reception
Scheduling, Problem Resolution, Quality Control, Inventory Control, Management

Strategy: *This individual's "job-hopping" history is effectively hidden by the umbrella treatment of employment history.*

Terry R. Smith

1018 Highland Street ▪ Steelton, PA 17113
(717) 939-6949

QUALIFICATIONS PROFILE

Extensive experience and practical knowledge of high-volume **Industrial Warehousing / Distribution and Manufacturing** environments. Hard-working, enthusiastic, dependable, and self-motivated; take responsibility to get the job done. Work cooperatively with a wide range of personalities. Excellent work history and attendance record. Computer skills. Take pride in achieving best possible results.

Special Achievement Award — Defense Depot Mechanicsburg Pennsylvania

Certificate of Recognition for 10 Years Successful Government Service

Certificate of Appreciation — Defense Logistics Agency

Material Handling Equipment Operation Award (Forklift) — 2 years

Material Handling Equipment **Safe Driver Award**

EXPERIENCE

MECHANICSBURG NAVY DEPOT, Mechanicsburg, PA, 1983–1999

Warehouse — WGG5 Step 5

Operated IMC warehouse forklift and sit-down crane. Experienced in shipping and receiving; weekend shift supervisor.

- Skilled machine operator; good sense of balance, distance, and eye-hand coordination.
- Well-liked, effective shift supervisor.
- Effectively executed shipping/receiving procedures and regulations.
- Worked well independently and as part of a team.

EDUCATION

HARRISBURG AREA COMMUNITY COLLEGE, Harrisburg, PA
Earned 36 credits / Liberal Arts

Completed 22 on-the-job training courses in safety and policy/procedures.

References Available on Request.

Strategy: *The most is made of limited work experience and education. Personal attributes and awards are highlighted to convey "soft skills" that will be important to employers.*

DOUG THOMAS

1234 South Park Street – Chicago, IL 60606

999-333-2222 – dsmith@yahoo.com

HVAC TECHNICIAN

Provide primary and specialized hands-on support for HVAC. Furnish routine and miscellaneous inspections regarding new installations, repairs, preventive maintenance, and procedures. Experienced with state-of-the-art equipment and technology. Learn quickly and follow directions. Work well with supervisors and peers. Conscientious worker who gives 100% effort.

EDUCATION

Ft. Collins Vocational-Technical Skills Center, Ft. Collins, CO
Industrial Building Maintenance — Diploma 1998
Basic-skills studies in Carpentry, Electrical, and Plumbing with special training in Heating and Air Conditioning maintenance. Hands-on training at off-site locations.

Computer Experience: Word, Excel, Access

North High School, Park Ridge, IL
Diploma, 1992

WORK EXPERIENCE

Heating and Air Conditioning Assistant
Hall's Heating and Air Conditioning, Chicago, IL
- Assisted owner with installation of new units, replacement of older units, and general troubleshooting on residential and commercial systems.
- Handled electrical work and made ducts from flat sheets of metal.

Park Maintenance Personnel
Colorado State Park, Ft. Collins, CO, 1997–2001
- Gutted and remodeled entire work center building.
- Hand-crafted wood park signs and laid cement pads for picnic areas.
- Installed fencing for 3- and 4-wheelers on 3.5-acre lot in 2 months.

Assistant Manager
Premier Carpets, Dallas, TX, 1994–1996
- Quickly learned all facets of carpet business.
- Trained new employees in cleaning, repairs, patching, and tack stripping.
- Balanced cash drawer and receipts; opened and closed store.
- Promoted from general employee to Assistant Manager.

Other positions held: Gutter Installer, Gas Station Attendant, Building Supply Routeman.

COMMUNITY INVOLVEMENT
Chicago Area Youth Football League, Coach

Strategy: *A clear summary gives this resume a sharp focus. Goals are supported by relevant experience and education. Dates are omitted.*

OLIVER ORTIZ

3083 43rd SW   Seattle, WA 98136   206.948.8088
oliver278@aol.com

PROFILE

Experienced in machine operations, customer relations, and organizing materials. Willing worker, able to work independently or as part of a team. Bilingual English/Spanish.

EXPERIENCE

Packager, Signature Packaging Solutions, Monroe, WA   2000–2002
- Packaged items for Starbucks, using variety of packaging machines.

Machine Operator/Molding, ABC Company, Seattle, WA   1996–1999
- Molded plastics on injection and compression machines.
- Mixed ingredients for plastics.

Delivery Driver, Rent-A-Center, Seattle, WA   1994–1996
- Delivered and picked up merchandise for customers.
- Assisted customers with concerns.
- Completed sales forms.
- Handled currency.
- Serviced damaged equipment.

Casual Mail Handler, United States Parcel Service, Hartford, CT   1992–1994
- Sorted and distributed mail to various departments.
- Weighed airmail and dispatched to appropriate airlines.
- Operated and maintained postage machines.

Returned Goods Clerk, Electrical Wholesalers, Hartford, CT   1991–1992
- Received goods.
- Stocked shelves.
- Picked and checked orders.
- Coordinated with purchasing departments.
- Kept records and inventory.

EDUCATION

Center for Professional Advancement, Capital Community College, Hartford, CT
Studied basic computers and job skills.

Strategy: *Use all relevant work experience, including Starbucks packaging job held while in prison, to show broad qualifications and job stability.*

RESUME 45: NANCY KARVONEN, CPRW, CCM, IJCTC, CEIP, CJST; GALT, CA

CHARLES IRONWOOD

806 East Walker Street   (530) 865-0607
Orland, California 95963   ironman@hotmail.com

NETWORK ENGINEER/TECHNICAL SUPPORT

SUMMARY OF QUALIFICATIONS

- ◆ Solutions-driven network engineer providing technical support to improve performance, operational efficiencies, and expense reduction.
- ◆ Flexible and focused, with unique analytical problem-solving ability.
- ◆ Solid theoretical knowledge of computer and network architecture and Microsoft Operating System.
- ◆ Excellent communication, team-building, and conflict-management skills.

EDUCATION

Butte Community College, Orland, California

Network Engineer: Windows NT, CompuVista Business Institute, Sacramento, California, 2002

Information Technology Certifications

MCSE	Workstation	Windows 95
MCP+I	NT Server/Enterprise	Windows 3.x
A+ Certified	Networking Essentials	**Windows NT**
Microsoft NT	Windows NT Server 4.0	Internet Info-Server
MS DOS 6.22	TCP/IP Implementation	Internet Explorer 5.0

ACCOMPLISHMENTS

- ◆ Resolved security issues on Windows NT involving group account policies and end users.
- ◆ Engineered effective Windows NT security structure and implementation in working networks.
- ◆ Implemented and routed network around TCP/IP protocol suite.
- ◆ Performed diagnostics, myriad configurations, and peripheral repairs.
- ◆ Installed software, provided peer-to-peer technical support, and consulted on LAN development.

WORK HISTORY

Computer Technician, Orland Health Care Center, Chico, California	1999–2002
Press Operator, Valley Industries, Chico, California	1998–1999
Painter, Hay Ho Painting, Orland, California	1997–1998

Strategy: *This individual gained computer training during his period of rehabilitation, and his resume focuses on relevant skills, certifications, and achievements.*

JERRY MCGUIRE

2020 Telegraph — Royal Oak, MI 48068

248-397-7704 — jmcguire@hotmail.com

SALES REPRESENTATIVE

Self-confident and motivated with good track record in sales and construction with start-up companies. Communicate clearly and effectively with people of diverse backgrounds. Use tact and patience when dealing with difficult customers. Goal oriented and persuasive. Areas of expertise:

- Budgeting
- Strategic Planning
- Problem Solving
- Relationship Selling
- Account Development
- Negotiation
- Customer Service
- Training
- Team Building

RELATED SALES EXPERIENCE

Sales Rep
Alpha-Omega Construction, Detroit, MI, 1999–2001
Start-up to high-growth residential, commercial, and farm building company.

Prospected new accounts utilizing variety of effective sales techniques including cold-calling, direct mail, and telephone campaigns. Emphasized service, quality, and price. Handled bids, accurately estimating materials and labor costs for remodeling and new construction. Located hard-to-find materials and supplies; arranged for on-time delivery. Kept records of jobs to determine profitability. Supervised construction crews of up to 65 people; hands-on building experience.

- Grew business from 7 employees to 65.
- Drove revenues from zero to more than $4,000,000.

Manager/Owner
McGuire Custom Golf Clubs, Royal Oak, MI, 1990–1998

Assessed golfers' level of expertise, utilizing knowledge of the sport, to design and build custom golf clubs. Promoted business through print advertising, networking, and customer service. Built and maintained client base and customer loyalty through quality product and service, resulting in high number of referrals.

- Slashed advertising budget 50% due to high referral business.

EDUCATION

Trenton High School, Trenton, MI: Diploma

Computer Experience: Windows, Microsoft Office, construction specific software, Internet.

Strategy: *Because the candidate's period of incarceration was short, the resume ignores the most recent two years and instead concentrates on prior experience that is relevant to his career goals.*

CAITLIN O'CONNOR

32 Garamond Street
Sacramento, CA 94205
916.374.8004
caitlin317@earthlink.net

MANAGEMENT PROFESSIONAL

Leadership   Training   Communication   Quality   Control

Dynamic management professional with effective verbal and written communication skills, exemplary organizational skills, and attention to detail. Able to multi-task, without sacrificing quality or timeliness of results. High level of discretion, familiar with risk management concepts and techniques, and proficient in variety of computer applications. Skilled in anticipating and resolving conflicts and problems. Effective at managing time and schedule of busy, demanding senior executive. Identified as a "key contributor" on evaluations each year. Received numerous performance awards. Fully trilingual, English/Spanish/German.

"It is reassuring to know that you will bring in a project on time or ahead of time, and done well." Agnes Schiraldi, Supervisor, describing actions leading to performance award.

COMPUTER SKILLS

WordPerfect, Word, Excel, PowerPoint, Access, Publisher, Front Page, Adobe Photoshop, Internet and Intranet Networking Systems. A+ Certification.

RELATED ACCOMPLISHMENTS

Airways Technical, Columbus, OH   1990–1999
Senior Technical Assistant / Credit and Collections Analyst, 1996–1999
- Transferred hardcopy microfilm order form into Word document that, in turn, allowed company to send microfilm orders via email rather than via fax; this saved company money for producing multi-copy form and telephone toll charges, as well as saving time. Worked with vendor to set up email procedure to ensure it was in place before actual orders were sent.
- Created variety of forms to expedite processing orders and record-keeping.
- Improved customer satisfaction by processing orders in a more timely manner.
- Filed and maintained historical record of price and cost. Completed financial project to enable Technical Publication Department to implement new policy for non-paying customers.
- Reviewed and analyzed requests for new or additional technical-publications materials from current and potential customers and company personnel. Determined eligibility, availability, and applicable charges.

Strategy: *The recent period of nonrelated work experience (completed while incarcerated) is relegated to page 2 so as not to detract from the strong experience and achievements of her early career.*

CAITLIN O'CONNOR

Page 2

Senior Technical Assistant / Credit and Collections Analyst, Continued

- Generated and processed customer invoices, refunds, and collections. Interfaced with internal and external personnel to provide, collect, clarify, and interpret information, explain or justify established prices, substantiate variations, and resolve discrepancies.
- Initiated authorization to fill approved orders and coordinate release of publications.
- Created charts to plot increase of revenues.
- Computerized maintenance of specialized records as directed, such as customer exception to distribution policies, customer responses to special offers, and policy changes. Accumulated and prepared records and statistics for planning purposes.
- Originally hired for data entry work, but within weeks was given considerably more responsibility when supervisor realized my skills.

Supplier Publication Coordinator, 1990–1996

- Created standardized forms for recording and maintaining data. Reduced vendor publication backlog through increased follow-up and training.
- Improved coordination of supplier publications and saved management time by delegating clerical tasks.
- Implemented training course for new recruits, speeding profitability.
- Contracted, coordinated, and maintained status of worldwide vendor publications.

ADDITIONAL EXPERIENCE

State of California, Dublin, CA
PC Service Technician   2000–2002
- Repaired and updated computers for state offices.
- Earned A+ certification.

EDUCATION

University of Michigan, Ann Arbor, MI
B.S., Business Management
Minors: Financial Management and MIS
3.89 GPA

Computer Institute, Cleveland, OH
Access I, II, III
PowerPoint I, II, III
Excel I, II, III

TOLLANY S. SOLU

1543 Esrands Court
Raleigh, North Carolina 27612

(919) 555-1212
tollanys@calatomail.com

INTERNATIONAL MANUFACTURING CONSULTANT
*Seeking Management-Focused Consulting Opportunities for U.S.-Based Companies Doing Business in Africa and Asia
International Food Processing — Chemical — Pharmaceutical Industries*

SUMMARY OF QUALIFICATIONS

- One of the only female executives on the continent of Africa to lead international manufacturing operations despite great challenges and brief political imprisonment during career.

- Proven, multi-year international management/leadership expertise with transferable skills from overseeing critical financial aspects in the manufacturing industry, including Controller-Level Leadership (Multi-Projects), Plant Management, Debt Reduction Strategies, Safety Program Design and Implementation, Manufacturing, Marketing, and Profit and Loss analysis.

- Regarded as an innovative, complete financial leader who successfully leads new strategic partnerships while managing teams on outsourced contracts with annual revenue in the millions of dollars.

- Strong production environment experience, operations management, and supervision of hourly employees. Able to review administrative and financial aspects of production plans as well as determine optimum business strategies in very difficult market, political, and economic conditions.

- Outstanding ability to establish strategic business plans that include evaluating and implementing leading-edge financial solutions while anticipating technology and personnel trends to meet a company's immediate and future needs.

- Able to direct financial-team activities that focus on design and implementation of new programs and strategies in financial areas that support leading-edge growth operations.

- Outstanding customer-driven financial solution management focus built through multi-year high-level partnering with international companies (U.S. and European primarily); track record of highly accurate forecasting, cost reductions/controls, and productivity enhancements across multiple corporate services and business areas.

- Transferable skill set for current positions includes:
  - *Strategic Planning/Initiatives*
  - *Controller/Financial Leadership*
  - *United Nations Liaison (Corporate)*
  - *Union Negotiations/Labor Experience*
  - *Corporate Cost/Budget Management*
  - *Food/Chemical/Pharmaceutical Expertise*
  - *Distribution Center Management*
  - *System Operational Evaluations*
  - *Safety Control/Design Issues*
  - *Cross-Functional Team Leader*
  - *Production Management*
  - *Political Experience/Sensitive Line Funding Issues*
  - *Production/Process/Procedural Troubleshooting*
  - *ISO 9002 Management*
  - *International Trade/Business Expertise*
  - *Total P&L Responsibility/Engineering Projects*
  - *Banking/Credit Relationship Development*
  - *Capital Program Management*
  - *New Market/Opportunity Development*
  - *Business Strategy/Channel Profitability*

EDUCATION

GEORGE WASHINGTON UNIVERSITY, MS, Political Science, May 2000
UNIVERSITY OF ALABAMA, BS, Chemical Engineering and Food Process Engineering, May 1996

PROFESSIONAL DEVELOPMENT

University of Chicago, Chicago, IL: three-month USAID-funded course in Plant Management
George Mason University, Fairfax, VA: three-month USAID course in Food Plant and Cost Management

Strategy: *This individual was a political prisoner in Africa; her personal and professional challenge is just hinted at in the Summary. Her compelling business background seemed strong enough, despite a four-year work absence, to more than interest employers in her abilities.*

RESUME 48, CONTINUED

TOLLANY S. SOLU	Page 2

PROFESSIONAL EXPERIENCE

CALATO SECURITIES LTD., Pretoria, South Africa
Managing Director, 1996–1998

Led this manufacturing and holding company with turnover of $212 million annually (aggregate value of over $300 million); held complete management responsibility for the company's three distinct business units with 280 employees, including Petroleum and Petroleum Products Distribution through three channels: gas stations/convenience stores (26); petroleum/fuel distributions; supply of cooking gas (butane) to institutions and retail outlets.

- Worked with contractors to produce goods to meet the company's orders; this work included close knowledge of land contracts with governments, parastatal organizations, and international relief agencies (to procure goods on their behalf). Goods included commodities to scientific equipment.
- Relief Distribution focused on international relief efforts in Sudan and Vietnam; successes included distributing hundreds of thousands of pounds of food to these war-torn and economically/politically and socially distressed areas. Designed and implemented an aggressive safety-first program to reduce time lost due to injuries.
- Successfully completed bid-proposal preparation to secure business by assessing competition and industry trend despite still built-in traditional conflicts within South Africa and its citizens.
- Strengthened working relations with employees and built the company from small to large.

Directly controlled comprehensive multi-unit management functions. Led cross-functional teams on the company's major projects. Oversaw organizational recruiting, training, and structure. Held P&L of technical department, which handled engineering projects. In this comprehensive management position, reviewed all employee performances and kept a hands-on, active role on all levels of personnel and financial management functions.

Held comprehensive controller/financial responsibilities for multimillion-dollar production and manufacturing division. Drove major initiatives and management enhancement strategies across multiple departments through initiatives in these areas: Safety, Quality, Finance, and Production Management.

CONAGRO-CHEMICALS, Cape Town, South Africa
Production Assistant (1989–1991); **Production Liaison** (1992–1993); **Production Manager** (1993–1996); **International Relations Specialist** (1992–1996)

- Helped company develop liaison relationship with Fortune 500 companies in the United States to keep funding and financial support during political upheaval and racial-segregation challenges following termination of Apartheid.
- Successfully increased ethanol and citric acid recovery by 67% through efficient process design and control.
- Reduced employees from 475 to 250 while simultaneously increasing production output through efficient use of new technology and overall cost reductions.
- Coordinated all operations and managed 250 employees for this facility, including ensuring ISO 9002 standards and EU-based food-safety procedures/standards.
- Directed both the Citric Acid and Ethanol (power alcohol) production divisions using molasses from sugar cane as the fermentation substrates. Successfully conducted pilot fermentations to determine optimal citric acid yields in line with different sources and different chemical clarification treatments of sugar juices (resulting in molasses of varying fermentation requirements).
- Improved production and operational reporting, which led to resolution of multiple manufacturing and operational delays.
- Increased raw material utilization capacity 68% while successfully negotiating lower-priced molasses supply from three neighboring sugar factories and U.S./European companies.
- Union work included solving workers' grievances and negotiating directly with unions to positive effect each time there was an issue; issues were resolved from management to floor workers — black and white/all cultures.

Led production improvements and initiatives that resulted in outstanding quality reputation, safety records, and reputation. Drove organizational changes that led to improved Best Practices SOP for the business across the board. Reviewed, standardized, and followed up to ensure these practices gained full support of all managers and other personnel. Held budgetary and P&L oversight. Change Agent Leadership included leading culture shift toward customer-focused teams, better race relations, and team goals throughout the plants.

RESUME 49: JANICE SHEPHERD, CPRW, JCTC, CEIP; BELLINGHAM, WA

Jamie Brownhouse

1234 New Town Lane
Issaquah, WA 98029
(425-904-8304)

Objective: Assistant Director, Center for Troubled Youth

PROFILE

Possess understanding of business protocol, a pleasant attitude, and skills required to succeed in the position. Willing to learn, work hard, and apply good work ethic.

Currently enrolled in business-management class; consciously trying to make a positive impact by tutoring young people. Ability and desire to effectively communicate to kids first-hand why they want to change their lives now, before they waste their youth.

QUALIFICATIONS

- Excellent numbers and financial-management skill.
- History of developing and maintaining loyal repeat customers.
- Excellent memory for names and faces.
- Proven strength in marketing without advertising.
- Skilled in recognizing and creating business opportunities.
- Demonstrated ability to successfully build upon limited resources.
- Spanish fluency.

EXPERIENCE

Men's Correctional Facility, WA, 1999–2002
Assigned position of **Kitchen Supervisor.**

- Directed activities and performance of 23 men in the preparation, service, and clean-up of meals for inmates.
- Applied strong leadership, conflict-resolution, and mediation skills. Monitored and kept records of kitchen inventory. Commended for consistently excellent management and job performance.

Self-Employed, throughout Washington State, 1995–1999
Pharmaceutical Sales

- Built and maintained loyal customer base.
- Created extensive contacts network.
- Managed cash flow.
- Kept accurate bookkeeping records.
- Polished communication and mediation skills.

Construction Laborer, part-time and seasonal work, various employers, 1987–1995

Developed finish carpentry skills and learned to operate heavy equipment such as bulldozer, caterpillar, dump truck, and cement mixer. Worked with crews with diverse backgrounds and personalities.

PROFESSIONAL DEVELOPMENT / EDUCATION

Business Management, Community College, WA, currently attending
Tutor/Advisor, Youth Group, Community Church
Street-wise, on-the-job training — illegal economy
Graduate, New Town High School, WA

Strategy: *Rather than gloss over troubled history, this resume makes a strong case for a life turnaround and skills learned through personal experience.*

CHAPTER 10

Resumes for People Returning to Work After a Sabbatical

Even when a work absence is voluntary, as in the case of an educational or personal sabbatical, the resume still needs to make a strong case for relevant qualifications and avoid any "red flags" from large gaps in employment. Many of these resumes highlight the sabbatical experience as a key qualification.

JOAN MARKS, M.SC.

2027 Oakwood Crescent ♦ Toronto, Ontario, Canada M1V 6G9 ♦ jmarks@starvision.ca
(416) 976-3756

OBJECTIVE: Committed to developing a career in translational research.

SUMMARY OF QUALIFICATIONS & SKILLS

- ♦ Strong academic qualifications at the post-graduate level.
- ♦ Lifelong interest in medical research—published thesis.
- ♦ Understanding of research techniques and technologies.
- ♦ Full range of laboratory research and laboratory management skills.
- ♦ Exposure to clinical research as a summer research assistant at the U of T Medical School.
- ♦ Proven skills in statistical analysis, assembling and organizing data.
- ♦ Supporting business experience with a strong management component.
- ♦ Able to plan and oversee projects from concept to conclusion—an efficient multi-tasker.

EDUCATION

University of Toronto, Department of Medical Science, Toronto, Ontario
M.Sc. Molecular Biology, 2002

> Coursework: Human Anatomy, Physiology, and Pharmacology
>
> Thesis: **Molecular Biology of Aging and Neurodegenerative Diseases**

Waterloo University, Faculty of Science, Waterloo, Ontario
B.Sc. Biology, 1992

PUBLICATIONS

"The Influence of Harvesting Technique on Measures of Disc Hydration". Canadian Journal of Physiology, Volume 78, #8, 1998

RESEARCH EXPERIENCE

Thesis (2000–2002)
Coordinated and implemented all aspects of thesis research project:

- ♦ Developed thesis statement; created and implemented the protocol.
- ♦ Managed lab and academic course time effectively.
- ♦ Applied for and obtained funding.
- ♦ Operated and maintained a variety of lab equipment.
- ♦ Delivered progress reports to advisor and peers.
- ♦ Ethically treated and cared for lab animals.
- ♦ Performed statistical analysis on results, compiled research, and successfully defended thesis.

(continued)

Strategy: *Advanced education followed a lengthy absence from related work, so only the most recent qualifications are included on page 1.*

Joan Marks, M.Sc.—Page 2

Additional Research Experience

Worked as a research assistant to professors and Ph.D. candidates (U of T Medical School) for four summers while completing undergraduate degree (1988–1992)

♦ **Virology:** Grew virus cultures.

♦ **Biochemistry:** Assisted in developing alternate kidney dialysis solutions to be used at the time of transplants.

♦ **Cardiovascular Pharmacology:** Studied the effects of anaesthetic on vascular tissue of rats.

OTHER PROFESSIONAL EXPERIENCE

Owner of Water Gardens Plus, a family business (1995–1998)

♦ Created a vision for the business and coordinated, with the assistance of the management team, day-to-day business operations.

♦ Grew the business from start-up to employing 15 personnel—doubled sales annually for 5 years.

Pharmaceutical Representative with Merck Pharmaceuticals (1992–1995)

Organized and managed a territory in Ontario.

♦ Helped launch a new cardiovascular drug and supported physicians prescribing the product.

♦ Educated pharmacists and doctors on the company's cardiovascular product line.

COMPUTER SKILLS

Microsoft Office: Word, Excel, and PowerPoint
Windows: 95, 98, 2000
Managed large volumes of data using spreadsheets and databases in research settings.

INTERESTS

Medical Research—Read medical periodicals and conduct Internet research on topics of interest.

Physical Fitness and Athletics—Participate in 10K and marathon races.

Volunteer Activities—Parent coordinator for the Junior Sailing Program, Toronto Sailing Club; chairperson for the Toronto Athletic Club Hockey Executive.

ELLEN F. DELREE

3678 Longwind Circle
Apex, North Carolina 27615
(919) 354-6633 H / (919) 752-4478 O
Delreeef@internet.net

DATABASE ADMINISTRATION / IMPLEMENTATION CONSULTANT
~ Seeking Senior Technical Support Position ~

Technology professional with excellent business operations and IT consulting and support skills. Utilize cooperative leadership, a consultative project management approach, and proven skills in Information Resource Management.

TECHNICAL SKILLS SUMMARY

FASTLINE	Installation & Configuration	**SELECTED TRAINING**	Introduction to Visual Basic
	Service Pack & Patch Applications		Perl Introduction
	Issue Troubleshooting & Resolution		Administrating Microsoft SQL Server 6.5
	Migration – Import/Export (NT)		Administrating Windows NT 4.0
	Master Scheduler & Poll Configuration		Transact SQL Programming
	Job Scheduler Job Setup & Scheduling		Introduction to UNIX
	Training & Security		UNIX Administration
	Batch Structure Processing		
SYBASE	Configuration	**REPORTING**	Cognos Administration
	Patches		Cognos Report Development
	Database Management		Impromptu 5.0
	Transact SQL Programming		Powerplay 6.5 (Open Analyzer)
	Backup & Restore		All FastLine DSS Tools
UNIX	HP UNIX & Solaris	**CODING**	C++ Maintenance
	Security		Perl Scripting
	Profile Scripts		
	Disk Partitioning		
	File System Setup		
DOCS	Visio	**NT**	NT Security
	PowerPoint		NT User Account Setup
	Microsoft Office Professional Suite		

GENERAL SKILLS

* IT Systems Administration
* Fluent in Russian
* Client Relations/Client Communications
* Technical/Reporting Consulting
* Crisis Resolutions/Problem Solving
* System Backup/Restoration Procedures
* Disaster Recovery/Security Procedures
* Senior Business Analysis
* Requirements Definition Work
* Programming/IT Project Management
* Operations Analysis/ Needs Analysis/Evaluations
* Network System Administrative Management
* Strategic Planning/Consulting
* SOP Development/Implementations
* User/IT Staff Training Initiatives
* System Installations/Configurations
* Senior Programmer Analyst
* Database Performance/Tuning

EDUCATION

NORTH CAROLINA STATE UNIVERSITY, Raleigh, NC
Master of Electrical Engineering and Technology Transfer, May 1991
Bachelor of Science in Information Technology with a Minor in Foreign Language Studies, May 1987

Strategy: *This "dot-commer" earned a large payout from the success of her prior company and returned from a personal sabbatical invigorated and ready for a new challenge. The resume uses a*

ELLEN F. DELREE

Page 2

PROFESSIONAL EXPERIENCE

TELECOMMUNICATIONS TECHNICIANS INTERNATIONAL, Raleigh, NC
Technical Support Analyst, 1995–1999
Key Project Accomplishments include:
- *Successful implementation of FastLine Modules including: Financials, Procurement, and HR.*
- *Provided a unique key tie between separate application systems.*
- *Restructured test system's database and restoration from backup.*
- *Provided client technical support and training for Sybase, HP UNIX, and FastLine 6.0/0.2.*
- *Continued support of FastLine System and trained new IT staff during multiple changes and growth.*
- *Updated system reports to contain divisions and train general ledger users how to make their own updates.*

- Served as key technical and reporting consultant, offering services for the implementation of Financial, Human Resources, and Procurement Modules for U.S. and Russian business operations.
- Responsible for the installation and configuration of Sybase, FastLine File Servers, FastLine job servers, and FastLine clients. Applied Service Packs and Patches to FastLine system.
- Performed UNIX, Sybase, FastLine, and NT administrative duties.
- Provided UNIX and NT scripting to assist with automating processes, including store procedures customizations.
- Set up and implemented backup and restoration procedures.
- Assisted with disaster recovery of the database system as well as updating security procedures.
- Troubleshot and resolved user requests, data, and system issues. Provided user and IT staff training as well as support for the FastLine environment. Documented FastLine system and developed new reports.
- Resolved payroll, HR, and custom reporting issues.

POWERSYSTEM, Cary, NC
Senior Programmer Analyst, 1993–1995
- Provided support on the FastLine Financials and Decision Support Modules.
- Performed UNIX, Sybase, FastLine, and NT administration duties.
- Migrated Finance system to new version.

MKKH SYSTEMS, Raleigh, NC
Support Analyst, 1991–1993
- Provided support for FastLine decision Support module: Query, Reporter, Management reporter, Structures, and Analyzer.
- Created and taught the first in-depth training class on Structures – started training developers and maintenance personnel, in addition to support staff.

BACKGROUND SYNOPSIS/QUALIFICATIONS

- *Demonstrated ability interfacing with users and management to gather requirements for new application projects.*

- *Prepare system environments such as applying UNIX patches, installing and configuring databases, NT file server space and patch level on NT systems at the required levels.*

- *Strong experience dealing with Sybase and SQL Server databases; experience installing, configuring, setting up startup and backup scripts, monitoring locked processes, recycling the server, and performing database disaster recovery for the test database.*

- *Excellent verbal and written communication skills, including the ability to plan, write, and present arguments and recommendations on the adoption of technology, workflow changes, project-management plans, and new technology integrations. Explain products or solutions to administrators, executives, and end users.*

- *Known for a very high level of customer service and satisfaction.*

References Available Upon Request

powerful visual presentation to convey her broad and deep skills and not "pigeonhole" her in the now-struggling telecom industry.

RESUME 52: ANN STEWART, CPRW; ROANOKE, TX

DOUGLAS G. BARNES

202 Santa Elena Boulevard
Austin, TX 78746
e-mail: dbarnes@texas.net

home (512) 330-9774
cell (512) 892-1483

Senior Management / Executive Profile

Results-oriented operations executive with diverse experience and strong record of achievement spanning four independent franchises. Projected MBA in International Business and Finance, December 2003.

- Manufacturing
- Warehousing
- Logistics
- Inventory Management

- Sales Management
- P&L Accountability
- Acquisition Management
- Team-Based Organization
- Community Leadership

- ISO 9000
- ERP, MRP, DRP, MPS, JIT
- Statistical Process Control (SPC)
- Theory of Constraints

Professional Experience

Education Sabbatical   2001–2002

Great Southwest Bottling Enterprises, Austin, Texas   1998–2000
Director of Operations

Accepted offer to lead Great Southwest Bottling Enterprise's flagship Austin operation within six months after acquisition of Tri-State Bottling Company. Led beverage production, syrup manufacturing, quality assurance, warehousing, inventory control, production planning, logistics, and transportation. Managed $145 million annual operating budget and $4.5 million in capital projects. Led organization of over 450 employees; produced 35 million cases annually.

- Increased plant productivity 15%, resulting in 10.5% profit growth.
- Implemented a Total Quality System for process improvement.
- Attained a 10% increase in quality index score after reviving a Statistical Process Control system that utilized automated data collection equipment and moving some of the test equipment out of the QA lab and into the hands of the line operators.

Tri-State Bottling Company, Oklahoma City, Oklahoma   1983–1998
Vice President of Operations, 1995–1998
Operations Manager, 1989–1995
Plant Manager, 1987–1989
Production Manager, 1983–1986

Successfully advanced career through three acquisitions; recognized with promotion after each. Led beverage production, syrup manufacturing, quality assurance, warehousing, inventory control, production planning, logistics, transportation, and fleet maintenance. Managed $120 million annual operating budget and $2 million in capital projects. Led organization of 400 employees.

- Played leadership role during Great Southwest Bottling Enterprises' acquisition of Tri-State Bottling Company.
- Developed a JIT system to service 28 distribution centers across the three-state area. Resulted in annual savings of $700,000 and the following reductions: material handling costs, 10%; accidents, 70%; turnover, 85%; inventory levels, 35%.
- Utilized the Theory of Constraints to avoid $3 million in capital costs and improve the output in syrup manufacturing by 15%.

Strategy: *The education sabbatical is addressed right up front, in the Professional Experience section, and the new degree is included in the Profile as well as detailed in the Education section on page 2.*

DOUGLAS G. BARNES, Page 2

- Championed a project team, primarily hourly employees and front-line supervisors, charged with purchasing and installing a high-speed production line. Achieved full production in 60% of projected time and with full product conversion cost 15% under budget.
- Developed an operator training and certification program that resulted in an overall productivity increase of 5%, reduced accident cost by 55%, and reduced turnover by 30%.
- Launched a contract packing business that contributed over $5 million annually to the bottom line.
- Successfully implemented Manufacturing Resource Planning (MRP) and Distribution Resource Planning (DRP) systems.
- Participated on the Tri-State Production Advisory Council, a prestigious, invitation-only group of senior- and executive-level managers and a think tank for coordinating efforts across the bottling network.
- Facilitated teaching of Covey Leadership Center modules across the Tri-State Bottling organization.
- Recognized with Tri-State's highest quality recognition, the President's Award, which was presented to the plant in 1993.
- Played key leadership role during Tri-State Bottling Company's acquisition of Texas Bottling Company in 1987; merged nine production plants into one over a period of a year and a half, which resulted in $15 million annual savings. Promoted to plant manager within six months of acquisition.
- Managed growth of Oklahoma City plant from 4 million cases to 25 million over a five-year period.

Education

University of Texas, Austin, Texas
Master of Business Administration, anticipated graduation December 2003 (Current GPA 4.0)
International Business and Finance

Bachelor of Arts in Business Studies, 2001 (GPA 4.0)

Continuing Professional Education

ERP, MRP, DRP, JIT, and Master Production Planning
Theory of Constraints, Clemson University

Covey Leadership Center — Facilitator Certification
    The Seven Habits of Highly Effective People
    Principle-Centered Leadership
    Four Roles of Leadership

Community Service

A strong advocate of Adult Education. Established a company-sponsored in-house program that guided people through obtaining GEDs, learning English as a second language, and gaining basic computer skills; provided tutoring for TASP and SAT testing. Coordinated college-level classes taught onsite and at the local universities.

Organizational Leadership: Texas Scholars Program, Adult Literacy Council, Oklahoma City Industrial Foundation.

Constance S. Baker

6260 Woolery Lane, Fort Lauderdale, FL 33316

Home: 954.265.9231 ■ Mobile: 954.401.1138
E-mail: cbaker@jitaweb.com

■ Summary

BUSINESS & OPERATIONS MANAGER – MULTI-SITE, TURNKEY OPERATION
Facility, Operations, and Administrative Procedures for a highly visible retail store

Intricately seasoned manager and "business connoisseur" with a polished history of utilizing word-of-mouth advertising for longevity, while incorporating diverse medias, unique marketing strategies, and a no-questions-asked service department. Pillar of the community and recipient of several awards — from area businesses and non-profit groups — throughout the state of Florida in recognition of the development and implementation of community and safety-conscious programs.

Planning / Program Development —
- Incentive / Sales Programs
- Customer Satisfaction Policies
- Special Events / Safety Training

Networking —
- Multimedia Advertising
- Press Releases / PSAs
- Public Promotions / Affairs

Administration —
- Front- and Back-Store Logistics
- Records Management
- Infrastructure & Processes

Personnel —
- Labor Relations / Staffing
- Operations Startup
- Workflow Optimization

■ Career Highlights

Created and implemented a "Head Smart" Program; sought area sponsors, volunteers, and media coverage designed to expose the realities of head injuries. Integrated a reward program for children wearing helmet protection, although no helmet law exists in the state of Florida.

Rallied and spearheaded the start of the Cindale Police Department Bike Program. Visited various departments, taught how to start the program, the equipment needed, soliciting startup funds, and citizen/community support.

Participated in the beginning stages of the Injury Prevention Center (IPC), designed to bring attention to accident rates and fatalities caused by lack of or improper use of equipment.

Involved in all facets of the business, from demographic selection, bank financing, and groundbreaking to store schematics and product lines — oversaw the purchasing and buying of each line based on store location and season.

Founding father of the Sunny Valley BMX Association, enabling Baker's store to form the area's first team that won national recognition for three consecutive years.

Focused on 100% quality customer care and vendor/supplier relations designed to increase productivity to augment long-term, strong business relations.

■ Professional Experienc

GENERAL MANAGER, 1984–2000
Baker's Bike & Fitness Company, Inc., Fort Lauderdale, FL
Operated family-owned bike and fitness business that grew from $65,000 in revenues to $3.5 million per year, including the addition of 5 store locations (50 employees), a mail order program, and warehouse facility. Oversaw all business logistics, from simplistic processes to complex administrative logistics, including on-site staff training, point-of-sale processes, advertising, marketing, new facility design, and cost management.

- Modified the product line to provide consumers with products pertaining to their lifestyles and needs (i.e., provided Mopeds in the '80s, BMX bike products in the '90s, and subsequently fitness products).

■ Training & Continued Education

Attended several classes covering software, sales motivation, operations, management, and time-management topics.

Strategy: *After taking a hiatus after selling the family business, this candidate was now ready to transition to a new job. An extended Summary and broad Career Highlights section add depth to the one job she held for her entire career.*

CHAPTER 11

Resumes for People Returning to Work After Relocating

Moving to a new area (or a new country) can present employment challenges for a "trailing" corporate spouse, military spouse, or immigrant. Often the period of unemployment is recent, so a chronological format can be used without detriment. As always, the key is to focus on relevant skills, achievements, and experience.

RESUME 54: BILLIE JORDAN; MAYSVILLE, NC

Nina Konrad

42 Forsythia Drive, Medford, NY 11763 — (631) 988-1004 — NK55455@Yahoo.com

Marketing Management Professional

Event Production & Marketing — Trade Show Coordination — Sales Management

Professional Training

Webster University, St. Louis, MO (Camp Lejeune, NC, campus)
- Began studying for Master of Business Administration degree in 8/00.

Fashion Institute of Technology, State University of New York
- Bachelor of Science degree received 8/98 with major in Marketing/Merchandising Management.

Kingsborough Community College, City University of New York
- Associate in Applied Science degree received 1/96 with major in Fashion Buying/Merchandising.

Relevant Courses

- Statistics
- Accounting
- Fashion Buying/Merchandising
- Market Research

- Marketing Strategies/Decisions
- Contemporary Retail Management
- Expository Writing

Professional Highlights

Talbots — New York, NY, and Wilmington, NC — *Assistant Store Manager*   11/96–5/02
- Managed up to 20 sales associates in a retail classic clothing store for business and professional women.
- Achieved sales goals daily and annually by maintaining customer service levels.
- Handled marketing events including direct mailings, in-store fashion shows, and events.
- Trained new associates, covering all aspects of the company manual and exposing associates to all areas of the operation.
- Designed and merchandised all window displays and sales floor daily.
- Conducted inventory bi-annually, prepared daily schedules, processed payroll data, and handled office duties including copying, faxing, and data entry.

Jim Marvin Enterprises — New York, NY — *Showroom Assistant*   9/97–8/01
- Assisted buyers in selecting merchandise at major trade show events in showrooms and convention centers.
- Conducted inventories and compared inventory data with customer needs.
- Prepared orders and assembled displays.
- Prepared flyers for direct mail and performed office duties including copying, faxing, and data entry.

Internship

Fashion Institute of Technology — 225 Fifth Avenue, New York, NY   9/97–1/98
- Mentored by the Vice President of Public Relations in a goal-oriented, evaluated position.
- Conducted market research through direct mailing, target marketing, creation and implementation of trade show specials, promotions, and window display development.
- Maintained exemplary client/tenant and home furnishing industry relations.

Skills

- Computer — Windows 98, Microsoft Office 2000, Word 8.0, Excel 8.0, Access 8.0, PowerPoint 8.0
- Language — Conversational Spanish

Strategy: *Because of a military transfer, this candidate found herself in an area where opportunities in the fashion industry are minimal, so she decided to start on an advanced degree. When another transfer brought her back to New York, she prepared this resume to reenter the fashion world.*

Sharon L. Wickins
13 Elm Road
West Middlesex, PA 16159

724-555-2858
swickins@aol.com

Career Objective: A **Sales** or **Customer Care** position employing my abilities to create a positive experience for the client while generating profits for the company

Professional Strengths Summary

- Able to direct others and clearly relate key concepts / goals.
- Build confidence in colleagues to garner results.
- Understand value of attention to detail combined with excellent time-management skills.
- Practice patience when dealing with difficult situations.
- Expertly adapt to the behavioral styles of others to maintain diplomacy and understanding.

Customer Service / Sales Qualifications

Track record for utilizing expert communication abilities to promote professionalism in customer care.

- Award-winning telemarketer with outstanding capability to lead successful sales campaigns.
- Communicate regularly with potential customers to assess needs / recommend appropriate services.
- Accurately quote current rates and prices.
- Develop superior product knowledge to increase strength of services.
- Accurately report sales statistics.
- Experienced with data-entry / record-keeping routines.

Employment History
(7⁺ years)

Aegis Communication	Don's Carpet / Upholstery Cleaning & Auto Detailing	West Middlesex Area School District
Port St. Lucie, FL	Port St. Lucie, FL	West Middlesex, PA
Telemarketer	*Assistant*	*Teacher's Aide*

Personal Development / Education

Peak Potential, Inc. (Sharon, PA)
Communication Styles Course

Sharon High School (Sharon, PA)
Diploma

Strategy: *A functional style is used to highlight relevant skills, while sporadic employment is summarized in a concise listing.*

Cheyenne A. Williams

22407 Wentworth Court
Mason, OH 45140
513-428-2599
cheyennewilliams@aol.com

Career Summary

Fifteen years of progressive sales, supervisory, and training experience.
Demonstrated and documented track record of exceeding sales goals.
Training, interviewing, hiring, and management experience.
Probing, negotiating, and organizational skills.
Business-to-business self-generated sales ability.
Effective territory-management skills.

Articulate and creative, offering innovative and practical solutions.
Assertive, self-motivated, goal-oriented, and efficient.
Adept at both oral and written communications.
Energetic and results oriented.

Professional Experience

Merck Scientific Products *(major distributor of lab chemicals, supplies, and equipment)*   Buffalo Grove, IL
Telesales Representative   March 1997–June 2002

- **Top performer, January 1998**

Responsible for the development of new and existing accounts within the Mid-Atlantic and Northeastern United States. Communicated with scientists, engineers, lab managers, quality-control managers, purchasing agents, and microbiologists for lab supplies, equipment, and furniture consultation and purchase. Coordinated technical assistance and support between the manufacturer and end-user. Conceptualized and pioneered a major vendor fair on-site at a large account while coordinating remotely. Negotiated a national contract for over $500K in new business revenue. Won an exclusive contract, locking out the competition. Managed territory by telephone, with occasional on-site visits. Increased stability of a difficult-to-manage territory within one year of assignment.

Global Search Consultants *(contingency recruiting firm)*   Oakbrook, IL
Sales Manager / Owner   1994–1997

Contingency recruiter for senior-management, middle-management, and various other positions in sales, marketing, finance, and human resources within restaurant and manufacturing industries. Initiated new business throughout the United States utilizing telephone and in-person presentations. Increased revenue to over $80K within the first two years of business. Responsible for accounting, purchasing, profit-and-loss statements, new business development, advertising, and public relations.

Strategy: *Relevant experience and notable achievements are highlighted in the extensive Professional Experience section, preceded by a Career Summary that includes both professional qualifications and personal attributes.*

Cheyenne A. Williams

Page 2

630-428-2599
cheyennewilliams@aol.com

Professional Experience, *continued*

Mediserv Products *(medical supplies and equipment)* — Chicago, IL
Medical Sales Representative — 1992–1994
- **Top performer June 1992, August 1992, October 1992**

Expedited sales of disposables, educational materials, and topical medications through detailing. Target market was OB/GYN and other medical specialties. Coached OB/GYN residents in the OR and outpatient clinical environments on the medical indications and insertion/removal of OB/GYN prosthetics. Utilized detailing, short lectures, journal reports, and demonstrations to generate new revenue. Territory responsibilities included time management, budgeting, sales projections, and forecasting. Turned a low-revenue territory around within 12 months.

Kodak Corporation *(office equipment and supply manufacturer)* — Oakbrook, IL
Marketing Representative — 1987–1990
- **Top performer May 1988, March 1989, August 1989**

Entry-level sales position with demanding quotas. Developed a customer base from 0 to over 200 companies, which generated revenues of over $400K annually. Increased sales solely from cold-calling activity. Actively conducted product demonstrations and formal slide presentations and prepared proposals for prospective customers. Coached and trained new hires, utilizing formal internal training methods and practical on-the-job training sessions.

Education

DePaul University — Chicago, IL
BS — Mass Media Broadcasting / Journalism — 1987

Mary Jenson

6610 Canyon Drive
Scottsdale, AZ 85251

mjenson@earthlink.net

Cell: 480/571-3986
Home: 480/966-1246

MORTGAGE LOAN OFFICER

A goal-oriented professional whose proven record of achieving productivity and service objectives has produced valuable results. Recognized as a contributing team member with outstanding analytical skills and high standards of quality customer service. Capable of expanding business in a highly competitive marketplace.

Highlights of Qualifications

› Prepare, analyze, verify, and approve loan applications
› Knowledgeable of loan products and loan approval processes
› Oral and written communication skills
› Problem-solving capability
› Public contact and interface
› Customer service abilities
› Bilingual: English/Spanish
› Skilled with accounting and financial procedures
› Ability to inspire trust, respect, and confidence
› Work independently and as a team member
› Develop effective working relationships with management and clients

PROFESSIONAL EXPERIENCE

<u>Alpha America Mortgage</u>, Palm Springs, CA
Senior Loan Officer, 1994–1998

Originated conventional real-estate loans and specialized in FHA loans, developing business and providing service primarily to the Hispanic community.

❑ Fulfilled corporate objectives and closed several loans per month.
❑ Accessed loan documentation and programs for placement with appropriate lender.
❑ Processed loans from conception to completion and followed through to timely closure.
❑ Reviewed loan applications, interviewed applicants, verified accuracy of documents, and arranged disbursement of funds.
❑ Assisted borrowers to understand the loan process and complete applications.
❑ Helped consumers qualify to purchase a home or to refinance an existing mortgage.
❑ Kept abreast of new mortgage products to meet customers' needs, including reverse-equity mortgages, shared-equity mortgages, and adjustable-rate mortgages.
❑ Met with customers, gathered data, answered questions, and processed required forms.
❑ Reviewed completed financial forms for accuracy and requested additional data if necessary.
❑ Requested credit reports from major credit-reporting agencies and ensured that the consumer met the lending institution's requirements.

Strategy: *Because this "trailing spouse" is seeking employment in her area of recent experience, a straight chronological resume works well for her.*

Mary Jenson Resume — Page 2

PROFESSIONAL EXPERIENCE (Continued)

<u>Internal Revenue Service</u>, Laguna Niguel, CA
Internal Revenue Agent, 1988–1994

Conducted intensive investigations of numerous individuals and corporations to resolve problems involving tax-law compliance.

❑ Interviewed individual taxpayers and corporate executives to determine validity of financial statements and performed detailed analysis of statements for accuracy.
❑ Upon completion of investigation, wrote reports recommending appropriate action.
❑ Attended ongoing training seminars to stay informed of federal taxation laws.
❑ Received Public Service Award for volunteering time to VITA, a program to assist underprivileged adults and senior citizens with tax preparation.
❑ Served as bilingual interpreter, assisting other IRS agents in telephone communications and correspondence with Hispanic taxpayers.

<u>University of La Verne</u>, La Verne, CA
Accountant, 1983–1988

Handled all accounting activity associated with university donations, including accounts receivable, bank reconciliation, general ledger, and year-end closing.

❑. Received commendation letter from Vice President for outstanding performance.
❑ Gained a broad knowledge of accounting as an assistant for the first three years.

EDUCATION and TRAINING

B.S., Business Administration — Accounting
University of La Verne, La Verne, CA, 1986

LICENSES

Enrolled Agent License, 7/94–Present

Real Estate License, 9/00
State of California

Notary Certification, 10/00

RESUME 58: JOYCE FORTIER, MBA, CPRW, JCTC, CCM; NOVI, MI

JOY BURDICK

1800 Henry • Birmingham, Michigan 48000 • (555) 223-1999 • jwburdick@yahoo.net

CAREER TARGET: PHARMACEUTICAL SALES

Dynamic professional with a strong medical background and experience in sales. Energetic and outgoing with great communication skills. Outstanding organization and time management abilities.

STRENGTHS AND SKILLS

- ➢ Highly creative, self-motivated professional with excellent interpersonal skills.
- ➢ Strong medical background obtained through education and work experience — familiar with medical terminology and diagnostics.
- ➢ Comfortable interacting with all levels of medical professionals, from physicians to nurses and specialists.
- ➢ Ability to conceptualize and generate new ideas, analyze problems and develop effective solutions.
- ➢ A dependable team player who relates well and works cooperatively with diverse personalities.
- ➢ Fast learner with demonstrated initiative and dedication to the achievement of organizational goals.
- ➢ Focus on providing exceptional service resulting in customer satisfaction and repeat business.
- ➢ Computer capabilities include: MS Word, the Internet and Outlook.

EDUCATION

B.S., *Physiology,* MICHIGAN STATE UNIVERSITY, East Lansing, MI
  Courses included: Biochemistry, Organic Chemistry, Physics, Anatomy and Biology

EXPERIENCE

THE GIRAFFE, CHARLESTON, IL   1999–2001
SALES ASSOCIATE

- ➢ Designed creative window displays for this children's clothing boutique.
- ➢ Sold merchandise to 70% of customers browsing during assigned shift, including many add-ons.
- ➢ Assisted owner with selecting merchandise for the shop.

GRACE HOSPITAL — EMERGENCY DEPARTMENT, DETROIT, MI   1991–1994
EMERGENCY MEDICAL TECHNICIAN   1993–1994

- ➢ Assisted nursing staff and physicians with invasive and non-invasive procedures. Averaged 40+ new admissions over any eight-hour period.
- ➢ Took basic vitals, and provided patient care and comfort measures.
- ➢ Charted procedures and maintained medical supplies for trauma 1 center. Know CPR.

UNIT CLERK   1991–1992

- ➢ Organized charting, and provided follow-up with patients' attending physician regarding various information.
- ➢ Utilized available resources and systems to efficiently facilitate work procedures.

Strategy: *This candidate used a relocation as an opportunity to refocus her career in the area of pharmaceutical sales. An extensive summary brings her experience and education together to create a strong introduction.*

RESUME 59: DENISE LUPARDO; LAKE FOREST, CA

RACHEL MAX

LEGAL ASSISTANT / PARALEGAL

8945 Town Court
Naperville, IL 60566
(630) 555-0945

OVERVIEW

Highly motivated legal assistant dedicated to professionalism and quality.
A proven record for providing dependable assistance as a team member in a
law environment.

SKILLS

- Aptitude for effectively interfacing with supervisors, professional staff, and clientele.
- Effective problem solver; prioritize and manage heavy workflow without direct supervision.
- Strong communication, grammar, and interpersonal skills.
- Knowledge of Corel WordPerfect, Microsoft Word, TimeSlips, and various software and office equipment.

EDUCATION

PARALEGAL CERTIFICATION (1991)
Focus: Litigation
University of California, Irvine, CA

GENERAL COURSEWORK
Focus: Business / Social Sciences
Irvine Valley College, Irvine, CA

EXPERIENCE

LEGAL ASSISTANT (1999–2002)
Smith & Jones, San Diego, CA
- Aided litigation partner in coordinating real estate transactions and corporate documents.
- Expedited preparation and editing of correspondence, discovery, and pleadings.
- Assisted counsel in preparing for court hearings, depositions, and trials.
- Responsible for maintaining court calendar, attorney's personal calendar, billing documents, and files.

PARALEGAL (1996–1999)
San Diego Management Company, San Diego, CA
- Responsible for daily review and organization of litigation files and calendar.
- Prepared corporate minutes and assisted with administrative support.
- Appointed to correspond with outside counsel regarding ongoing litigation.
- Reviewed and supervised monthly billing statements of outside counsel.

LEGAL ASSISTANT / PARALEGAL (1993–1996)
Little, Marcus, & Preston, San Diego, CA
- Drafted discovery motions and correspondence, prepared court forms for filing and service, and maintained court calendar.
- Prepared deposition summaries and maintained files.

PARALEGAL (1991–1993)
Gold Coast Management Company, San Diego, CA
- Assisted with the preparation, filing, and service of litigation documents.
- Prepared unlawful detainer pleadings, court forms, and motions for Bankruptcy Court.
- Monitored court calendar and prepared miscellaneous office correspondence.

PAST/PRESENT AFFILIATIONS

California Association of Independent Paralegals
California Real Estate Licensure

Strategy: *Relevant education, certification, and recent experience make for a strong resume for this relocated spouse. The design is eye-catching.*

HANNAH MANDEVILLE

203-484-9823   12 Iris Terrace, North Branford, CT 06471   hannah@vsmail.com

PROFESSIONAL OBJECTIVE

Sales/Management

PROFESSIONAL PROFILE

- Profit-minded, bottom-line driven professional focused on results, quality, and teamwork.
- Highly motivated, goal-directed team member/mentor with strong leadership abilities and traits.
- Valued by employer for extraordinary contributions to building peak annual revenues.
- Number one ranked Team Manager/Leader in the nation for four consecutive years.
- Respected by others for knowledge, consistent performance, and witty, caring personality.

EXPERIENCE

CORPORATE CREATIVES, Alexandria, Virginia   **1996–2002**

Team Manager/Leader, 10/97–9/02
- Reporting to franchise owner, entrusted to manage all facets of day-to-day operations with accountability for and compensation based on annual profit performance. Mentored and motivated employees to perform at highest levels to ensure customer satisfaction and retention.

Key Results:
- Provided sound leadership in establishing vision and direction to achieve desired goals.
- Fostered cooperation among team members, contributing to a productive work environment.
- Exceeded annual growth goals, with averages at 18% to 22%.
- Retained key accounts in a highly competitive and cyclical market — accomplished through networking, sales prospecting, and outstanding customer focus.
- Collaborated with clients, identifying budget parameters and vision to deliver superior-quality end product; successfully maintained 68% of total sales orders per month.
- Recipient of *National Excellence in Leadership Awards:* 2002 — Gold; 2001 — Gold; 2000 — Gold; 1999 — Gold; 1998 — Silver; 1997 — Bronze.
- Active member of Business Council; completed various seminars on Leadership/Management.

Customer Service Representative, 6/96 – 10/97
- Hired by owner to perform entry-level duties: assisted walk-in customers; phone quotations; prospecting; data entry. Performed daily account reconciliation of sales and cash register; followed through on a myriad of details, ensuring customer satisfaction; made thank-you calls and wrote personal notes of appreciation; managed project deadlines and quality assurance.

EDUCATION

Bachelor of Arts — Art and Design — Regents College, Albany, New York, May 1996
- Emphasis: Drawing, Art History, and Sociology
- Dean's List — Five Semesters
- Personally paid for over 75% of college education

"Hannah is one of those rare individuals you discover (and hire) once in a lifetime. I would not be where I am today — for certain — without her vast contributions and commitment to our company."
- Eliott Ramsey, Owner/General Manager, Corporate Creatives, Alexandria, Virginia

Strategy: *A straight chronological format is enhanced with a strong profile and a quote from her past employer.*

RESUME 61: JOYCE FORTIER, MBA, CPRW, JCTC, CCM; NOVI, MI

KAUSHA SWETH

888.444.0909   473 Scarlet Drive, Novi, MI 48300   Ksweth@hotmail.com

MARKETING • PROJECT MANAGEMENT • MIS MANAGEMENT

Self-motivated professional with a unique combination of skills in marketing, project management, and technology. Proven results: increasing company revenue, developing cost-saving programs, developing new markets, and building product awareness.

SUMMARY OF QUALIFICATIONS

- Attuned to ever-changing needs of business; service oriented with strong intuitive and analytical abilities.
- Astute in identifying areas in need of improvement, with the vision to develop and implement successful action plans.
- Excellent program/project and general business management skills.
- Creative in problem-solving and cost-cutting issues.
- Work cooperatively on teams, as well as independently, toward excellence and quality in corporate objectives and goals.
- Creative and knowledgeable with marketing campaigns, always meeting project deadlines.
- Strong management and organizational skills.
- Able to set goals, prioritize tasks, structure operations, and handle multiple projects simultaneously.
- *Computer skills:* MS Office, Oracle, Visual Basic, Web Development.

EXPERIENCE

MARKETING STRATEGIST (VOLUNTEER)   AMERICAN CANCER SOCIETY, Southfield, MI   1995–Present
Work on the no-smoking campaign, *The Great American Smokeout*, consulting with prospective advertisers and developing strategic advertising concepts to promote the campaign.

SENIOR EXECUTIVE, CLIENT SERVICES   PRESSMAN ADVERTISING & MARKETING, Bombay, India   1990–1991
A leading financial advertising firm in India.
Analyzed the competitiveness of existing products, developing new technologies and redefining market niche. Restructured PR strategies and created new sales collaterals, and advertising and trade-show materials to support market expansion. Handled financial advertising for stocks and mutual funds.
- Directed successful media campaigns, including ad layouts, media buying, and cost analysis.
- Completed major projects within budget through proper planning and coordination of resources.
- Monitored the status of various projects, tracking costs and manpower utilization and keeping management informed of project status at all times.

EXECUTIVE OF CLIENT SERVICES   NAC ADVERTISING & MARKETING CO., Bombay, India   1989–1990
A major advertising company in India.
Prepared strategies for media campaigns and materials for local, regional, national, and global advertising. Handled client servicing, market research, production, copywriting, business development, and press conferences. Developed sales-promotional materials such as POP displays, trade-show exhibits, circulars, catalogs, booklets, and direct-mail advertising. Handled many major clients in India.

MARKETING EXECUTIVE   HINDUSTAN BREWERIES & BOTTLING, LTD., Bombay, India 1986–1989
Supplier of beer to exclusive clients in India and abroad.
Handled marketing, sales, advertising, and PR. Coordinated with distributors to supply major hotels and nightclubs in Bombay. Managed PR programs, launching materials to increase awareness, recognition, and market share. Outperformed competition by sponsoring sporting events and holiday parties.

EDUCATION
Master of Arts, *International History,* UNIVERSITY OF BOMBAY, Bombay, India
Master of Arts Candidate (50% complete), *Advertising & PR,* MICHIGAN STATE UNIVERSITY, Lansing, MI
Post-Graduate Degree, *Management,* BOMBAY UNIVERSITY, Bombay, India
Bachelor of Arts, *Clinical & Industrial Psychology,* MITHIBIA COLLEGE OF ARTS & SCIENCE, Bombay, India
Seminar, *Import/Export Management,* Bombay, India
Computer Skills, COMPULEARN, Southfield, MI
Workshop, *Public Speaking for Executives*

Strategy: *In addition to extensive professional experience in India, this immigrant/trailing spouse had volunteer experience in the U.S. that was relevant to her career in marketing.*

SONNY H. FARAJ
CIVIL ENGINEERING PROFESSIONAL
1408 Sutton Place ▪ Ann Arbor, MI 48109 ▪ Residence: 734.773.4978 ▪ Office: 734.773.8002

Strong leader with extensive experience in lifecycle project management — from design, development and testing to completion. International and updated BSCE credential; recipient of multiple awards for engineering excellence.

PROJECT EXPERIENCE

Land Reclamation & Bridges
- Paved road construction & infrastructure
- Vehicle bridge construction
- Concrete lining for canals
- Open and covered drains
- Land leveling

Dams & Lakes
- Excavation
- Filling & compacting
- Intake, escapes, weirs, regulators and culverts
- Pumping stations
- Drains

Buildings & Steel Structures
- Foundation design and soil investigation
- Concrete piles
- Brick & reinforced concrete construction (homes, schools)
- Steel structures (garages, factories, warehouses)

Project: Reconstruction of Concrete Riverbed Surrounding Ancient City
Role: **Executive Engineer**
- *Challenge:* High ground water level throughout site plan.
- *Actions:*
  - Opened side drains along canal and incorporated pumping stations.
  - Excavated the river in cross sections.
  - Converted open drains to cover drains.
  - Began lining while operating pumping stations to eliminate uplift pressure.
  - Removed pumping stations; filled canal with water.
- *Results:* Time saved = 40%

Project: Issyk Kul Riverbed Land Reclamation
Role: **Executive Engineer**
- *Challenge 1:* Collapse of cover field drain sides due to high water level and collector drains not working sufficiently.
- *Actions:*
  - Integrated pumping stations; drained water from collector to main drain.
  - Decreased ground level on field drain alignment to reduce risk of collapse.
- *Results:* Time saved = 20%

- *Challenge 2:* High temperatures and evaporation of soil moisture led to hairline cracks in canal concrete lining.
- *Actions:*
  - Wet canal section before lining.
  - Reduced time cap between trimming and lining.
  - Decided to lay concrete at night instead of daytime.
- *Results:* Time saved = 15%

Project: Haddad Hiram Development
Role: **Resident Engineer**
- *Challenge:* Develop irrigation structure (head regulators, intakes, syphones culverts) cost and time effectively for various locations.
- *Actions:*
  - Redesigned structures as pre-cast units.
  - Developed pre-cast plants at site locations.
- *Results:* Reduced cost 30%

Strategy: *A project format is used to show extensive, relevant experience as well as quantifiable results. All experience is from his career in Kyrgyzstan. He has supplemented his educational credentials since coming to the U.S.*

PROFESSIONAL HISTORY

Executive Engineer
GREATER CENTRAL ASIA RECLAMATION COMPANY – OSH, KYRGYZSTAN (1989 to 2001)

Led the development of project plans throughout Asia and the Middle East, as well as site investigation, structure irrigation, materials testing, dams and intake structure, and lake, drain and canal excavation. Also provided quantity estimation.

Resident Engineer
ISSYK KUL PROJECT – ISSYK KUL, KYRGYZSTAN (1980 to 1989)

Planned design and edited original drafts for concrete structures and filling and compacting projects. Provided design and cost negotiation consultation for Pellicar Company (Greece) and Sribona Company (Russia).

Supervising Engineer
ARGA AGRICULTURAL DESIGN & CONSTRUCTION COMPANY – BISHKEK, KYRGYZSTAN (1977 to 1980)

Supervised building site of steel and concrete structures; provided soil testing expertise.

Estimating Engineer
PRINCIPAL CONSTRUCTION COMPANY – BISHKEK, KYRGYZSTAN (1975 to 1977)

Responsible for cost analysis and quantity estimation.

EDUCATION

B.S. — Civil Engineering (2002)
University of Michigan
Ann Arbor, Michigan

B.S. — Civil Engineering (1977)
University of Bishkek
Bishkek, Kyrgyzstan

Other courses:
Scientific and technical training in integral reclamation, project planning and business administration.

Awards detailed upon request.

SONNY H. FARAJ
1408 Sutton Place ▪ Ann Arbor, MI 48109
Residence: 734.773.4978 ▪ Office: 734.773.8002

RESUME 63: GINA TAYLOR, CPRW; KANSAS CITY, MO

48 w. 103rd street, Neehaw, Kansas 66203
(913) 721-9626

freddie nella

uniquely qualified for

on-air talent — radio imaging — commercial voiceover — documentaries — music production – acting

- ❖ personable, articulate, and professional with elements of uniqueness
- ❖ proven ability to adapt quickly to challenges and changing environments
- ❖ poised in public speaking and widely experienced in communications
- ❖ comfortable with powerful personalities and celebrities
- ❖ great communicator; "in-the-trenches" experience

voiceover/radio imaging talent

prestige communications, Lancashire, United Kingdom 1993–2001
- ➤ **radio imaging** — Radio One, Lancashire; Radio Five, Sheffield

sasson communications, Lancashire, United Kingdom 1993–1997
- ➤ **voiceover** — Norwegian Cruise Line
- ➤ **voice** — International Balloon Festival, Glasgow, Scotland

on-air talent

metro radio group, Sheffield, United Kingdom 1985–1993

radio five
"night magic" *(late night romance)* **10:00 pm–2:00 am**
- ➤ #1 adult 25-54 program, 1995

radio seven
"night magic" *(late night romance)* **9:00 pm–12:00 midnight**
- ➤ #1 adult 25–54 program (from 7th), capturing 36% of viewing audience, 1993
- ➤ "People's Choice Award," 1995
- ➤ "Citation of Excellence," Category: Local Radio, 1994

"Saturday night oldies"
- ➤ #1 adult contemporary, Saturday night

metro — Sheffield
"sweet fa"
- ➤ News, traffic, guest interviews, live broadcast, music programming…the whole thing!
- ➤ Weekly radio documentaries.

acting (actors equity #10256)

Movies: "Paper Marriage," London, United Kingdom
Television: "Spender" and "the rays," London, United Kingdom
MC: "The World Disco-Dancing Championships," London, United Kingdom

personal data

Military (12 years): British Airborne Forces, Special Forces
Active Duty: Malaysia, Indonesia, Kenya, Oman, Jordan, and Falkland Islands
Well-Traveled: Far East, Middle East, Europe, Eastern Bloc, Scandinavia, North Africa, Canada, Caribbean

Strategy: *This immigrant from the U.K. needed a strong resume to show his qualifications for his professional career in broadcasting. The resume is strong visually, as well, due to an appropriate graphic and interesting name treatment.*

CHAPTER 12

Resumes for People Returning to Work After Retirement

Whether financially strapped or simply bored, retirees returning to work need to deal with a period of unemployment as well as the possibility of appearing "too old." Unless the retirement has been very short, a functional format is often the most effective approach.

RESUME 64: SHEILA ADJAHOE; UPPER MARLBORO, MD

LILLIE K. SIMPSON
732 Boxhall Way, Hartford, Connecticut 06120
(860) 432-8973   LillieKSimpson@aol.com

OBJECTIVE

An administrative assistant position in the SEE Program.

HIGHLIGHTS

- 34 years of government experience at various administrative levels.
- Extensive college-level business courses.
- Outstanding follow-up skills; goal-driven; always seek to bring projects to completion.
- Self-starter who sees what has to be done, then does it.
- Recipient of many Outstanding Service Awards.

RELEVANT SKILLS AND EXPERIENCE

OFFICE TECHNOLOGY

- Keyboarding skill of 50 wpm.
- Mastery of MS Office Suite (Word, Excel, Access) and Windows 95 environment.
- Expertise in various other software packages including SAS, WordPerfect, CODAP, SPSS, PROFS, Harvard Graphics, and Lotus 1-2-3.

ADMINISTRATION

- Developed organization and command budgets.
- Recommended distribution of bulk software purchases.
- Scheduled training classes and served as an instructor.
- Coordinated and conducted monthly Information Management Office meetings.
- Served on personnel screening and selection panels.
- Organized CODAP conferences.
- Processed travel orders.

LEADERSHIP

- Supervised 7 to 9 employees as Team Leader for the Configuration Management and Requirements Team.
- Served as lead officer in the development, implementation, and operation of CAPRMIS (Capability Request Management Information System) for the Personnel Information System Command.

WRITING

- Wrote policy statements, procedures manuals, and programs of instruction.
- Wrote the user manual for the PERSINSCOM (Personnel Information Systems Command) system.
- Wrote Comprehensive Analysis Reports for the Army, Navy, Airforce, and Marines.

WORK HISTORY

1982 – 1994	**Program Analyst**	Department of Army, Washington, DC
1980 – 1982	**Management Analyst**	Department of Navy, Washington, DC
1976 – 1980	**Administrative Assistant**	Department of Army, Washington, DC

EDUCATION

Montgomery Jr. College, Rockville, Maryland
    Associate Degree in Business Management/Personnel Administration
    Additional coursework in Business Management and Personnel Administration
Strayer College, Washington, DC
    Courses in Business Administration

Strategy: *Present a strong Relevant Skills and Experience section that perfectly keys in on the skills she wants to use in her second career.*

SUSAN LYNN GARDNER

538 Sky Road
Paramus, NJ 07133
(201) 369-3267
SLGardner@hotmail.com

SUMMARY OF QUALIFICATIONS

In-depth experience in the following areas:

- **Billing and Invoicing** — Managed accounts payable and accounts receivable invoices at the Hudson Generating Station of Public Service Electric and Gas. Evaluated invoices for accuracy and checked material orders. Worked with statistical documentation.

- **Computers** — Familiar with Lotus 1-2-3, WordPerfect, and Word for Windows; knowledge of customized mainframe payroll systems (APPO Operating System).

- **Clerical Administration** — Performed payroll functions, word processing, data entry, and various secretarial duties. Reported to regional business manager and site manager. Implemented special financial projects as needed. Distributed petty cash funds.

- **Customer Relations** — Interfaced with distribution employees and procurement analysts. Communicated with managers regarding payment and approval of bills. Worked as part of a clerical team encompassing generating-station personnel and field personnel. Served as a Member of the Corporate Committee for APPO Users. Analyzed current systems for defaults and made recommendations for the future. Served as the generating station Notary.

- **Personal Strengths** — Developed excellent communication skills. Enjoyed helping employees and working with people in all areas. Known as a cooperative team player and a diligent, responsible employee. Career encompassed 14 years of increasing responsibilities and promotions in the administrative areas of a major utility company.

PROFESSIONAL EXPERIENCE

1980–2001 **NEW JERSEY UTILITIES**
Madison and Clark Generating Stations
Administrative Clerk "A" — Senior Level/Staff Support
Offered an early-retirement package after 20 years of service.

Promoted three times to the highest administrative step. Worked closely with the APPO Project Team. Demonstrated expert knowledge of DWAC and PACE Accounting Systems. Responsible for vendor relations and various financial duties. Maintained contact with station supervisors, ordered all supplies for the station, and performed related secretarial duties.

EDUCATION

GREATER NEW JERSEY COUNTY COLLEGE, Newark, NJ
AS in Liberal Arts
Continuing Education: Customer Service, Effective Speech and Writing

Strategy: *After 20 years with one employer, this individual took an early-retirement package but quickly grew bored. The functional format is effective at highlighting her skills.*

John T. Richardson

100 Elm Drive • Orchard Park, NY 14127 • 716/555-2121

QUALIFICATIONS

- 30 years of Management, Sales, and Customer Service experience.
- Stable employment history with more than 25 years at same local company.
- Background in production and printing.
- Possess mechanical aptitude with experience in basic repairs/maintenance.
- Keyboarding/data entry skills.
- Known for loyalty, honesty, enthusiasm, willingness to learn, interpersonal/communication skills, and sense of humor.
- Use creativity in approaching new situations and solving problems.

HIGHLIGHTS OF EXPERIENCE

Production Management

- More than 20 years' experience overseeing, planning, scheduling, and tracking the use of human and physical resources in a production environment.
- Supervised departmental activities as well as all factory operations (four departments), directing the activities of a small staff and later four production managers and their staffs totaling 120 employees, operating in a 24x5 environment with monthly sales of $500K.
- Monitored expenses to remain within budget guidelines and effectively utilized time and equipment to achieve sales goals.
- Applied solid organizational abilities to meet the demands of these positions.

Personnel Management

- As a manager, performed diverse human-resources functions, including interviewing, hiring, disciplining, terminating, training, motivating, scheduling, and performance assessment.
- Used interpersonal, analytical, and decision-making skills effectively on a daily basis.
- Developed a pre-employment screening tool that tests basic language, math, and reasoning skills, which is still in use by the company today.

Customer Service & Sales

- For the last 10 years of my career, assisted customers with questions, problems, and orders via telephone.
- Handled assigned accounts (including one of the company's largest accounts, $3 million in annual sales) as well as inquiries from potential new customers.
- Contacted forms dealers and brokers to market the company's services and expertise.
- Designed business form solutions to meet diverse customer needs, specializing in complex numbering and mailer forms.
- Entered orders, following through production to completion and keeping customers informed of status.
- Maintained excellent customer relationships, resolved problems effectively, and served as a resource to other customer-service and sales team members.

Strategy: *This is another example of a purposely low-key resume, written so as not to overwhelm readers with his qualifications and experience. The functional style pushes all dates to page 2.*

John T. Richardson — Page Two

EMPLOYMENT	SUPERIOR FORMS INC. — Buffalo, NY	1968 to 1997

Senior Customer Service & Sales Representative
Press, Collator & Bindery Liaison
Factory Superintendent
Foreman, Collator Department
Foreman, Bindery & Hand Assembly Department
Equipment Operator/Shipping Clerk

ELM DRIVE BINDERY — Orchard Park, NY   1979 to 1992
Owner/Operator
- Home-based company servicing forms manufacturers who required hand or piecework, such as labeling and stringing.

U.S. AIR FORCE   1964 to 1968
Airman First Class/Personnel Specialist
- Honorable discharge

AFFILIATIONS   Member, Circle of Support for DDSO Client involved in NYS OMRDD Self-
Determination Pilot Program
Member, Erie County Traumatic Brain Injury Support Group &
NYS Head Injury Support Group
Volunteer Driver, DDSO

EDUCATION   Graduate: St. Thomas Military Academy — St. Paul, MN

HAROLD C. JACKSON

PO Box 184, Barton Hill Road, Albany, New York 12203 • Tel: 518-325-9969 (Home) / 518-325-4212 (F.D. HQ)
Email: Jackson@mindspring.net

MANAGEMENT PROFILE

PUBLIC SAFETY / CODE ENFORCEMENT / FIRE SUPPRESSION & PREVENTION / EMERGENCY MEDICAL SERVICES

Accomplished Senior Manager combining strong management skills with expert capacity to build and nurture cohesive, productive teams to achieve optimal levels of performance.

QUALIFICATIONS SUMMARY

➢ Extensive background and training in all facets of emergency operations including fire, emergency medical, and hazardous-material handling.

➢ Recognized for consistent ability to identify opportunities to employ innovative processes and procedures to revitalize operations and affect bottom-line results. Strong ability to identify, analyze, and solve problems.

➢ Flexible leader and expert strategist delivering unique change management initiatives. Explore innovative paths and procedures to achieve outstanding results. Initiate good conceptual ideas with practical applications.

➢ Demonstrated ability to effectively influence key decision makers. Take decisive action based on well-documented facts. Excellent ability to cope with stressful situations and multiple priorities.

➢ Strong leadership skills with a genuine interest in growth and development of staff, inspiring team members to achieve success through developing individual strengths.

➢ Excellent interpersonal skills and capacity to optimally utilize all channels of communications. Innate ability to effectively communicate goals and interplay of ideas and concepts to convey clear understanding of the corporate mission and philosophy.

CORE COMPETENCIES INCLUDE:

Project Management	Strategic Planning	Operations Management
Team Leadership	Staff Training / Development	Problem Analysis / Resolution
Process Reengineering	Inspection / Code Enforcement	Purchasing
Budget / Finance	Grant Writing / Administration	Liaison Skills

MASTER OF DEVELOPING AND IMPLEMENTING STRATEGIC PLANS AND OPERATIONS INITIATIVES THAT ACHIEVE RESULTS.

PROFESSIONAL CAREER PATH

Albany County Fire Department, Colonie, NY   1980–2002
Fast-track promotion through increasingly responsible positions commencing as Firefighter and ultimately leading to Battalion Chief.

DIRECTOR OF EMERGENCY MEDICAL SERVICES — BATTALION CHIEF
SHIFT COMMANDER — CAPTAIN
ENGINE COMPANY OFFICER — LIEUTENANT
EMERGENCY MEDICAL TECHNICIAN — ENGINEER
FIRE FIGHTER
Supervised Emergency Medical Services comprising 45 EMTs and paramedics at three fire stations. Participated in the direction of all aspects of personnel relations including hiring, disciplinary actions, training, development, and evaluations. Served as incident commander at medical emergencies and structure fires. Coordinated all phases of emergency medical service (EMS) and served as Chairman of EMS Operations Committee. Wrote and implemented EMS protocols.

Continued…

Strategy: *This recently retired fire chief is looking for a second career. The Management Profile makes his target crystal-clear.*

HAROLD C. JACKSON

Page 2 of 2

➤ Planned, organized, and executed EMS training, testing, and recertification for 63 EMTs. Served as Emergency Medical Services Training Officer.
➤ Catalyst in the conceptualization of paramedic program for Albany County Fire Department. Aspects of state licensure became model for other fire departments.
➤ Instrumental in developing a medical-director contract that became model for other EMS agencies.
➤ Orchestrated groundbreaking legal interlocal agreement with neighboring fire department to share personnel, which enhanced public relations and augmented learning opportunities for firefighters.
➤ Established and launched Fire Cadet Program (paid internship) to allow 17- to 21-year-olds to participate in fire service through a comprehensive training and mentoring opportunity.
➤ Appointed as Venue Commander during Lake Placid 1980 Winter Olympics.
➤ Streamlined process to provide medical oxygen to EMS through small cylinders, eliminating rental fees and **saving 50% on oxygen cost.**

EDUCATION

Associate of Applied Science in Fire Science
SUNY at Albany — Albany, New York

Associate of Science Degree
Sienna College — Latham, New York

CERTIFICATIONS

Fire Science Officer II
Apparatus Driver / Operator
EMT and CPR Instruction
EMT-Basic National Standard Curriculum

Fire Fighter I, II, III
Fire Inspector I — Fire Instructor I
Hazardous Materials
EMS Training Officer

PROFESSIONAL DEVELOPMENT COURSEWORK

Managing Emergency Medical Services
Leadership and Decision Making
Pesticide Fire and Spill Control
Preparing for Incident Command
Handling Hazardous Materials Incidents
Life Safety Code
Leading People Effectively
Aerial and Quint Operations & Tactics
Weapons of Mass Destruction
Public Information Officer
Fire Service Communications
Executive Analysis of Multiple-Venue Operations

Advanced Incident Command
Hazardous Materials Incident Analysis
Incident Command
Commanding the Initial Response
Servicing Fire Extinguishers
Conducting Basic Fire Inspections
Stewart Rose Fire Training
EMS Leadership Course
Supervising Today's Workforce
Advanced Leadership Issues in the EMS
Fire Service Organizational Theory
Emergency Medical Services Special Operations

AFFILIATIONS

New York State Fireman's Association
National Fire Academy Alumni Association
New York State EMT Association
District 2B Inter Hospital Committee
New York State Fire Chief's Association
New York State Department of Public Safety Division of Community Emergency Management

Raymond S. McComb

229 Berenger Court #578
Chicago, Illinois 60329
(630) 886-1141 ▪ RSMcComb@msn.com

> *"...You are the most highly organized engineer I have met...the thoroughness of your work and your dependability are excellent...your assumption of responsibility for assignment scheduling and accomplishment is outstanding..."* — James Turner, Former Dept. Chief, Orbital Sciences Corporation

Executive Profile

High-energy, results-driven professional blending formal education in Civil Engineering with in-depth experience in Mechanical Engineering focusing on project engineering. Exceptional leadership, management, and relationship-building skills; foster team unity and project cohesion across all levels of staff, management, and customers. Technically fluent, rapidly assimilating cutting-edge technologies, ideas, and processes. Reputation for unsurpassed loyalty, dedication, professional ethics, and integrity.

Areas of Expertise

- Project Lifecycle Management
- System Testing & Qualification
- Change Management
- Budgeting / Cost Control
- Product Development
- Component Design
- Production Processes
- International Sales
- Team Building & Leadership
- Operations Improvements
- Strategic Problem Solving
- Contract Administration

Selected Engineering Contributions

- Directed four Integrated Product Development (IPD) design teams to develop ECS components for Japanese Experimental Module (JEM) program of International Space Station project.

- Full authority for engineering budgets ranging from $100,000 to $3 million.

- Leader of "Tiger Team" to resolve high rejection rate on new vendor castings, saving loss of 500 castings, avoiding recall of 115 delivered units, and restoring customer confidence.

- Reduced design costs by transferring schematic preparation from design department to project engineering. Verified feasibility of transfer, established departmental and design procedures, and conducted training of personnel.

- Represented division in two-year technical definition and sales campaign with three major Japanese contractors for the Japanese Experimental Module (JEM). Resulted in first-phase contracts of more than $3 million and potential for final qualified hardware contracts exceeding $55 million.

- Led division in five-week renegotiation of $228 million corporate contract with Space Station contractor.

- Established project administration position to monitor, report, and control individual project department budgets, reducing workload of centralized engineering administrator.

- Created and filled unique position of Engineering Business Manager for International Space Station, monitoring all business, financial, and technical program activity.

- Recipient of engineering excellence awards for impact on manufacturing production and delivery: "F-18 Outstanding Customer Relations Award," Northrop Corporation, and "Valued Ethics and Trust Award," Japanese consulting firm.

- **"...Your ability to relate to the various personalities with whom you come in contact, your positive attitude and your written communication skills are valuable assets for your future development..."** — Frank Taylor, Former Group Manager, Orbital Sciences Corporation

Strategy: *To help this retired engineer return to employment, the resume eliminates dates and focuses on his engineering background and specific achievements. Quotes make a strong statement about his engineering skills.*

Raymond S. McComb

Page 2

Professional Highlights

PROJECT ENGINEER / PRODUCT DEVELOPMENT — Orbital Sciences Corp., Tempe, AZ (16 years)

Key contributor in six separate aerospace programs culminating with assignment as engineering program manager for sale of control components to Japan, a joint partner in International Space Station with Boeing. Excelled in four additional special assignments, achieving success through versatility of strategic planning, organization, and implementation. Program engineer for component development on major subsystems and development engineer for individual valve systems.

Built track record of consistent program success to contribute to company's long-term success. Managed all phases of Integrated Product Development (IPD) for control system components manufactured for multiple environments in both aviation and space-related applications. Oversaw all phases of proposals, design, development, testing, qualification, and initial production.

SENIOR ENGINEER — Northrop, Aircraft Division, Hawthorne, CA (3 years)

Fast-track promotion from product-support analyst to senior engineer, designing and manufacturing environmental control and fuel subsystems for F-18 tactical aircraft program. Gained expertise in project management from OEM viewpoint, coordinating engineering actions with component suppliers. Functioned in additional roles of engineering project coordinator for subsystem design, engineering change-board coordinator, and logistics-support analyst for ECS system design.

Additional Experience

Computer Consultant — JL Enterprises, Columbus, IN
Customer Service Representative — United Airlines, Chicago, IL
Transportation Specialist — Werner Enterprises, Omaha, NE
Officer / Instructor Pilot — United States Air Force

Education & Training

Bachelor of Science in Civil Engineering
Purdue University, West Lafayette, IN

Master in Business Administration Degree Program in Computer Information Systems
Arizona State University, Tempe, AZ

Management Training

Total Quality Leadership (TQL), Integrated Product Development (IPD) team procedures, and ISO 9000/9001 Conversion Requirements for international markets.

AutoCAD R14 Professional Level Training — Ivy Tech State College

Technical Expertise

Capable of rebuilding personal computers, upgrading existing equipment to include latest technologies.

Microsoft Office Suite, Technical Management Programs, AutoCAD Design Products, and various support and educational software.

Certifications

Licensed Commercial Pilot with Flight Engineer Certification

RESUME 69: BILLIE JORDAN; MAYSVILLE, NC

Katherine D. Taylor

10 Blue Bird Ct., Cove City, NC 28562 • (252) 441-2322 • cell (252) 719-2939 • kdt@yahoo.com

Manufacturing/Production/Office Management

Results-driven professional with 20 years' management experience in manufacturing with consistent achievement in productivity and quality, personnel management, and team building. Aggressive, with exceptional ability to motivate team workers.

Accomplishments

- Developed "World Class Manufacturing" Training Program for the Kinston plant.
- Managed the transfer of the Quality Assurance Lab from Kinston to Cove City.
- Participated in the implementation of Demand Flow Technology into the Cove City plant.
- Received Silver and Gold Cup Awards for $100,000 and $250,000 company savings, respectively.

Career Highlights

Classic Faucets, Incorporated, Cove City, NC
1976–2002

Warehouse Supervisor (Goldsboro and Cove City) (2001–2002)
   On special assignment to supervise on- and off-site warehouses including activities of team leaders, shipping and receiving attendants, and salaried shipping/receiving clerks. Managed the Kanban System providing inventory to the appropriate locations.

New Products Materials Planner, Cove City (2000–2001)
   On special assignment with the Materials Department to assist in getting components approved and manufactured for a significant number of new products according to scheduled lead-time requirements.

Senior Quality Assurance Supervisor, Cove City (1995–2000)
- Transferred the Quality Assurance Systems Laboratory to Cove City and assumed supervisory responsibility for the dimensional, functional, fit, cosmetics, and bill-of-material audits to ensure good product for the customer.
- Trained technicians, clerks, and auditors at the new location in the use of all instruments and processes.
- Maintained compliance with all standards agencies such as the International Association of Manufactured Plumbers Organization, Canadian Standards Association, American National Standards Institute, and the International Standards Organization.
- Produced all necessary reliability reports.
- Developed all job descriptions and method sheets for this department.
- Managed quality holds for the corporation, new product approvals, and releases.

Strategy: *The two recent "special assignments" cover significant job changes that caused this candidate to take early retirement from her company. The standard chronological format effectively showcases her career progression.*

Page 2

Production Supervisor, Kinston (1980–1995)

- Supervised final assembly, cartridge subassembly, brass buffing, brass polishing and tipping, subassembly of components, ring and seat buff, spout buffing, CNC buffing, brass, and black nickel plating.
- Managed 60 to 200 operators, machinists, buff house operators, and material handlers.
- Coordinated the schedule and job assignments of all operators with production and materials management.
- Identified and managed outsourced tooling suppliers.
- Developed budget and ensured compliance.
- Supported activities of self-directed work teams.
- Coordinated machine run-offs on a timely basis.

Technical Skills

Quality Equipment: Calipers, Comparators, micrometers, flow meters

Processes: Nickel, brass, and zinc plating; injection molding; screw machines; PVD (Physical Vapor Deposition); buffing; silver-solder brazing; sonic welding; air-decay testing; water functional testing; vibratory finishing processes; and die casting

Machinery: Bodine, Kingsbury, Astro, Fusion, Vibramatic, Cincinnati Milicron, packaging/bagging machines

Education/Training

Industry Training—Variety of courses in Management/Supervision; Process Training; Materials Management; Quality Management; Demand Flow Technology & Business Strategy Workshop and Advanced Mixed-Model Workshop; and Systems, Applications, and Products (SAP-integrated business systems solutions—7 modules)

American Society for Quality Certificates—Reliability Engineering, Introduction to Quality Engineering, Understanding QS 9000 Implementation and Auditing, Introduction to Quality Management, and ISO 9000 Quality Systems Documentation

Computer Training—Microsoft Word, Excel, Access, PowerPoint, WordPerfect, Cullinet, Lotus Norton Commander

Central Carolina Community College, Sanford, NC, Industrial Management Curriculum 1983–1988

Affiliations

American Society for Quality — Member from 1995 to 2000

WALTER G. KAMINSKI
Cellular Phone: (262) 871-5645

May through December	January through April
3233 Oak Tree Court	2223 North 60th Street
Brookfield, Wisconsin 53005	Scottsdale, Arizona 85402
Residence Phone: (262) 781-4665	Residence Phone: (480) 567-9745

BUSINESS & INVESTMENT CONSULTANT
Long-Term Growth ... Profit Building ... Business Development
COMMODITIES/STOCKS ... LAND DEVELOPMENT ... PROPERTY MANAGEMENT ... FRANCHISING

A visionary, innovative, and goal-oriented business-development professional with 30+ years of cross-functional expertise in sales, marketing, administration, and management. Excellent interpersonal communication, presentation, and training skills. A strong mentor with the ability to teach "out of the box" thinking. Demonstrated competency in the following areas:

- Executive Leadership
- Startups & New Ventures
- Market Timing & Market Positioning

- Market Research & Analysis
- Executive Road Shows
- Stockholder Relations

PROFESSIONAL EXPERIENCE

GOLDEN MUFFLER SHOPS — Wisconsin & Arizona   1975 to 2000

OWNER/FRANCHISEE
Owned 8 franchises in 2 states, oversaw general management team, and developed new business opportunities.

METROPOLITAN LIFE INSURANCE — Milwaukee, Wisconsin   1966 to 1975

GENERAL AGENT
Monitored agent sales activity and assisted with training and regulatory compliance issues. Developed prospect lists, identified sales opportunities, and presented/sold insurance and investment plans to individuals within the Southeastern Wisconsin territory.

INVESTMENT EXPERIENCE

- Seat Holder and Active Floor Trader on Chicago Board of Trade, Mercantile Exchange, Chicago Board of Options Exchange, and New York Cotton Exchange, 1971 to 1999.
- Speaker at international investment conventions discussing hard currency, gold, silver, and oil. Quoted in the *Wall Street Journal*.
- Property Owner/Manager of residential and commercial properties in Milwaukee, Arizona, and Costa Rica.
- Land Developer of residential and commercial property in Cedarburg, Wisconsin.

EDUCATION

Bachelor of Business Administration: Marquette University, Milwaukee, Wisconsin
Continuing Education: Numerous Investment Conferences worldwide from 1971 to present

COMMUNITY ACTIVITIES

Milwaukee City Development — Led redevelopment efforts of Market Street commercial area in conjunction with Richard Rudwell of the UW–Milwaukee School of Architecture.
Milwaukee Country Club, Member

Strategy: *This retired professional was seeking a consulting position with a high-profile start-up firm. As such, a brief qualifications overview presents his expertise without overwhelming the reader with details.*

Jonathan Amin

15826 67th Drive, Apt. 12K
Hillside Way, NY 11513
Phone: 718-335-9338 ▪ E-mail: JAmin@aol.com

Professional Overview

Active, broadly talented professional offering enthusiasm for challenges, aptitude for new ideas and situations, and uniquely diverse life and career experiences. Expert in all aspects of business administration through more than 25 years of successful business ownership. Strong leader in community and professional organizations. Keen mind motivated by diversity and complexity of activities.

Value Offered

Experienced Business Manager & Administrator
- Managed all aspects of a successful practice including hiring and supervising staff, directing sales and marketing, purchasing, record keeping, and financial control.
- Delivered top-notch customer service as an optometrist, building strong repeat-patient and referral-based business.

Organizational Leader
- Long-standing officer and director, 2 years as president of Optometric Council of New York State.
- Championed causes for organization, liaising with New York State legislators to influence pending legislation.

Creative Mastermind & Wordsmith
- Wrote and edited monthly column for industry newsletter, giving due attention to current standards in grammar, punctuation, and common usage of the English language.
- Conceived and encoded more than 500 cryptograms to date, surpassing common cryptoquotes in complexity and devising impediment to code-breaking of cryptograms with computer programs.
- Self-published two pocket-book-sized, 59-page volumes of "Original Cryptograms," each containing 250 cryptograms. Market and sell first volume through website.

Multi-talented, Hands-on Expert
- Fully familiar with Medicare, Medicaid, and other third-party insurance programs from both sides —provider and beneficiary. Experience gained through own optometry practice and assisting close family member through two complicated surgeries.
- General contractor for extensive office renovations, hiring laborers, designing layout, drawing floor plans, calculating room areas, purchasing furniture, and selecting accessories.

Active Community Contributor
- Member of Queens County Democratic Committee for 2 years.
- Current Advisory Board member of Hillside Way Jewish Center.
- Chairman of United Jewish Appeal —Federation of Jewish Philanthropies Appeal, Hillside Way Division, for 3 years.

Career & Academic Experience

Optometrist —General Vision Services, New York, NY (1997–1999)
Business Manager / Optometrist —Dr. Jonathan Amin, Optometrist, New York, NY (1975–1996)

B.S., Optometry —Columbia University, New York, NY
B.A. —Ohio State University, Columbus, OH

New York State Optometry License

Strategy: *For this 80-year-old retiree, the world of work still beckons. Because he is very flexible about his career choices, a Value Offered section outlines key areas of expertise to interest employers.*

CHAPTER 13

Resumes for People Laid Off, Downsized, or Otherwise Out of Work for More Than Six Months

These resumes were written for people whose unemployment was involuntary and probably caused by a tight job market or lack of opportunity due to serious downsizing in their area. A gap of less than a year will not usually derail a job search because an average transition can take six months or more. So usually there's no need to deal with the gap on your resume. For this reason, an effective approach is a chronological format preceded by a strong summary that encapsulates key qualifications. But you'll see examples of excellent functional-format resumes in this chapter as well.

MARTY L. GRAYSON

10 Peace Street
Ayden, NC 28590
Home (252) 535-0400 mlgrayson@coastalnet.com

FOCUS

To obtain a responsible and challenging administrative support position

HIGHLIGHTS

Software	Office Machines	Strengths
• Word, Excel	• Copier	• Organized
• Access, PowerPoint	• Fax	• Customer-Service Oriented
• SAP, Culinet	• Computer	• Fair
	• Printer	

CAREER EXPERIENCE

King Incorporated   1980–2001
Ayden, NC

Shipping Coordinator (Began as Production Operator, then promoted to Quality Control Technician, Inventory Control Clerk, Shipping Clerk, and Shipping Coordinator)

- Supervised shipping personnel including loaders, administrative processors, and finished-goods transport personnel.
- Trained, cross-trained, and ensured compliance with shipping procedures.
- Ensured smooth material flow from manufacturing to shipping and from one shift to another.
- Maintained manifest shipping accuracy of 99%.
- Processed over/shorts on a daily basis and reconciled the shipping bin daily.
- Maintained adequate supplies of oil, fuel, stretch film, and pallets.
- Maintained a safe work environment, including the battery charging area.
- Followed budget guidelines and developed cost reductions.
- Communicated with accounting, distribution centers, and supervisors.
- Served as First Aid Attendant and Fire Brigade Member, 1983–1999.

Strategy: *After being downsized, this individual took the opportunity to refocus her career toward an administrative role.*

MARTY L. GRAYSON — Page 2

Home (252) 535-0400 mlgrayson@coastalnet.com

EDUCATION

Pitt Community College, Greenville, NC

Received the following certificates 1985–1987: Orientation & Study Skills, Introduction to Personal Computers, Lotus 1-2-3, Harvard Graphics, Bookkeeping, Math Concepts, Business Mathematics, Quality Assurance Concepts, Shop Math, Industrial Blueprint Reading, Precision Measurement Concepts, Instruments, Statistical Process Control

Pamlico Technical College, Bayboro, NC

Introduction to Computers and Data Processing, 1985

CERTIFICATES

SAP Training (Systems, Applications, and Products—integrated business systems solutions) — 2001

Team Leader Training — 2001

Ambulance Attendant — 1990–1994

CPR Training — 1990–1994

First Aid Attendant — 1991

Emergency Medical Services Seminar — 1991

Aeromedical Safety for Emergency Response Teams (East Care) — 1989

RECOGNITION

Operation Filter Team promoting a new kitchen faucet (water filter) at various Lowe's locations in NC: Represented Team in Charlotte — 2000

President's Achievement Award — 1992

Perfect Attendance Awards — 1986, 1987, and 1989

CIVIC/COMMUNITY INVOLVEMENT

Desabelles (Shrine Club Ladies Unit), Greenville, NC — Treasurer 2000–2001

Pitt County Shrinettes, Shrine Club, Ayden, NC — President 1985–1986

Raised funds for crippled children in Ayden and Greenville for more than 20 years

RESUME 73: PETER HILL, CPRW; HONOLULU, HI

JEFFREY J. LEE

586 4th Avenue • Honolulu, Hawaii 96822
(808) 555-8785 • jjlee@email.net

GENERAL MAINTENANCE MECHANIC

Air Conditioning • Refrigeration • Electrical • Plumbing

19 years of broad-based maintenance experience. Promoted through increasingly responsible decision-making positions. Place priority on safe working environment.

CERTIFICATIONS AND TRAINING

ESCO Institute
UNIVERSAL, TYPE I, TYPE II: Certificate No. 4755890002365, Section 608
MOTOR VEHICLE: Certificate No. 47523456, Section 609

Sears Extension Institute
Basic Refrigeration, Advanced Refrigeration, Central Air Conditioning,
Understanding and Using Test Instruments

Hawaii Hotel and Restaurant Industry
Basic Refrigeration, Blueprint Reading, Plumbing

RELEVANT EXPERIENCE

WAIKIKI INTERNATIONAL RESORT   **Honolulu, Hawaii**
(formerly Hawaiian Hotel at Waikiki Beach)

General Maintenance 1st Class	1996–2001
Maintenance 2nd Class	1988–1996
Maintenance Trainee	1982–1988

Accountability and Accomplishment Highlights

• Performed comprehensive property-equipment checks, service, and repair to ensure normal guest service and building operations.

• Collaborated with foreman to handle recurring challenge of air in chilled-water air-conditioning system. Conceived innovative solution to bleed air from system, resulting in reliable and efficient operation.

• Given authority to select new fan-coil units for major room-renovation project. Met with competing vendors and made suitable product recommendations to hotel management.

Strategy: *To position this individual for a specific opportunity, this resume presents an experienced and knowledgeable air-conditioning maintenance professional.*

JEFFREY J. LEE
Page 2

SEARS, Hardware department   **Honolulu, Hawaii**

Sales Associate   **1980–1988**

Sold hardware products, educating customers on tool operation and uses. Performed minor tool repairs.

EDUCATION

Associate in Science Program
Refrigeration and Air Conditioning
Honolulu Community College — Honolulu, Hawaii

Associate in Science Degree
Merchandising Mid-Management and Hotel Operations Mid-Management
Kapiolani Community College — Honolulu, Hawaii

RECOGNITION

"Your alertness and quick response to the smoke exiting from the compactor aided in averting a possible fire from occurring…I would like to add my personal thanks for being such a conscientious and valued employee."

Letter of Commendation — April 1994
General Manager Brian Usher

"Your quick response and bravery beyond the call of duty were instrumental in the proficient handling of the fire emergency. We are truly proud of your performance and feel privileged to have you at the Hawaiian Hotel."

Letter of Commendation — September 1992
Executive Assistant Manager Tommy Feshler

"…in recognition of outstanding and valuable service to the Hawaiian Hotel."

Certificate of Recognition — September 1982
General Manager David Donaldson

~ References Furnished On Request ~

Rick Weston

142 Fort Macon Road, Newport, NC 28523 (252) 794-2824

Machinist

Career Highlights

Machinist — 1996–2001   Jones Enterprises, Inc., Newport, NC

- Determined the sequence of operations from blueprints and drawings to manufacture products for the pharmaceutical industry.
- Machined parts to specifications using metal-working machine tools.
- Designed fixtures and tooling.
- Assembled parts into units with tools.
- Laid out and verified dimension of parts using precision measuring instruments and mathematics.
- Calculated and set machine controls.
- Selected, aligned, and secured fixtures.
- Measured, examined, and tested completed parts.
- Cleaned and lubricated tools and equipment.
- Conferred with engineering and manufacturing.
- Restored out-of-operation equipment.

Sales / Stock Associate — 1994–1995   Riverwalk Hardware, Newport, NC

- Assisted customers in finding desired items.
- Processed sales transactions—cash and credit cards.
- Priced coded stock.
- Stocked merchandise for sale and display and maintained cleanliness.

Machine Skills

Metal and Wood Working Machines

- Manual Milling Machine
- Flex/Arm Tapping Machine
- Grinder
- Jointer
- Manual Lathe
- Wood Lathe
- Band Saw
- Radial Arm Saw
- CNC Hurco 40/20 M
- EDM Machine
- Table Saw

Education and Certifications

Journeyman Certification, North Carolina Apprenticeship Council, North Carolina Department of Labor — November 2001

Cartaret Community College, Morehead City, NC — Advanced Machinist Degree, 1996

Morehead City High School, Morehead City, NC — Graduated 1991

Strategy: *After being laid off, this job seeker needed a strong resume to be competitive for similar positions with other companies in the area.*

RESUME 75: BILLIE RUTH SUCHER, MS; URBANDALE, IA

STEPHEN D. MARACICH

17 Egrett Bend, Unit 8
Chicago, Illinois 60618

smaracich@yahoo.com

773-841-9354 Cellular
877-922-4023 Business

PROFESSIONAL OBJECTIVE

Outside Sales/Account Executive

PROFESSIONAL QUALIFICATIONS

- Successful sales/customer relations experience with a Chicago-based Fortune 500 company.
- Effective relationship-builder who is personable and caring; aggressive in pursuit of new accounts.
- Outgoing personality with strong commitment to developing and maintaining solid customer base.
- Goal-oriented team player who is ethical, versatile, and has what it takes to do a job well.
- Well-liked by others and known as a fast learner who works hard, has drive and ambition, is efficient, and believes in providing extraordinary customer service; competitive by nature.

EXPERIENCE

DOLINVEST, Chicago, Illinois   12/00–5/02
- Senior Corporate Account Manager
  Managed over 350 accounts for this financial services firm. Accountable for all facets of cold-call prospecting, account profiling, and meeting demanding sales and call goals. Position downsized.

Key Results:

- Exceeded sales goals for 12 consecutive months.
- Increased profit margin by at least 8.5% each month.
- Provided timely responses and business solutions to customer inquiries to ensure business retention in this highly competitive market.
- Performed duties with efficiency and productivity; named "Employee of the Month" four times.
- Increased sales 128% in 12-month period, while improving overall profits by 34% during time of organizational transition.

Regiss Pet Clinic, South Bend, Indiana   9/00–12/00
- Veterinary Assistant — during college

Passport Restaurant, Grand Rapids, Michigan   5/00–9/00
- Server/Bartender — during college

EDUCATION

B.S. Notre Dame, South Bend, Indiana, December 2000
• Major: Business Marketing • Minor: Corporate Communication
• Captain, Football Team; First Team All-American

Professional Sales Training: Three months of extensive sales training sponsored by Dolinvest.

Computer Knowledge: Network 2 Certified; Word, PowerPoint, Excel, Access, and Outlook.

Strategy: *Despite a short tenure with his most recent employer, this laid-off sales professional was able to come up with strong achievements that helped create a focused, effective resume.*

RESUME 76: PETER HILL, CPRW; HONOLULU, HI

MICHAEL WILSON
94-332 East Main Street ◆ Kailua, Hawaii 96797
Home: [808] 555-1298 ◆ Cellular: [808] 555-6598 ◆ E-mail: mwilson@oceannet.com

---

NETWORK MANAGER / ENGINEER
Expertise Includes: WANs ◆ LANs ◆ WLANs ◆ VPNs ◆ Servers ◆ Firewalls
Cisco Certified ◆ Thorough Knowledge of OSI Model and TCP/IP

Seasoned Network Administrator with 14+ years of broad-based IT experience. Skilled at planning, implementation, and oversight of network infrastructure upgrades and maintenance. Background includes demonstrated ability to solve problems quickly and completely without risking system reliability. Adaptable to organizational and industry change. Driven professional with high level of personal integrity.

TECHNICAL PROFICIENCIES

CISCO: Catalyst 5500/5000/6500/3500 switches — 3600/2600/7513/4000 routers — Aironet 340/350 wireless bridges — Cisco Works 2000 — VPN Concentrator 3005

SERVERS: Win2K — WINS — Windows NT (dual and multiple domain models) — PDC — BDC — DNS — DHCP — RAS — SQL — SNA — Novell — Microsoft Exchange — MS Proxy Server

PROFESSIONAL CHRONOLOGY

Network Analyst   Honolulu, Hawaii
Island Hospital   1998–2002

❖ Handled all network improvements including 2001 upgrade from flat model to hierarchical routed system that resulted in increased security and additional broadcast control.
❖ Managed 14-clinic wide area network. Configured, planned capacity for, and maintained WAN, incorporating facilities on all major islands. Converted all outpatient clinics from DSL to frame relay.
❖ Oversaw network infrastructure and horizontal cabling project, collaborating with Cisco Systems to design and implement new LAN GB backbone. Integrated wireless network utilizing state-of-the-art bridges and NICs.
❖ Accomplished cutting-edge upgrade, replacing Fast Ethernet with progressive Gigabit Ethernet, positioning backbone to handle new standard.
❖ Installed and maintain hospital's VPN connection.
❖ Configured and oversaw Windows 2000 Active Directory domain.
❖ Managed and administered user migration from Novell to Windows 2000 domain.

Network / Facilities Manager   Honolulu, Hawaii
Local Link Networks, Inc.   1997

❖ Planned and constructed firm's internal and external networks. Configured and maintained Internet and VPN routers.

Strategy: *This resume clearly positions the individual as an experienced techie with a solid network-administration background. Accomplishments showcase his problem-solving expertise.*

MICHAEL WILSON

Page 2

- ❖ Configured and installed Microsoft SQL servers in Microsoft Clustered environment, including Active/Passive and Active/Active Failover SQL Cluster designs.
- ❖ Managed Windows NT dual domain, Microsoft Exchange server, and Proxy server.

Decision Support Systems Analyst   Honolulu, Hawaii
Channel Medical Services   1994–1997

- ❖ Provided all levels of PC support as Team Lead for User Support Center.
- ❖ Managed and maintained Cisco routers and switches.
- ❖ Administered organization's RAS, Windows NT, Novell, Microsoft Exchange, and SNA servers.

PC / Programmer Analyst   Honolulu, Hawaii
XYZ, Inc.   1991–1994

Performed network management, installing and administering Novell Netware. Handled claims system database program support. Carried out hardware and software maintenance. Performed JCL and COBOL batch programming.

TECHNICAL TRAINING AND CERTIFICATION

Cisco CCNA 2.0 Certification, June 2001

Data Communications Systems: Design, Implementation, and Management, December 1997
Island High Tech Park — Honolulu, Hawaii

NetWare 3.11 Systems Manager / NetWare 3.1x Advanced Systems Manager, July 1996
Valley Community College — Honolulu, Hawaii

EDUCATION

Associate of Science, Data Processing, 1991
Valley Community College — Honolulu, Hawaii

❖ *References Furnished On Request* ❖

JOHN B. URATA

3131 Carmel Road • San Diego, California 92109
Home: (858) 555-0234 • Cellular: (858) 555-0235 • E-Mail: ju_arborist@plantnet.com

Seeking Position in...

URBAN FORESTRY / TREE CARE

Tree ID and Selection • Plant Health Care • Tree Hazard Assessment • Tree Appraisal

ISA Certified Arborist with demonstrated ability to plan and implement ecosystems that include trees. Extensive knowledge of San Diego area trees, geography, and climate. Absolute dedication to professionalism and ongoing education. Outstanding communication skills. Computer proficiencies include Word, Excel, Access. Speak Japanese and some Spanish. Ethical, observant, and thorough.

CERTIFICATIONS, TRAINING, AND RESEARCH

ISA CERTIFIED ARBORIST: License No. WC-12345 (2001)
CALIFORNIA CERTIFIED NURSERY PROFESSIONAL: License No. 12345 (1983)

American Society of Consulting Arborists (ASCA) Consulting Academy:
Report Writing and Professional Practice Workshop (Feb. 2002)

ArborLearn: *Online Tree Appraisal Course* (Jan. 2002)

Utah Community Forest Council: *Tree Hazard/Appraisal Workshop* (Dec. 2001)

Self-Directed Research in Japan: *Performed private study on significance of trees and flora as well as
their influence in Japanese cultural, political, commercial, and religious life.
For future publication.* (1993–1995 and 1997–1999)

RELEVANT EXPERIENCE

Landscaper / Gardener   2000–2002
Private Estate of Mr. John Doe   Rancho Santa Fe, California
Five-acre, multimillion-dollar property

- Oversaw 130+ trees (10 to 15 species), single-handedly performing ongoing ecosystem and landscape management. Also included 7,500-square-foot lawn and rose garden.
- Planned and implemented 5-month mission to prepare landscape for private wedding. Project was total success.
- Implement organic-gardening procedures. Recycle majority of green waste.
- Successfully performed comprehensive redesign of rose garden.

Nursery Sales Associate   1992–1993
Williams Gardens   Corona Del Mar, California
Retail gardening and home-decorating store with 50 employees

- Performed sales and customer service functions, educating public on basic planting decisions and offering troubleshooting tips.

Strategy: *The headline section at the top of the Qualifications Summary section showcases this individual's core competencies and knowledge. Essential certifications and training are highlighted in a key center section.*

RESUME 77, CONTINUED

JOHN B. URATA
Page 2 of 2

- Maintained nursery grounds and stock. Oversaw seasonal sales promotions of roses and bulbs.
- Gave widely attended gardening seminars.

Nursery Sales Associate   1980–1986
Flower Ridge Nurseries, Inc.   Santa Ana, California
Retail nursery with 15 employees

- Planted trees, shrubs, bedding plants, and grass in residential gardens and commercial lots.
- Handled wholesale purchasing and customer deliveries.
- Led rose-pruning workshops.

PROFESSIONAL AFFILIATIONS

American Society of Consulting Arborists (new)   San Diego Horticultural Society (since 2000)
International Society of Arboriculture (since 2000)   American Horticultural Society (since 1996)
California Urban Forestry Council (since 2000)

EDUCATION

Business Management Certificate Program
University of California at San Diego Extension, *anticipated completion 2004*

Master of Science, Education, 3.5 GPA
California State University at Fullerton, 1997

Bachelor of Arts, English, 3.3 GPA
California State University at Long Beach, 1989

Associate of Arts, Ornamental Horticulture
Orange Coast College — Costa Mesa, California, 1984

OTHER EXPERIENCE

English Teacher, New Day School — Sendai, Japan   1997–1999
Japanese Language Teacher, Park Villa High School — Park Villa, California   1996–1997
ESL Instructor, Rancho Diego Community College District — Orange, California   1996–1997
English Teacher, AEON Intercultural Corporation — Toyohashi, Japan   1990–1995

• • •

Gary Douglas

191 Alley Way • Atlanta, GA 30043
770/555-1212
garyd@yahoo.com

Qualifications Summary

Strong Leadership • Full Project Lifecycle Management • Technical Management
Sales & Presentation Skills • Risk Analysis • Auditing & Security • Web Development
Negotiations • Problem Solving • Team Motivation • Results Orientation • Interpersonal Skills

A dynamic leader with excellent qualifications in driving new business development initiatives and managing diverse multimillion-dollar projects that position commercial enterprises for prosperity and technological advancement. Known and respected for having outstanding presentation, negotiation, mediation, and closing skills, and for applying the practices of the Project Management Institute's "Project Management Body of Knowledge." Innovative solutions provider offering client-centric solutions. IT trendsetter and mentor producing a large network of accomplished team members.

Telecommunications Expertise
Metropolitan & Long-Haul Networks • Managed Wavelength Services
Long-Distance Networks • Data Networks • Voice & Data Protocols

Internet Expertise
Internet & Intranet Design • Content Development
E-Commerce • Affiliate Marketing • Ad-Hoc Reports

Auditing & Security Experience
User Authentication • Access Management Security Policies • Disaster Recovery
Contingency Planning • Security Policies & Procedures • Information Assurance
Controls Auditing • Risk Assessment & Management

Professional Experience

NORWAY COMMUNICATIONS, Alpharetta, GA   2000–2002
Senior Systems Engineer
Managed multimillion-dollar optical system deployments by leading cross-functional teams on several concurrent customer engagements across the U.S. and Canada.

- Closed a $1.5M contract in equipment and engineering services by carefully reassessing customer requirements and internal software release issues, and by developing a workaround solution that kept the customer's delivery timeline intact.
- Led and trained a team of engineers in a flawless European network implementation resulting in the customer purchasing over $10M of additional equipment for overseas deployments and a cost savings for our European counterparts of $120K.

Strategy: *Affected by a downturn in the telecommunications industry, this individual positions himself as a senior-level manager with diverse experience in communications, software, and professional services.*

RESUME 78, CONTINUED

Gary Douglas • Page 2   770/555-1212 • garyd@yahoo.com

Professional Experience, continued

MANNER AFFILIATES, Atlanta, GA   1999–2000
Senior Project Manager

- Secured a multimillion-dollar contract with a major retail grocer by establishing and documenting an effective project-management process that included procedures for managing software development releases.
- Facilitated project-status meetings for issue determination/resolution.
- Identified and mitigated project risks.
- Implemented MS Project web interface for more efficient tracking of project status.
- Advised Chief Technology Officer on business planning and strategies.

MK&P CORPORATION, Atlanta, GA   1998–1999
Associate, Operational Systems & Risk Management

- Proposed and implemented a corporate intranet solution generating over $300K in revenue.
- Led and developed junior associates into highly efficient and productive team members of the intranet application-development team.
- Performed assurance audits resulting in two major clients accepting proposal recommendations to improve IT operations with annual cost savings of $60K and $85K respectively.

IBM, Atlanta, GA   1996–1998
Supervisor/Analyst, Network Operations (1998)
Project Manager/Lead Negotiator (1997–1998)
Access Network Manager (1996–1997)

- Led a team of 25 members and successfully negotiated an agreement that enabled entry into the local service provider market.
- Successfully negotiated reform to access network-payment agreements that accounted for an increase of over $1.5M annually to company's bottom line.
- Participated in company's leadership-development program, for which less than 1% of 120,000 employees are selected.

Education

Iowa State University of Science and Technology, B.S. in Industrial Technology

Professional Training
Situational Leadership / Stephen R. Covey Effective Leadership
Interpersonal Effectiveness and Listening Skills / Effective Project Management
Network Architecture / Nodal Services / ASB High-Speed Data Networking Curriculum
Internet Development and Architecture / Networks Optical Products Training

Leadership Recognition

2001 recipient of the Outstanding Team Member Award for Leadership
Selected for prestigious Leadership Development Accelerated Executive Program

GEORGE FRANIK

International and New Business Development / Relationship Management
Market and Competitive Analysis / Multilingual

8444-A International Way
San Diego, California 99129

(855) 543-4613
gf31@pacbell.net

NEW BUSINESS SPECIALIST

Sales and marketing professional with effective combination of analytical and interpersonal skills. Proven international trade expertise, especially in Europe and Asia, with emphasis in strategic planning *and* market development *and* client relationships. Advanced skills in solving key account challenges through designing country-specific sales / marketing strategy and recruiting in-country sales professionals.

Strengths include: (1) client relationship management / communication with client-company top officers; (2) strategic business planning, sales planning, market planning, and product development and management; (3) advertising, marketing, media relations, and corporate image development. Fluent in English, French, German, Dutch.

- Impressive ability to create business opportunities.
- Consistent history of accomplishments in new business / new market development.
- Top performer; ready and eager for new challenges.

Company Affiliations:

The Gap	The Limited Group	Blockbuster	Adidas
Wal-Mart	Food Lion	Home Depot	Nike

PROFESSIONAL ACHIEVEMENTS

VP MARKETING AND SALES   B.F.A., INC., SAN DIEGO / TOKYO / PARIS / BEIJING, 1995–2002

Directed domestic and international sales for $250-million world leader in high-technology motion and presence sensors. Prepared all objectives, budgets, and forecasts. Coordinated marketing and sales for Europe and Asia, advertising and promotion activities, distribution channels, product positioning, market-management, market surveys, and competition monitoring. Served as liaison with strategic partners. Developed corporate image.

- **Led sales team to #1 position in the world.**
- **Increased sales from $14 million to $52 million in three years.**

MARKETING MANAGER   BARNES TEXTILES, RICHMOND, VA, 1993–1995

Managed all marketing activities in the United States. Prepared marketing plans, developed corporate image, coordinated advertising and promotional projects, communicated with outside agencies, managed market share, performed market surveys, and monitored competition.

- **Contributed to repositioning that resulted in #2 position in the United States.**
- **Increased sales by $16 million in 12 months.**

MANAGEMENT CONSULTANT   KCL, BRUSSELS, BELGIUM, 1992–1993

Completed management-consulting assignments for Fortune 1000 companies. Specialized in diagnostic analysis, strategic business plans, and establishing key relationships.

EDUCATION

MBA with an emphasis in Marketing
BS Economics and Management

University of Richmond, Richmond, VA
Vrije University, Brussels, Belgium

Strategy: *The candidate's strengths are emphasized in the top half of this resume; high-profile company affiliations are highlighted and key achievements are boldfaced. This is a concise one-page presentation for a senior executive.*

Michael Henry

14 Windsong
Long Beach, CA 92310

310/668-9337
Email: mhenry@home.com

PROJECT / DESIGN ENGINEER

HIGHLIGHTS OF QUALIFICATIONS

- Project Management
- Research and Development
- Total Quality Management
- Product Development
- Creativity / Innovation
- Integration Techniques
- Budget / Schedule Compliance
- Planning / Attention to Detail
- Production / Manufacturing
- Military Programs

- Resources Management
- Military Compliance
- Quality Assurance
- Technical Liaison
- Specifications
- Product Improvement
- Systems / Component Design
- Process / Procedure Standardization
- Communication Skills
- Problem Resolution

PROFESSIONAL EXPERIENCE

THE BOEING COMPANY, Long Beach, CA
Senior Engineer, 1989–2002
▸ Planned, scheduled, conducted, and coordinated detailed phases of C–17 Aircraft fuel system technical projects.
  - Superior project skills in orchestrating, organizing, and managing.
  - Strong background in aircraft fuel systems and components.
  - Expertise in aircraft component design and specification.
  - Aircraft systems design and development knowledge.
  - Extensive laboratory testing experience.
  - Troubleshooting and fault isolation techniques on aircraft.
▸ Provided technical and field support to staff in production, manufacturing, technical, and engineering environments.
▸ Designed and coordinated parts for a new center-wing fuel system, including preparation of specifications, scheduling, and qualification of new parts. Achieved desired goals by working closely with staff at Parker Hannifin.
▸ Recognized for superior performance, quality, effort, and teamwork.

NAVAL WEAPONS STATION, Seal Beach, CA
Mechanical Engineer, 1982–1988
▸ Project engineer for quality assurance, reliability, and environmental testing of complex missile systems and subcomponents.

NAVAL CIVIL ENGINEERING LAB, Port Hueneme, CA
Mechanical Engineer, 1980–1982
▸ Conducted research and development of alternative-energy systems for incorporation at Naval facilities.

EDUCATION

Bachelor of Science Degree, Mechanical Engineering, 1979
California State University, Long Beach, CA

Strategy: *This resume clearly presents strong qualifications gained over more than a decade with Boeing. The Highlights of Qualifications section contains a detailed key-word list.*

LAURIE HOLT

6400 3rd St., Lubbock, TX 79416   LS52000@aol.com   806.792.3988

CAREER PROFILE

A 20-year progressively responsible professional career in management, marketing, and HR. Consistently met or exceeded company goals, significantly impacting profits. Advanced rapidly based upon demonstrated results in customer service / satisfaction, selection and training of personnel, merchandising, sales growth, organization, and leadership. Professional qualifications include:

- Management / Organization
- Team Building / Leadership
- Public Relations / Promotions
- Strategic Planning / Implementation
- Administrative Policies / Procedures

- Public Speaking
- Sales / Marketing
- Customer Service
- Community Outreach
- Human Resource Affairs

Experienced in MS Excel, Word, and PowerPoint; Quicken and Windows 98

PROFESSIONAL EXPERIENCE

ADMINISTRATION / MANAGEMENT: *Program management, planning, development, budgeting, and supervision*

- Organized, detail-oriented, and skilled in managing multiple tasks, as evidenced by supervising three department managers and 60 employees; ensured that all aspects of the departments ran effectively—merchandising, personnel, and sales plan / budget.
- Controlled shortages and inventory, exceeding company standards.
- Passed all store audits at satisfactory or above ratings.
- Earned **Team Leader of the Month** for the District.
- As interim store manager during a change in leadership, created a positive yet hard-driving environment.

"Laurie, you have added back to the Odessa store an atmosphere that is congenial and positive again… A great turnaround from the previous level of morale…you accept challenges head on, as when you stepped into the acting Team Leader position."

—Ed Meath, Mervyn's District Manager

SALES / MARKETING: *Customer relations, presentations, advertising, and marketing*

- Degreed in Marketing: completed comprehensive training in advertising and marketing.
- Awarded Merchandiser of the Year from District Manager.
- Developed innovative "survivor game" that boosted credit solicitations so that goals were met at 110%—recognized as a store leader in driving profits.
- Applied marketing concepts to achieve departmental sales success that met or exceeded company goals.

"Laurie led her teams effectively to drive sales. She has very high standards and holds her teams accountable for results."

—Phyllis Guthrie, District Team Leader

HUMAN RESOURCES: *Personnel selection, hiring, training, and development*

- Hired, trained, and developed over 2000 employees.
- Scheduled weekly over 60 personnel and reviewed time sheets for submission to payroll.
- Managed employee performance.

"…worked to performance-manage the Support Team Coordinator to help improve our in-stock numbers and get better results from that team."

—Phyllis Guthrie, District Team Leader

Strategy: *To help this laid-off retail manager transition to a new field, this resume highlights transferable skill areas in a functional format. Quotes following each section provide a "testimonial" to her abilities.*

RESUME 81, CONTINUED

LAURIE HOLT

806.792.3988	Page 2	LS52000@aol.com

PROFESSIONAL EXPERIENCE (continued)

- Administered medical benefits.
- Maintained and documented personnel files.
- Conducted safety meetings and managed workers' comp claims.
- Assisted with college recruiting program, interviewing and hiring college graduates; **four of the recruits became successful district team leaders.**

"Laurie took on college recruiting with the STL and helped select new management trainees for our district. She learned to asses the candidates and know if the match was right for our stores."
— Gina Baugh, Store Manager

COMMUNITY: *Event planning and coordination*

Spearheaded numerous community and company outreach events:

- Directed the Community Closet, assisting 25 women from Women's Protective Services over a two-day period with personal improvement and interview training.
- Organized March of Dimes Walk-a-Thon for employees; increased participation over a 10-year period by 133%.
- Organized and implemented "Child Spree," a one-day event bringing 25 to 40 children to the store and soliciting donations for school attire from other businesses to help with the effort; helped 800+ children over a 16-year period. Project showed a 200% increase in donations and numbers of children served within 6 years.

EMPLOYMENT HISTORY

Experience includes retail team leader, operations manager, interim store manager, area manager, department manager, buyer, and sales and visual merchandising. Excellent record with former employers, Mervyn's in Odessa, Midland, and Lubbock (1985–2001); Cross & Cross, Alpine (1983–1985); and C.R. Anthony's, Alpine (1978–1983).

EDUCATION

BBA, Marketing, Sul Ross State University, Alpine, TX, 1984

Received scholarships and worked throughout university studies.

Completed additional 16 graduate hours after completing degree.

Graduate of hundreds of hours of professional training, workshops, and seminars on topics such as ADA, EEO, interviewing, leveraging diversity, DISC Dimensions of Behavior, decision-making, management, marketing, sales, and others.

Excellent Professional References Provided Upon Request

Kevin Yost

Page 1 of 2

850 Ninth Ave. #3P, New York, NY 10023
yostk@attglobal.net

Home: 212-980-2985
Cell: 917-455-4120

Health Services Administrator

**General Primary Care / HIV-AIDS / Health Promotion Programs
Substance-Abuse Treatment / Diverse Patient Population**

- Successful track record of delivering quality care while championing operational efficiencies.
- Expertise in management information systems and data analysis.
- Experience with budgeting, fiscal policy, third-party reimbursement, purchasing, training, research studies, OASAS funding/program regulations, and Joint Commission on the Accreditation of Healthcare Organization (JCAHO) standards.
- Effective supervisor with solid decision-making, interpersonal, and communication skills.
- Master's degree in Public Health from Columbia University.

Relevant Experience

ALBERT EINSTEIN MEDICAL CENTER, Bronx, NY

20+ years

Administrative Director, Substance-Abuse Treatment Program
Oversaw business operations of $6 million substance-abuse treatment program with on-site continuity and general primary care. Accountable for resource acquisition & allocation, quality-control initiatives, capital projects, and MIS. Participated in research studies of health services costs and utilization.

Administrative Director, Methadone Treatment Program
Supervised funding and operation of $3.1 million Methadone Maintenance Treatment Program, providing care to 900 patients in 3 clinics with a staff of 60. Served as on-call administrator for both drug-treatment program and entire medical center.

Unit Supervisor, Methadone Program
Accountable for administration of clinic treating 150 patients. Involved budget administration, personnel management, quality assurance, and regulatory compliance.

Counselor/Assistant Supervisor
Treated 75 heroin addicts maintained on methadone or in varying stages of detoxification. Confirmed eligibility and assessed needs of applicants. Prepared and maintained patient charts. Assumed management responsibilities during supervisor's absence.

SELECT ACHIEVEMENTS: OPERATIONS

- Improved consistency of clinical care and streamlined business operations by consolidating three methadone treatment clinics, with different standards and operations, into a unified treatment program. Developed policy & procedure manuals, job descriptions, and forms.
- Instrumental in creating a model program for substance abuse clinics to address AIDS-related issues early in the emergence of this epidemic. Secured funding for health educators who trained staff and patients on HIV transmission and risk reduction.
- Substantially improved the physical environment of the clinics, minimizing health risks (due to inadequate ventilation and asbestos) and increasing privacy, security, and space utilization. Obtained capital funding from governmental and private sources.
- Pioneered the successful "one stop shopping" model of substance-abuse treatment and general and HIV-related primary care services. Provided 10,000 primary-care encounters annually without losing money. Planned and implemented all aspects of linking these services from obtaining a license to establishing computer systems.
- Created a quality-assurance program that eliminated charting deficiencies and resulted in excellent reports from federal, state, and hospital review teams.

Strategy: *The challenge for this health-services administrator, who was laid off following a merger, was to present both specific and more general skills and downplay his age. His achievements are broken into functional areas to improve readability.*

Kevin Yost

SELECT ACHIEVEMENTS: MANAGEMENT INFORMATION SYSTEMS

- Introduced and maintained systems for collecting data from multiple locations, validating it, and importing into a database used to support business and academic projects.
- Automated the weekly process of patient Medicaid coverage verification, reducing man-hours from 24 to 2.
- Initiated billing commercial insurance carriers for methadone maintenance treatment and collected $50,000 in the first year.
- Streamlined the Medicaid accounts-receivable management system and brought in $75,000 to $100,000 per year in non-routine billing for methadone treatment.
- Created a system to produce data reports that have practical application in day-to-day clinic operations (such as a monthly alpha listing of all patients by caseworker) and support adherence to federal and state documentation requirements.
- Collected $30,000 to $50,000 annually through generating NYS OASAS-approved sliding-scale invoices for self-insured patients.

Teaching/Training Experience

PC/MIS Consultant, Data Tamers, New York, NY	1989–Present
Lecturer, New York University, New York, NY	1987
Lecturer/Field Instructor, St. John's College, Bronx, NY	1982–1986

Education

Master of Public Health, Columbia University School of Public Health, New York, NY
Bachelor of Arts, New York University, New York, NY

Memberships

American Public Health Association
American Society of Law, Medicine, and Ethics
New York Academy of Science

VICTORIA DESOUSA, MBA

Suite 420 – 80 North Shore Drive, San Francisco, CA 90480
Phone: 444.666.9696 E-mail: vdesousa@AOL.com

SENIOR SALES EXECUTIVE

Results-driven professional with an exemplary record of developing strategic initiatives to enhance sales. Initiate action and thrive on challenge. Entrepreneurial in business approach; able to seize opportunities; demonstrate excellent networking skills. Build profitable rapport with peers, management, consultants, clients, and other stakeholders. Capable of critically evaluating and responding to diverse sales patterns and trends. Recognized as an inspirational, motivational manager who celebrates diversity and proactively leads and challenges a sales team. Tactful and diplomatic communicator able to disseminate ideas and generate action across all levels of an organization. Exude energy and enthusiasm. Consistently meet or exceed sales targets. Critically analyze the marketplace with respect to feasibility and profitability.

PROFESSIONAL EXPERIENCE

Premier Giftware Inc., Dallas, Texas   1988–2002
Held the following 5 progressively responsible positions prior to downsizing:
DIVISION SALES MANAGER, BAY AREA, San Francisco   1998–2001
* Directly accountable for generating the following unprecedented revenue growth in Premier Giftware's second largest sales base in the United States.

	2001	**2000**	**1999**
Revenue Increase	$453,787	$945,718	$2,023,620
Order Count Increase	2,584	3,326	3,332
Average Order Increase	$4.74	$1.73	$8.09
Area % Increase vs. National	2.6% to 1.2%	4% to 2.7%	9.4% to 7.1%
Renewal Rate %	70.2% to 100+%	72.3% to 100+%	83.2% to 100+%
Rep. Count Growth	2.9%	3.1%	3.5%
Fundraising	54.2% vs. 2000	47.7% vs. 1999	199.7% vs. forecast

* Won the following prestigious awards for impressive sales strategies, team leadership, and overall revenue growth.

2000	**1999**
National Leader – "Best Decile" (coverage & productivity)	National Leader – "Staff Gain"
2nd Place – "World Sales Leader"	3rd Place – "World Sales Leader"

* Directed 21 geographically dispersed Sales Managers within the Northern California territory.
* Oversaw recruitment, training and development, and human-resource issues.
* Selected by corporate head office to initiate, administer, and test Premier Giftware's MLM project.
* Devised, implemented, and monitored the territory's $7 million operation budget.
* Created unique and aggressive marketing strategies, coupled with motivational incentive programs, designed to elevate sales.
* Initiated partnerships with community groups to facilitate fundraising and escalate Premier Giftware's profile and market share.
* Acknowledged by staff for instilling confidence, enthusiasm, and encouragement to deliver an optimum performance.
* Pinpointed community and trade events, using sales booths to promote the "Great Buy, Great Sale" plan and achieving phenomenal sales activity and growth.
* Planned, organized, and facilitated staff-appreciation banquets for the presentation of awards.

Strategy: *This resume takes an aggressive approach and clearly and precisely portrays sales results in a striking table format.*

VICTORIA DESOUSA, MBA   **PAGE 2**

MANAGEMENT ASSOCIATE   1998
- Acknowledged by senior sales management for producing outstanding results in the 1998 fourth quarter in the following areas:

	1998
Revenue Increase	$202,217
Order Count Increase	1,576
Renewal Rate %	81.8% to 100+%
Rep. Count Growth	6.3%

DIVISION SALES TRAINER   1992–1998
- Seconded to New York for four months after selection by Vice President-Sales, West Coast, to develop comprehensive manuals and training courses for the U.S. marketplace.
- Developed and delivered the "Premier Giftware National Recruiting" seminar and trained Premier Giftware personnel to implement program across the country.
- Taught Sales Managers in a classroom or field environment: Prospect Marketing, Presentation Skills, Planning and Organizing, and Understanding Business Opportunities for Growth.
- Selected to test the new Representative Development Program; provided training to National Sales Managers; played the key role in the national launch of the "Train the Trainer" program.

NATIONAL SALES TRAINER   1990–1992
- Conceived and designed the "District Manager Guide to Premier Giftware," an informative manual still utilized by Premier Giftware 12 years later.
- Recognized as the youngest National Sales Trainer in the U.S.
- Devised and conducted the week-long Premier Giftware Training Modules I and II, provided to District Sales Managers semiannually.

DISTRICT SALES MANAGER   1988–1990
- Named "Sales Manager of the Year" in 1988 for a 19% revenue increase in territory, one of only 3 in the Western U.S.
- Achieved "The Circle of Excellence" in 1989 for a 32% revenue increase, the top 10% in the U.S.
- Employed, trained, motivated, and managed 450 independent Sales Consultants.
- Surpassed sales and profit objectives established by senior management in 1988 by 2.9% and in 1989 by 33.1%.

EDUCATION

California State University, Fullerton, CA   1996
MASTER OF BUSINESS ADMINISTRATION

California State University, Fullerton, CA   1990
BACHELOR OF ARTS — Mass Communications

Fashion Institute of Hollywood, CA   1985
DIPLOMA — Mass Merchandising

Selected courses, workshops, and seminars have included the following subjects:

Leadership	Instructional Techniques	Six Thinking Hats
Train the Trainer	Instructor Training	Motivating for Impact
Action Writing	Managing People, Process & Performance	Dealing with Difficult People
The Leadership Grid	Behavioral Interviewing	Instructional Design

GRANT WILLIAMS

215 Hampton Place
Loveland, OH 45050
(513) 664-0348
chetlowry@yahoo.com

SUMMARY *of* QUALIFICATIONS

Project Management
    Planning
        Organization
        Work Plans
        Subcontractors
    Control
        Budget/Schedule
        Documentation
    Execution
        Communications
        Quality Control
        Technical Quality
        Health & Safety

Supervision & Team
Leadership

Motivational "We Can
Do It" Attitude

Training & Career
Development for Field
Operations Personnel

Working Superfund
Knowledge
    RCRA, TSCA,
    CERCLA,
    SARA, UST, CWA

Emergency Response/
Crisis Management
    Site Assessments
    System Design &
        Installations
    Solidification &
        Stabilization
    Cleanup & Shutdown
    Electrical & Plumbing
        Maintenance

Contaminants Experience
    Hydrocarbons
    Pesticides
    Toxic Metals
    Explosives
    Radioactive Materials
    PCBs

Hard-charging **OPERATIONS MANAGER** with 20+ years of sound environmental-project experience in all aspects of planning and implementing site remediation and closure while reducing costs and achieving regulatory compliance. Strong leadership skills demonstrated by an instinctive ability to guide and motivate a diverse workforce to work at optimum levels in a fast-paced environment.

PROFESSIONAL EXPERIENCE

XYZ CORPORATION (formerly ABC CORPORATION), Cincinnati, OH
A member company of the Fortune 1000 XYZ Group, XYZ CORPORATION is a leading environmental- and facilities-management firm with 8,000+ employees at 83 nationwide locations.

Operations Resource Manager *of* Craft Labor   1998 – 2002
- Directed a craft labor pool of 1500+ with 14 staff coordinators' assistance.
- Deployed key field workers to numerous ongoing projects, maintaining a 98% billable rate at XYZ *and* ABC during the merger.

ABC REMEDIATION SERVICES CORPORATION, Cincinnati, OH

Regional Operations Manager   1996 – 1998
- Established objectives and directed 300+ field personnel in a 13-state Midwest region, maintaining a 93% billable rate as Regional Operations Manager.
- Organized interview and training process for multiple candidates for local projects as well as resource offices.

Site Superintendent   1984 – 1996
Investigated, analyzed, and identified objectives for remedial actions/cleanups; monitored project teams; managed outside liaison affairs with contractors and regulatory-agency personnel to successfully complete disposal actions.

- USACE IT Industries/Bakercorp Superfund Site, Chicago, IL
  Coordinated remediation of 50,000 tons of lead-contaminated soil from 150 residential sites two weeks ahead of schedule and $500,000 under budget, leading to additional remedial activity of $1M per month for XYZ. Awarded USACE North Central Division "Best Safety Program for Large Construction Contractor," 1995.
- Other Cleanup Sites USACE: Nitro, WV; Cincinnati, OH
                          USEPA: Chicago, IL

Senior Electrician   1981 – 1984
- Installed electrical, plumbing, and gas systems in decontamination, office, lab, and project sites.
- Maintained electrical and plumbing systems: equipment, controls, and pumps.

EDUCATION/SPECIALIZED TRAINING

UNIVERSITY *of* FINDLAY, Findlay, OH
    B.S., Environmental Safety and Occupational Health Management

Certified Hazardous Materials Management Training, University *of* Findlay
OSHA: 40-hour Supervisors' Training; 40-hour HAZWOPER Training
        40-hour Site-Safety Training; 8-hour Annual Refresher Course
Approved USEPA Response Manager for EPA Regions I, II, III & V
Nuclear-Reaction, Chemically Contaminated First Aid for Self & Victims, and
        Related Decontamination Procedures

Strategy: *The left-column summary contains easily skimmable key-word qualifications. The resume is concise, yet packed with achievements and relevant experience.*

CHAPTER 14

Resumes for People Returning to Work After Additional Education

Some professionals temporarily exit the workforce to complete a degree. They then re-enter their careers with additional credentials and qualifications. The challenge for these people is to choose the most compelling information to present on their resumes, so that both education and experience are appropriately emphasized. In most cases, the Education section, which showcases the new credentials, should appear before the Experience section.

WENDY M. CROFTON

20 Juniper Drive   Home: 215-549-6688
Huntingdon Valley, PA 19006   wmcrofton@hotmail.com   Cell: 215-674-4973

PROFILE

Dynamic, creative designer offering extensive experience in a wide variety of venues: special events, theatre / stage, and retail. Scope of knowledge includes set design, lighting, and sound effects. Resourceful, flexible individual, with an ability to effectively solve problems quickly, and a consistent, sharp eye on "the big picture."

EDUCATION

WEST CHESTER UNIVERSITY, West Chester, PA
   B.A. Candidate, Technical Theatre   **January 2001 to Present**
      Relevant Courses: Scene Design, Scene Building, Costume Construction

JOHN MOORE UNIVERSITY, Liverpool, England
   Fashion & Textile Studies   **1980 to 1982**
      Relevant Courses: Fashion Design, Textile Design, Color, Life Drawing, Fine Art, Art History,
      Communication Art, Fashion Drawing, Apparel Fabric, Fashion Show Production, Silk Screen, Painting,
      Etching, Woven Design, Print Design

ST. HELENS COLLEGE OF ART & DESIGN, St. Helens, England
   Art & Design Studies   **1978 to 1979**

EMPLOYMENT

EVENT COORDINATOR   **1999 to 2001**
Center Stage Events, Narberth, PA

Planned and executed all logistics for exclusive, large-scale corporate, political, and social events.

- Carried out the opening welcome party at the Music & Arts Academy for the 2000 Republican National Convention's California delegates, an event featuring a cocktail gathering, entertainment, and dessert, coffee, and cordials on the stage.
- Coordinated a brunch for 1,000 guests at Radiance Square, featuring former First Lady Nancy Reagan as keynote speaker.

EXECUTIVE DIRECTOR   **1993 to 1999**
The Main Events, Philadelphia, PA

Directed sales, managed a sales team, and personally conducted presentations, using design and space-planning expertise to successfully communicate themes and concepts to clients.

- Organized the opening of the Hawaii National Convention Center. Supervised set construction. Coordinated the five-day series of events, most notably the opening black-tie gala with 2,000 guests and an outdoor lei-tying ceremony with local government figures. Led a team in coordinating long-distance equipment transport as well as local rentals.
- Conceived and facilitated the stage and ambient lighting design for the opening of the Atlantic City Convention Center, transforming the convention hall into an elegant event space. Subsequently carried out numerous logistical duties, including managing communications with rival unions.
- Directed a major event for Young & Watson, L.L.P., the 25th anniversary of their Entrepreneur of the Year. Incorporated lighting and special sound effects to keep interest high. Designed lighting, sound, and a set intermingling the Philadelphia skyline and the Entrepreneur award itself. Finally, constructed a laser tunnel as a guest passageway from dinner to dessert and dancing.

Strategy: *Experience relevant to this candidate's current goal and recent education is appropriately highlighted, but education is positioned "front and center" for maximum impact.*

WENDY M. CROFTON

Home: 215-549-6688   wmcrofton@hotmail.com   Cell: 215-674-4973

EMPLOYMENT, CONTINUED

EXPO / EVENT PLANNER   **1992 to 1993**
Philadelphia Society Magazine, Springfield, PA
Provided support to the art department by functioning as a liaison between graphic designers and clients, communicating clients' wishes, and presenting artists' renderings. Additionally, coordinated special events.
- Staged the magazine's first-ever bridal expo, an event in conjunction with Macy's, in the Doubletree Hotel in Philadelphia. Attended to all logistics from event inception through completion: conducted space planning and layout for convention booths, obtained commitments from wedding-gown vendors to provide pieces for fashion shows, planned fashion shows, and coordinated all food and bakery vendors.

SALES / ART DIRECTOR   **1991 to 1993**
Cultural Decor, Fairless Hills, PA
Promoted and coordinated customized theme decor for corporate and private events for clients including Coca-Cola, Tropicana, the Philadelphia 76ers, and the Philadelphia Mayor.

STORE MANAGER   **1988 to 1991**
Fashionista, Philadelphia, PA
Designed front window displays and in-store merchandising for this women's business-casual apparel retailer. Directed and trained a staff of 20. Managed promotions.
- Surpassed all sales goals for the first time in the store's history.
- Won acknowledgment company-wide as an authoritative resource for all the stores; selected to compile daily, weekly, and annual figures for eight stores in the region.

BUYER / MANAGER   **1982 to 1988**
Expressions, Philadelphia, PA
Selected and purchased high-quality, exclusive women's apparel. Supervised and trained retail sales staff.
- Led store to exceed all revenue goals.
- Provided integral support for product-line expansion from one primary offering to diversified lines of clothing, successfully introducing more than $500K in inventory.

AFFILIATION

Philadelphia Chapter Executive Director, International Special Events Society, 1993 to 1999

RESUME 86: JEWEL BRACY DEMAIO, CPRW, CEIP; ROYERSFORD, PA

CYNTHIA A. CANNON

10 Spring Mill Road ▲ Wyncote, PA 19061 ▲ 610-497-6715 ▲ cannongirl@aol.com

PROFILE

Approximately eight years of professional experience in office, benefits, and financial management, in preparation for work in financial training or consulting. MBA Candidate. Core competencies: business management, financial systems automation, budgeting, cash-flow analysis, statistics, and payroll and benefits. Computers: Peachtree, Quicken, Microsoft (MS) Office, PICK Mainframe, Java & ColdFusion Programming, the Internet, and email.

EDUCATION

MBA CANDIDATE, Concentration: Finance & MIS 2000 to Present
Drexel University Philadelphia, PA

- ▲ GPA: 3.7
- ▲ Relevant Courses: Mergers & Acquisitions, Risk Management, Capital Budgeting, Computer Networking

BS, GENERAL MANAGEMENT, AND BS, GERMAN FOR INTERNATIONAL TRADE 1994
Indiana University of Pennsylvania Indiana, PA

- ▲ Cum Laude
- ▲ Studied Abroad in Germany at Duisburg University, Duisburg, Germany; proficient in German
- ▲ Management Student of the Year, 1994

PROFESSIONAL EXPERIENCE

BOOKKEEPER 1997 to 2000
Philadelphia Police Union, Dental, Optical, & Prescription Fund Philadelphia, PA

- ▲ Executed financial management procedures such as forecasting cash flows, reconciling bank accounts, and preparing financial reports for quarterly audits for this insurance fund with a $14 million annual budget. Monitored COBRA eligibility.

- ▲ Upgraded financial procedures from a manual system to automation, thus directly contributing to an immediate reduction in administrative expenses. Administered the 401K plan. Recorded vacation, personal, and sick days.

LIFE INSURANCE COORDINATOR 1996 to 1997
United Order of Firefighters, Lodge 5 Philadelphia, PA

- ▲ Automated the system, providing for the first time a clear and accurate reconciliation of payments received from the city and subsequent premium payments to insurers. Partnered with a bookkeeper in utilizing the updated, computerized records to submit to the city for payments in arrears for approximately 200 members.

- ▲ Organized efforts to simplify the claims process for families of slain officers. Acted as a liaison between families and insurers. Won recognition for this work from surviving spouses, who wrote to the editor of the union magazine.

OFFICE / BUSINESS MANAGER 1993 to 1995
Dynamic International Corporation Indiana, PA

- ▲ Provided control over this entrepreneurial company's finances. Instituted budgeting and cash flow procedures so that employees could be paid biweekly, not intermittently, monthly, or bimonthly as finances previously allowed.

- ▲ Implemented the first health-care benefits plan for this 10-year-old firm. Researched, analyzed, and compared plans, then secured the most advantageous plan for the employees.

Strategy: *A clean, one-page format allows equal presentation of education and relevant experience.*

RESUME 87: SALOME A. FARARRO, CPRW; MOUNT MORRIS, NY

HELENE CARSON

111 East River Road • Rochester, NY 14623
585-334-9900 • carson@email.com

- ▶ **Medical Billing Specialist** completing certificate program.
- ▶ Will pursue credentials from American Health Information Management Association (CCS and CCS-P) and American Academy of Professional Coders (CPC and CPC-H).
- ▶ Dedicated self-starter who enjoys challenges, including learning and applying new skills.
- ▶ Diverse career has included varied opportunities to work independently, in teams, and as a manager, all of which have contributed to development of these key abilities:

  - Detail focus
  - Organization
  - Coordination
  - PC proficiency (MS Windows and Office 2000, Internet, e-mail)

  - Research
  - Communication
  - Customer service
  - Maintaining confidentiality

EDUCATION

Medical Billing Specialist Certificate Program: Monroe BOCES — Rochester, NY; completion anticipated July 2003. *A 19-week professional training program, which includes:*

- ICD-9 & CPT-4 Coding
- Basic & Advanced Medical Terminology

- Introduction to Insurance Plans/Forms
- Introduction to Medisoft

AAS, Optical Engineering Technology: Monroe Community College — Rochester, NY

HIGHLIGHTS OF EXPERIENCE

Contractor/Self Employed   2000–2001
- Assisted relocating individuals in their employment searches in the US and Canada by researching and contacting appropriate potential employers through Internet, e-mail, telephone, and direct mail.
- Compiled reports of key data.
- Honed computer and research skills.

Hospitality: Italian Gardens — Rochester, NY   1985–1999
- Held every position (front and back end) in this family-owned restaurant.
- Applied exceptional customer service, organization, and coordination skills.

Business Manager/Owner: Silhouette Flower Shoppe — Rush, NY   1990–1994
- Oversaw all facets of daily operations, including floral design, wedding coordination, staffing, purchasing, and bookkeeping.
- Expanded service and delivery area.
- Added four wire services and managed third-party ordering process.
- Participated in wedding shows that resulted in a three-fold increase in wedding-related business.
- Enhanced retail sales area of the shop with a wider gift line and selection of plants/flowers.
- Substantially improved bottom-line revenue over previous ownership and sold business for profit.

Optical Engineering Technician: Eastman Kodak Company — Rochester, NY   1981–1985
- Assisted engineers with quality assurance of confidential and cutting-edge photographic prototype development projects within the Consumer Products division.
- Tested equipment in controlled and simulated "consumer use" environments.
- Consistently received highest performance ratings and raises.

Optical Technician: QXL Corp. — Freeport, NY   1980–1981
- Assembled, inspected, and tested critical optical components for YAG lasers in a sterile setting.

*Extensive community service/volunteer experience that has demanded and enhanced
leadership, planning, coordinating, and teaming abilities. Information available upon request.*

Strategy: *This job-seeker's experience is mostly unrelated to her recent training as a medical billing specialist, so a strong summary is essential to clearly identify her target.*

SAUL E. DOMINGUEZ

6907 84TH Street
Lubbock, TX 79424
sdomingu@ttacs.ttu.edu

Residence: 806.794.1420
Fax: 806.798.3233
Mobile: 806.789.2023

CAREER PROFILE

Dynamic management professional with experience in diverse industries including restaurant and banking and credit services. **B.A. Degree** with fluency in Spanish and English. Solid ability to drive organizational change with a **notable record of accomplishments in developing businesses and increasing sales** while effectively managing the organization. Demonstrated achievements in:

- **Strategic Business Planning**
- **Training and Development**
- **Finance & Budgeting**
- **Leadership & Management**
- **Marketing & Business Development**
- **Customer Service, Clientele Development & Retention**

EDUCATION

Bachelor of Arts Degree, Texas Tech University, Lubbock, TX • December 2001

- Majored in Political Science with a minor in **Spanish.**
- Graduated with a **3.7 GPA** and **cum laude honors.**
- Selected to Golden Key National Honor Society.

Significant classes include Public Relations and Mass Communications.

Graduate of management training classes for Norwest Bank and public relations courses.

PROFESSIONAL EXPERIENCE

University Student—full-time, **TEXAS TECH UNIVERSITY,** Lubbock, TX • 1997 to 2001

Resigned full-time position and relocated to Lubbock to earn an undergraduate degree.

Troubleshooter, **LEA COUNTY ELECTRIC CO-OP,** Lovington, NM • 1994 to 1997

Maintained primary and secondary electrical lines over a 30-square-mile area, working with a seasoned team of 30 crewmen for one of the largest electrical co-ops in the nation.

- Personally resolved non-payment issues with clients.
- Corrected line problems successfully and in a timely manner as a team member.

Owner / Manager, **RISTRAS RESTAURANT,** Lovington, NM • 1993 to 1994

Developed successful Mexican restaurant with eight employees in a town of 6,000.

- Opened with a base of $10K and produced **$180K in sales.**

Manager, Credit Manager, **NORWEST FINANCIAL,** Roswell, NM • 1987 to 1994

Promoted to Branch Manager after two years as Credit Manager. Selected and trained five employees and serviced clients within a 30-mile radius. Figured profit and bad-debt projections; established and met or exceeded goals. Solicited area businesses and provided a range of financing options for their customers. Conducted all initial interviews of new accounts.

- **Increased business from $4.5M to $6.5M.**

Strategy: *Prior experience was much lower-level and only marginally related to current targets, so the Career Profile and Education sections are of primary importance. Note how the education is again*

SAUL E. DOMINGUEZ, PAGE 2

Residence: 806.794.1420
sdomingu@ttacs.ttu.edu

Fax: 806.798.3233
Mobile: 806.789.2023

PROFESSIONAL EXPERIENCE (continued)

NORWEST RESULTS (continued)

- Managed over 1,200 accounts, personally increasing business by 10%.
- Developed and instituted a system to manage bad debts daily.

Recruited by manager to join Norwest Financial as one of four credit managers. Manually pulled credit files and made direct calls to verify employment. Made excellent loan judgments utilizing Norwest's rating system. Initiated collections either in person or via telephone on accounts as warranted.

- "Cold called" businesses and professional offices, increasing client base for credit services.

Branch Manager, COLLECTRITE, Roswell, NM ▪ 1983 to 1987

Led nine collectors to establish winning records for privately owned collections company whose clients included hospitals and physicians in the eastern New Mexico area.

- Branch grossed over $100K yearly with **a 30% profit margin.**
- **Led the nation as branch with the highest profit and the lowest bad debt margin** for two years.
- Developed and presented educational seminars on collections for private physicians and their office staff; utilized skits and charts to add interest and visual appeal.

CERTIFICATIONS

Previously held insurance licensures include: Accident and Health, Life, Unemployment, and Auto.

COMMUNITY

Volunteer in Mothers Against Drunk Drivers (MADD) activities, fund-raise for State Trooper Association, and assist families in need with meals at holidays.

TECHNOLOGY

Proficient in Windows 2000, MS Office 2000, and acquainted with other software programs.

LANGUAGES

Dual fluency in Spanish and English.

briefly mentioned under "Experience," to let readers know what he has been doing for the last four years.

Suzanne Robinson

568 Big Walnut Drive
Westerville, OH 43081

614-746-5890
SB3309@aol.com

IT Programmer / Analyst

Qualifications

Recently updated technical skills with DeVry Information Technology degree supported by five years of practical programming experience. Strong organizational skills combined with teamwork and attention to detail ensure high-quality project deliverables. Experience in Hogan Umbrella Systems, CIS, MVS, JCL, COBOL, C++, and SQL.

Technical Skills

Programming Languages: C++, SQL, COBOL
Database Applications: Hogan Umbrella Systems, CIS

Education

DeVry University	Columbus, OH
BS in Information Technology	2002
C++ Programming Courses	
Phoenix Community College	Phoenix, AZ
COBOL Programming Courses	1985–1986
Grand Canyon College	Phoenix, AZ
BS in Business Administration	1979

Professional Experience

First National Bank of Arizona, Phoenix, AZ   1973–1991
Senior Programmer Analyst (1987–1991)
Programming responsibility for Hogan Umbrella Customer Information System (CIS) for an $11 billion bank.

- Created, coded, tested, and implemented CIS job streams to meet needs of various business units.
- Coordinated with ten business units and the Technology Department's application-support areas to ensure the three Hogan CIS databases supported the CIS needs of the Bank and its 2.1 million customers.
- Supported reorganization of the Real Estate Department when dealing with severe loss exposure by developing a new reporting system utilizing the existing Real Estate system and CIS.

Strategy: *This resume appropriately highlights recent education as well as prior practical programming experience. On page 2, community involvement highlights this candidate's organizational and team-work skills that are necessary for successful programming projects.*

Suzanne Robinson

Page 2 of 2

First National Bank of Arizona–continued
Programmer I (1986–1987)
Created ad-hoc reports for the Bank's Marketing Department after analyzing their needs. Created, coded, tested, and ran job streams utilizing CIS and six bank applications to generate one-time reports for marketing analysis and planning. Bank applications included: demand deposits, savings deposits, certificates of deposit, charge card, installment loans, and real-estate loans.

Computer Programmer Trainee (1986)
Studied COBOL and JCL utilizing in-house training courses while supporting computer staff on the Helpline and in the Print Pool.

Branch Auditor (1984–1985)
Audited bank branches and departments for compliance with bank and federal regulations through on-site visits and report analysis.

Data Security Administrator (1973–1984)
Facilitated Problem Management Meetings to identify, review, and correct data-security problems. Modified IBM's Problem Management System to detect and identify problems in the data center. Adapted data elements and reports for the data center's needs.

Community Activities

Worthington Academy Publishing Center   Worthington, OH
Manager   1999–Present
Manage the daily activities of the Publishing Center to support the lower and middle schools. Organize the volunteers to ensure projects are delivered by deadlines. Manage expectations of teachers and administrators to meet needs within the center's defined budget.

Worthington Academy Parent-to-Parent Program   Worthington, OH
Facilitator   2000–Present
Organize and facilitate meetings with parents of middle- and upper-school students to recognize potential problems with teenagers and methods of handling situations. Member of Parents' Association of Worthington Academy responsible for obtaining budget support for the program.

RESUME 90: SHARON PIERCE-WILLIAMS, M.ED., CPRW; FINDLAY, OH

DIANNE IGLEHART

215 Hampton Drive
Perrysburg, OH 43551
(419) 425-3480
diglehart215@aol.com

★ **Recreation *and* Tourism/Special Events Coordinator** ★
A Team Player with Excellent Interpersonal Skills

PROFILE

A detail-oriented, high-energy individual with strong planning, organizational, and leadership skills demonstrated through the ability to successfully communicate with many different age groups and ethnic backgrounds in various community, church, and school programs while multi-tasking with integrity and efficiency. Qualified by:

Verbal & Written Communications   Problem-Solving Skills
Project Development & Management   Microsoft Office Proficiency
Professional Development   Self-Starting Capabilities
Time Management   Community Leadership/Public Speaking

EDUCATION

BOWLING GREEN STATE UNIVERSITY, Bowling Green, OH
M.Ed. Recreation *and* Tourism/Special Events   Graduation: December 2002

Graduate Assistantship with Dr. Toni Williams, funded by the BGSU Center for Policy Analysis and Public Service grant, to study and promote the economic development of tourism along the Lake Erie shoreline (Fall 2000); collaborated with graduate research team to develop a marketing strategy for the Detroit Pistons (Spring 2001).

OHIO STATE UNIVERSITY, Columbus, OH
Bachelor *of* Science Degree *in* Biology

OHIO STATE UNIVERSITY, Columbus, OH
Allied Medical Postgraduate Certificate Program *in* Medical Technology

Completed a five-quarter medical technology program and passed the American Society of Clinical Pathologists (ASCP) certification exam.

PROFESSIONAL CONFERENCES

• *Your Ticket to Success: An Educational Seminar & Workshop on Event Management,* 2001
     The keynote speaker was Dr. William Ross, Director of the Event Management Program at George Washington University in Washington, DC.

• *Pelee Island Conference: Wave of the Future,* 2000
     Island economic and tourism development were among many of the issues discussed at this premier Canadian tourism conference.

• *Conference on Tourism: Soaring into the Future,* Ohio Travel Association Annual Meeting, 2000
     The keynote speaker was Scott Wilson from Southwest Airlines.

• *The Business of Nature: A Disciplined Approach to Nature-Based Tourism,* 2000
     This workshop featured William Kiper from the Texas Nature Tourism Association.

Strategy: *This resume portrays a well-rounded individual whose transferable skills will make her "trainable" in any workplace situation pertaining to her recent education.*

RESUME 90, CONTINUED

DIANNE IGLEHART

215 Hampton Drive
Perrysburg, OH 43551
(419) 425-3480
diglehart215@aol.com

Page 2

PROFESSIONAL AFFILIATIONS & ACTIVITIES

Ohio Travel Association, Member
National Parks *and* Recreation, Student Member
American Society *of* Clinical Pathologists
Toledo Service League, **President** (2 years), Chairman of several committees (8 years)
Special Olympics **Chairperson** of 1st local event for Ohio Valley School & Industries
William Shakespeare Club, **President** (3 years), 18-year member
Editor and Publisher of St. Joseph Hospital Newsletter (2 years)
Editor and Publisher of Toledo Enrichment Program Newsletter (2 years)
Editor and Publisher of Toledo High School Music Booster Newsletter (2 years)
Twig 25 member (6 years), **President** (2 years)
Volunteer in the Toledo City Schools (18 years)
Just Say No Club **Advisor** (5 years)
Church Council, 2001, and former Sunday School teacher (4 years)
Harmony House current volunteer (2 years)
CASA/GAL Advocate, sworn in by Judge Pierce, November 2001

WORK EXPERIENCE

9/01 – 12/01   TOLEDO CITY SCHOOLS, ***Substitute Teacher,*** Toledo, OH
    Substitute for all grade levels in the Toledo City School system.

12/99 – 12/00   VICTORIA'S SECRET, ***Sales Associate,*** Toledo, OH
    Part-time sales associate at Franklin Park Mall.

10/97 – 1/00   ST. VINCENT MERCY MEDICAL CENTER, ***Phlebotomist,*** Toledo, OH
    Part-time phlebotomist in the main hospital, ER, nursery, surgical, and
    outpatient areas.

4/94 – 4/98   LILY BAY GIFT COMPANY, ***Sales Associate,*** Toledo, OH
    Part-time sales associate in upscale gift and home furnishings store.

1/72 – 3/77   ST. JOSEPH HOSPITAL, ***Medical Technologist,*** Columbus, OH
    Full-time medical technologist in the Chemistry and Immunology laboratories
    immediately following post-graduate certification from Ohio State University.

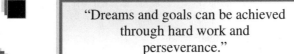

"Dreams and goals can be achieved
through hard work and
perseverance."

RESUME 91: SUSAN GUARNERI, NCCC, LPC, CCMC, CPRW, CEIP; LAWRENCEVILLE, NJ

John Joseph Derry
176 Woodhaven Drive, Eatontown, NJ 07724 • (732) 927-5555 • JJDer@bol.com

Web Applications Management
e-Commerce • B2B • Project Management

KEY QUALIFICATIONS

✓ **Technical Strengths:** Up-to-date, diverse training in e-Business Management coupled with years of experience in analytical / technical process-engineering profession.

✓ **Project Coordination and Teamwork:** Highly productive in team environments as both member and team leader. Efficient in handling multiple project priorities.

✓ **Communication:** Able to communicate technical information in an easily understandable way. Recognized for relationship building with team members and clients. An effective listener.

✓ **Personal Attributes:** Innovative problem solver. Committed to goal achievement. Dependable.

EDUCATION

☑ Cybersoft Internet Professional — CIP 1, Cybersoft, Inc., Woodbridge, NJ
August 2002, **Certified e-Business Architect, e-Business for Managers**
December 2001, **Certified Cybersoft Communications 1000** including Fundamentals of Networking, Database, Web Development, Web Design, Multimedia, and Internet Business

☑ Bachelor of Science, Industrial Engineering, Connecticut Institute of Technology

TECHNICAL SKILLS

e-Commerce: e-Business and B2B Infrastructures and Consumer Payment Protocols
Applications: ERP, e-Procurement, Selling Chain Management, Customer Relationship Management
Software Tools: MS Word, HTML, FrontPage 2000
Operating Systems: Windows NT, Windows 95, 98, XP

PROFESSIONAL EXPERIENCE

1988–2000   ENGINEERING SYSTEMS, INC., Astro Space Division, Eatontown, NJ
Manufacturing Engineer, Production Engineering Department

Provided assembly documentation and engineering floor support throughout all phases of production flow, including fabrication, assembly, and test operations, for the manufacture of diverse satellite products contracted by major government clients (USSA and the U.S. Air Force).

ACCOMPLISHMENTS

- Promoted to Team Leader for new equipment installation and upgrades. Performed research and analysis and tested in production mode. Full authority to sign off fully tested equipment.

- Reduced cycle time by 30% through the development of assembly and test tolling. Improved recycle characteristics and cut hazardous emissions into the atmosphere by 40%.

- Collaborated with 60-person design-engineering team to ensure that designs were producible in the manufacturing environment. Provided cost-effective manufacturing recommendations.

- Trained 8 entry-level engineers in 4-month period to prepare efficient, labor-effective work plans for a multi-line production floor in an 80,000-square-foot facility.

Strategy: *Leading with a clear headline announcing his new career field, this is a concise yet powerful resume for a career transitioner who recently retrained in e-business. Accomplishments that play up his technical skills, project orientation, and teamwork abilities are appropriately included.*

RESUME 92: BEVERLY BASKIN, ED.S., MA, NCCC, LPC, CPRW; MARLBORO, NJ

PETER J. KANE

131 Poplar Street
Ridgewood, New Jersey 08770

(908) 567-0912
pjkane@aol.com

SUMMARY

Increasing responsibilities in the following areas:

Accounting and Finance

- Accounts Receivable
- Payroll
- Tax Accounting
- General Ledger

- Accounts Payable
- Budget Analysis
- Cost Accounting
- Computers

Security

- Loss Prevention
- Facilities Management
- Investigations

- Safety
- Conflict Resolution
- Asset Recovery

ACCOUNTING

Hands-on experience in accounting and related financial areas including the completion of numerous courses at Middlesex County College and Rutgers University. Knowledge of Lotus 1-2-3, Quicken, and Microsoft Word.

LOSS PREVENTION

Checked equipment and vehicles and performed administrative tasks related to security and investigations for Ford Motor Company. Surveyed property and developed security reports. Provided employee training regarding safety, loss prevention strategies, and asset recovery.

FACILITIES MANAGEMENT

Performed security functions, including guarding property against illegal entry, fire, and damage. Protected visitors and employees at Ford Motor Company from physical harm. Prepared reports of irregularities and noteworthy occurrences.

DISPATCHING

Screened incoming calls and dispatched proper services to the Police, Fire, and First Aid Departments. Worked as a former Communications Dispatcher for the New Brunswick Township Police Department.

NEGOTIATIONS

Trained in crisis and conflict management. Enjoy working with the public, employees, and vendors. Possess the ability to assess situations and create win-win business negotiations.

EXPERIENCE

1991–1998

- Ford Motors, New Brunswick, NJ
  Security and Maintenance Administration

1990

- Supermarkets General Corporation, Woodbridge, NJ
  Quality Assurance Clerk

1987–1990

- Monroe Township Police Department, Jamesburg, NJ
  Communications Dispatcher

EDUCATION

Rutgers University, New Brunswick, NJ
Major: Accounting, Expected Graduation December 2002

Strategy: *The functional style is used here because the candidate has no prior experience that relates to his recent education and current goals.*

CHAPTER 15

Resumes for People Returning to Work After an Entrepreneurial Venture

People who have run their own businesses but decide, for a variety of reasons, to return to "corporate America" face a unique challenge: how to present multifaceted entrepreneurial experience so that the resume is focused on a specific area of expertise. This is particularly difficult because so often an entrepreneur wears "many hats." As you view these resumes, you'll see that instead of trying to tell everything they've done while running their businesses, these entrepreneurs focused on the activities and achievements that are relevant to their current career targets.

Robert Simons

458 Laurel Court
Fort Worth, TX 76114
(817) 826-7818
audioguru@yahoo.com

Audio Electronic Engineering Technician — 14 years

Transforming Ideas into Actions

- Broad-based technical expertise and creative problem-solving abilities.
- Adept with Analog, Digital, Mixed Signal, and Microprocessor Circuitry.
- Accomplished musician (jazz drummer) with an exceptional musical ear and strong knowledge of audio and acoustic theory and techniques.
- Committed to ongoing professional development through networking, education, and membership in the Audio Engineering Society, Acoustic Society of America, and the Percussive Arts Society.
- Demonstrated competencies in:

Troubleshooting	Electronic Circuit Schematics
Service & Repair	Data Book Interpretation
Analytical Thinking	Training
Design & Development	Prototyping
Testing & Measurement	Simulating
Quality Control	Customer Relationship Management

Technical Skills

Hardware
Audio Precision Portable One Plus

Tektronix TDS 210 Series Digital Storage Scope with Fast Fourier Transform (FFT) Module

Hewlett-Packard 8903B Audio Analyzer

Hewlett-Packard 34401A Digital Multimeter

Tektronix PS 280 DC Power Supply

Hewlett-Packard 6209B DC Power Supply

X86-based Machines from 486 to Pentium III

Power Macintosh PC G3

Software
Multisim 2001 SPICE Circuit Simulation

MicroSim 7.1 PSPICE Circuit Simulation

IMSI TurboCAD 8.0 Standard

Microsoft Word & Excel 2000

Microsoft Internet Explorer 6.0

Microsoft Outlook 6.0

Netscape Navigator 6.2

Operating Systems
Windows 2000 Professional

Windows NT 4.0 Workstation

Windows 3.11; 98/95

Windows 6.22 Disk Operating System (DOS)

Macintosh OS X 10.1

UNIX System V

Professional Experience

Electronic Engineering Technician / Principal   1992–Present
Trident Sound Works, Fort Worth, TX
Manufacturer and Service Provider of High-Performance Audio Equipment

Founded business to create, customize, and repair audio products for professional musicians, audio engineers, and the high-fidelity consumer market. Accountable for all phases of product development from concept to design to manufacturing.

Select Achievements
- Designed and manufactured:
  - Single-Ended High-Fidelity Vacuum Tube Amplifiers using SPICE Models to aid in prototyping.
  - Portable power supplies for use with Digital Audio Tape (DAT) field location recordings where light weight, low noise, and extended recording time are essential. Engineered for Sony DAT players.
  - High-performance, low-noise power supplies using Solid State and Vacuum Tube circuitry for use within audio circuits.
- Retained by professional musicians to customize sound and resolve complex technical issues.
- Consulted on recording-facility layout for Acoustic Wave Productions. Involved designing room acoustics, ergonomics, wiring, and recording-equipment modifications.
- Established a joint venture with R&J Sound to contribute electronics expertise.

Strategy: *Technical achievements, rather than business-management activities, are emphasized in the Professional Experience section. The left-column Technical Skills summary is an effective way to present*

RESUME 93, CONTINUED

Robert Simons
Page Two

audioguru@yahoo.com

Senior Electronic Audio Technician, Servicing Department   1987–91
Harp Audio West, Phoenix, AZ
  Exclusive Provider of Car Audio Products for Jaguar

Rapidly promoted to senior-level Electronic Audio Technician. Accountable for all phases of troubleshooting analog, digital, mixed-signal, and microprocessor circuitry from module to board to component level. Specialized in the repair and modification of Surface Mount Device (SMD) circuits. Served as Assistant Manager of Quality Control Department.

Select Achievements
- Acquired over 8,000 hours of troubleshooting experience that enhanced efficiency in diagnosing and solving problems.
- Prevented loss of millions of dollars by identifying issues with products before distribution. Reported findings to design engineers.
- Streamlined quality-control testing process, which significantly reduced return rate and improved customer satisfaction.
- Executed Circuit Board Modifications (Power Supplies, Radio Frequency, and Audio Output Circuitry) that increased product reliability.
- Reduced number of backordered audio units 96% within three months.
- Selected to lead and train small teams of electronic technicians.

Education

Two-Year Diploma in Electronic Technology (600+ hours lab time)   1984
Hawk Technical Institute, Grainville, PA

what is essentially a list. (You can also see a Web version of this resume at www.newleafcareer.com/samples/index.html.)

RESUME 94: ANNEMARIE CROSS, CEIP, CPRW; HALLAM, VIC, AUSTRALIA

 JASMINE THORPE

8012 Sadie Lane • Belleville • Michigan 48112   Ph: (734) 332-6587 • (734) 306-6684

PROFESSIONAL PROFILE

Highly motivated, solutions-focused **Office Manager** with extensive experience and an impressive record of achievements within all facets of office administration, bookkeeping, secretarial, HR, and general office management. Combine strong computer literacy with proficiency to implement strategic operational initiatives that enhance productivity, quality, client service, technology, and overall bottom-line performance.

☑ Proven expertise in all facets of office management and bookkeeping, including financial and executive reporting utilizing latest technology and accounting software.

☑ Outstanding organizational, administrative, and time- and resource-management skills. Ability to set and achieve priorities and manage multiple projects in tandem without compromise to quality. Perform well in busy work environments.

☑ Strong leadership qualities, directing a cohesive team of professional staff, with a strong work ethic and philosophy to lead by example. Promote facilitation, support, and flexibility to surpass company objectives and client expectations.

☑ Exceptional interpersonal and communication skills, with proficiency to instill confidence and build and maintain strategic business/client relationships, while interfacing positively with people of diverse backgrounds.

CORE COMPETENCIES

- Office Management
- Client Interaction
- Diary Management/Scheduling
- Receptionist/Telephonist
- HR Generalist Functions

- Bookkeeping and Accounting
- Executive Support
- Correspondence Preparation
- Administration and Clerical
- Shorthand and Dictaphone

PROFESSIONAL EXPERIENCE

AQUA OFFICE SERVICES   1994–Present

Office Manager

Hands-on management role, providing on- and off-site bookkeeping, secretarial, and administrative support to businesses across diverse industries. Clerical and secretarial duties involve answering phones, filing, shorthand, and dictaphone typing. Set up and train end-users on QuickBooks/MYOB accounting software in either one-on-one or group settings. Complete taxation reporting; interface with accountants as required. Author company profiles, correspondence, sales/promotional materials, and management reports. Evaluate, develop, and implement office procedures; maintain office operational efficiency through ongoing coordination and follow-up. Troubleshoot computerized financial records requiring investigation and rectification of incorrectly recorded information.

☑ Captured significant increase in office efficiency through creation and implementation of documentation systems that eliminated unnecessary procedures.

Continued…

Strategy: *This resume "hides" the candidate's business-owner status and focuses on key skills related to her career target.*

RESUME 94, CONTINUED

JASMINE THORPE   Page 2

☑ Earned reputation as expert troubleshooter and problem solver; requested by many companies to review and restructure accounting software systems. Uncovered and tracked staff members' embezzlement of company funds totaling $20K.

☑ Directed major software conversions and computer upgrades; accomplished tasks without disruption to work output.

SUPERWAY, INC.   1988–1991

Office Manager

Sole management, coordination, and hands-on performance of entire bookkeeping, administration, clerical, reception, and secretarial procedures. Controlled financial information on both manual and computerized systems; input data; reconciled and generated reports for senior management and accountant; managed accounts payable/receivable. Secretary to managing director, accountant, general manager, and sales manager; diary management, travel arrangements, and correspondence preparation. Product costing. Budget preparation and monitoring. Payroll and personnel management including calculation of hourly rates and overtime; pay reviews; superannuation; and personnel file management.

☑ Set up and managed international financial records for Superway. Held full responsibility for P&L and executive reporting.

☑ Collaborated in conversion of accounting software system (QuickBooks) with minimal disruption to operations. Instrumental in troubleshooting; identified and implemented several software conflict-resolution procedures. Created and executed accounting-journal entries to rectify incorrect reporting.

OUTSTANDING PERSONNEL   1987–1988

Temporary Outplacement Assignments

Administration, reception, and bookkeeping support for diverse clientele.

☑ Requested personally for repeat assignments by a number of high-profile clients.

☑ Streamlined bookkeeping performance through implementation of effective accounting methods and by refining documentation-handling processes.

☑ Coordinated setup/installation of new computer systems and accounting software packages, involving conversion of all company data and ongoing facilitation of troubleshooting issues.

PROFESSIONAL DEVELOPMENT

Diploma of Business (Human Resource Practice)	2002
Cert IV in Business (Human Resource Operations)	2002
Cert II in Business (Office Admin)	2000
Diploma of Business (Accounting)	1999

TECHNICAL EXPERIENCE

• MYOB • QuickBooks • Microsoft Office Professional • Microsoft Outlook
• IBM PCs • Apple Mac

– Professional references available upon request. –

PAUL M. CLARK

500 Park Avenue
Dallas, TX 75234

(972) 280-7240
mclark@msn.com

Information Technology Professional

**Offering a broad range of technical experience and skills and
a strong desire to return to an I/T support role.**

Hardware	Server:	Compaq and Hewlett-Packard (HP)
	Desktop:	Hewlett-Packard (HP), Compaq, Dell, and IBM
	Midrange:	IBM AS/400

Software   Novell Netware, Microsoft Windows NT, Windows 95 & 98, OS/400, SNADS, TCP/IP, and RPG400.

Certifications   Novell 200, Networking Technologies, Microsoft M803, Administering Microsoft Windows NT 4.0, Microsoft 770, Install/Configure Win NT 4.0.

PROFESSIONAL EXPERIENCE

1999 – Present   **Clark Software Distribution · Dallas, Texas, owner**
Metroplex Technology Systems · Fort Worth, Texas, partner
Entrepreneur
Plan and manage all aspects of the business including goal setting, marketing and sales, financial planning, operations, and reporting.

1997 – 1999   **Security Technology Southwest Division · Dallas, Texas**
Regional Support Services Manager

Managed I/T support services in the Dallas Region: server administration, desktop/server training, LAN technical support, regional vendor management, and product evaluation; deployment of desktop hardware, operating-system software, office-applications software, anti-virus utilities, server operating-system software, backup utilities, and server anti-virus utilities.

- Under the direction of the vice president of regional support services, established organizational goals based on business needs; defined project priorities; played leadership role in planning, strategy, and status sessions with vice president and functional managers. Managed up to $5 million annual I/T budget.
- Managed 24x7 operation in client/server environment; supported over 30 servers in a corporate network of over 500.
- Provided I/T services to over 2,800 users in the Dallas Region.
- Set corporate standard for servers and for desktop hardware and software configuration (30,000 desktops).
- Led development of first Building Server Administration Operations Manual implemented company-wide.

Strategy: *After two not-very-successful attempts at entrepreneurship, this individual decided to reenter the workforce. The boxed summary clearly communicates his interests and expertise.*

RESUME 95, CONTINUED

PAUL M. CLARK, page 2

1992 – 1997   **Security Technology Retirement Services Company** · **Dallas, Texas**
Systems Manager, 1994 – 1997
Project Manager, 1992 – 1993
Project Leader, 1992

Supported the Institutional Retirement (401K) record-keeping business. Resolved diverse problems and developed, enhanced, and implemented client/server applications, client/server hardware, mainframe business applications, AS/400 business applications and hardware, network communications, and the corresponding operating systems software.

- Promoted from project leader, managing small to medium-sized projects, to project manager, then to systems manager responsible for establishing organizational goals, defining project priorities, and participating in planning, strategy, and status sessions with vice president and functional managers.
- Automated Microfiche Data Routing process, saving $200,000 and reducing turnaround time from 5–7 days to 2–3 days.
- Implemented desktop PCs at Cincinnati, Ohio, site; removed mainframe terminals.
- Designed, developed, and implemented new AS/400 computer room and its infrastructure.
- Recognized with Outstanding Service Award for managing successful move of 1,000+ users to two new buildings (500+ each).
- Led Client Service Operation Forum, a traveling road show designed to communicate technology direction to upper management of Security Investments business community.

EDUCATION

DeVry Institute · Irving, Texas
Computer Science
Certificate of Completion, 1983

Brookhaven College · Dallas, Texas
Business Administration coursework, 1977 – 1980

Significant corporate continuing education:

       Technical Skill-Building
       Project Management
       Strategic Coaching
       Performance Management

RESUME 96: LINDA WUNNER, CPRW, CEIP, JCTC; DULUTH, MN

Matthew Christopher

55 Dunwoody Street
St. Paul, Minnesota 55121
(651) 555-0716

OBJECTIVE

SALES — Using strong sales ability, business savvy, and business-building track record to drive revenue and profits for a growing company.

QUALIFICATIONS

- Proven sales performance: Built successful company from ground up to revenues of $500,000.

- Talent for building and leveraging business relationships.

- Detail orientation and ability to follow up and follow through.

- Rock-solid reputation for quality workmanship and honesty.

- Ability to interact with all people from day laborers to company presidents.

EMPLOYMENT

Matthew Christopher Construction, Duluth and St. Paul, MN
OWNER, 1980 to 2000
Subcontractor, Oneida Realty Company, 1997 to 2000
Shareholder/Member, Builders Commonwealth, 1990 to 1997

- Built successful business ($500,000 in sales, 1998) based on honesty, performance, follow-up, word of mouth, and recommendations.

- Personally generated all new business — cold-called, followed up on referrals, and delivered winning sales presentations amid heavy competition.

- Effectively supervised employees and subcontractors, adapting leadership and motivational strategies to elicit top performance and ensure projects completed on schedule.

EDUCATION

St. Paul Technical Vocational Institute, St. Paul, MN
ARCHITECTURAL DRAFTING AND DESIGN, 1980

COMMUNITY

Hockey Coach, Pee Wees and Termites

Strategy: *Targeting sales positions, this resume highlights the candidate's sales achievements as a business owner. The striking graphic illustrates sales growth.*

Cheryl McKinney

14775 Downing Ct.
Beaverton, OR 97006

cheryl@hep.com
(503) 680-4243

Sales Executive / Recruiting Director / Marketing Professional

Professional Summary

Outstanding sales and marketing executive with over 12 years of professional sales, management, recruiting, counseling, coaching, and business development experience. Able to work independently and as part of a corporate management team to accomplish objectives. Skills and traits include:

- ❑ Outstanding consultative sales
- ❑ New business development, new market identification
- ❑ Marketing and advertising experience
- ❑ Inside and outside account management
- ❑ Highly organized and self-directed
- ❑ Self-motivated and persistent
- ❑ Particularly adept at finding creative solutions to problems
- ❑ Able to handle all aspects of running a business/office

Select Achievements

❑ Entrepreneurial experience: Founded Hardware Engineering Professionals recruiting agency:

- ▪ Developed successful client relationships with start-up companies to Fortune 500 companies.
- ▪ Became recognized as an agency that delivers and was frequently called upon by companies such as Hewlett Packard and Intel Corporation to fill their difficult positions.
- ▪ Managed and operated all business activities including marketing, advertising, client development, and candidate recruitment.
- ▪ Successfully expanded agency focus from software engineering to hardware engineering and independently acquired the technical knowledge necessary to successfully recruit in a highly technical and specialized field.
- ▪ Developed company web site.

❑ Top Account Executive for Premiere Software and HNC Software. Consistently achieved or surpassed monthly and annual sales goals.

Select Client Companies

Hewlett Packard ▪ Intel Corporation ▪ Sequent Computer Systems ▪ Informix Software
Neurocom International ▪ Electro Scientific Industries ▪ Amdocs ▪ Microsoft
Dynamics Research Corporation ▪ Pyramid Systems ▪ Super PC ▪ Tektronix, Inc.

Strategy: *An effective design, selected achievements, and big-name clients draw attention to this candidate's sales qualifications in a high-impact manner. Good organization keeps the resume readable despite its length.*

RESUME 97, CONTINUED

Cheryl McKinney
Page 2 of 3

cheryl@hep.com
(503) 680-4243

Work Experience

Recruiting Director/Manager
Hardware Engineering Professionals, 1996 to Present

Provide recruiting services to clients, performing both contract and permanent placement. Specialty areas are Software to Hardware Computer Engineers and various supporting staff. Develop client relationships. Source through leads, referrals, cold calls, and the Internet. Perform on-site visits, applicant interviews, and reference checking.

Recruiting Director
Trinity Corporation, Trinity Engineering, 1995 to 1996

Recruited engineering professionals to fill open positions for client companies. Targeted client companies and established client relationships by frequent phone contact and on-site visits. Interviewed candidates in person and over the telephone. Matched candidates to open positions. Involved in the entire process of placing a candidate from initial interview to offer and acceptance.

Account Executive
Premiere Software, 1994 to 1995

Sold a programmer's editor for the Windows environment, maintenance, and other software-development tools to software developers and engineering managers across the U.S. and Canada. Demonstrated top sales performance and increased total company revenue. Usually exceeded quotas and was awarded numerous monthly and year-end bonuses. Developed a number of sales strategies that helped increase sales.

Sales Consultant
Northwest Software Partners, 1991 to 1993

Sold software-engineering contract services to high-technology companies across the U.S. and Canada by telephone. Developed client relationships, overcame objections to hiring off-site contractors, promoted the services and skills of individual engineers, and established contracts. This position was part-time while completing Master's program as a full-time student.

Sales Engineer
HNC Software, Inc., 1989 to 1990

Marketed compilers for C, C++, Pascal, debuggers, assemblers, Source Control Tools, software support, and seminars by telephone across the U.S. and Canada. Provided some on-site product demonstrations, developed sales strategies, provided feedback to engineering/sales support.

Software Engineer
Tektronix, Inc., 1983 to 1988

Lead software design and implementation effort for a release of the TekCASE Analyst, a computer-aided software (CASE) tool for structured analysis. Product was on VAX/VMS, VAX/UNIX, and other workstations. Researched, introduced, designed and implemented new features of the product, ported it to the IBM PC, and performed other product analysis, design, evaluation, and maintenance functions.

Cheryl McKinney
Page 3 of 3

cheryl@hep.com
(503) 680-4243

Other Professional Experience

College Instructor. Computer and other courses.
Part-time. January 1989 to March 1993.

- ❏ "Creative Career/Life Planning Workshop" Portland Community College
- ❏ "Introduction to Computers" Portland Community College
- ❏ "dBASE III+" Portland State University
- ❏ "DOS and WordPerfect" Clackamas Community College

Personal Accomplishments

- ❏ Member of Toastmasters public speaking club (CTM, VP Public Relations).
- ❏ Valedictorian of 1975 high-school graduating class: Redmond, Oregon

Education

M.A. Counseling Psychology, 1993
Lewis and Clark College, Portland, Oregon
GPA: 3.78
Emphasis on Career Counseling

B.S. Computer Science, 1983
Portland State University, Portland, Oregon
GPA: 3.85

References Available

Ready to relocate

JOHN R. CORLEY

100 Spring Avenue, Bern, Alabama 36340 — N45K34@aol.com — 334.555.5555

WHAT I CAN OFFER LANCE, INC., AS YOUR NEWEST DISTRICT SALES MANAGER

❑ **Sales ability** that ignites stagnant markets.

❑ **Customer service** that increases market share.

❑ **Communication skills** that get competitive intelligence.

❑ **Team-player approach** that helps your sales force.

❑ **Dedication to build relationships** that position you as the "sole source."

RELEVANT WORK HISTORY WITH EXAMPLES OF PROBLEMS SOLVED

❑ **Owner** and **On-Site Manager,** Ace's Total Package Store, Bern, Alabama   95–Dec 01
This 2,300 ft² store generated $1.0M in annual sales in a small, isolated market dominated by four large competitors.

Supervised an inside sales force of two full-time and four part-time employees. Maintained an inventory of about $81K.

Turned around a 30-year-old business that was losing $35K a year—despite five years' efforts by the previous manager to save his business. Literally got my hands dirty by restoring every part of store from the floor up. *Payoffs:* **Profits rose** rapidly to **$100K** annually in just five years.

Practiced, every day, **customer service our competitors just couldn't beat.** *Payoffs:* **Recaptured patrons who** had avoided the store for years and **had to drive by four larger competitors** to get to my front door—even though our prices were 2% higher.

Gained competitive intelligence from the best possible source—my competitors' vendors. Although I was last on their route, they valued the genuine hospitality I offered by treating them as customers. *Payoffs:* Their inside tips let me buy at bargain prices, lower the cost of inventory, and sometimes **beat competitors' promotional campaigns.**

Built and maintained legendary customer service. Example? Drove 14 miles to fill a demanding order from a new customer—at our busiest time. *Payoffs:* This **customer** not only **drove out of her way to shop with us** but **sent others** to us as well.

❑ **Sales Representative** *promoted over seven eligibles to* **Territory Manager** *and given additional responsibility as* Southeastern Coordinator for the Tide Racing Team and Director of P & G's participation in Alabama's Special Olympic Team, Procter & Gamble, Central City, Alabama.   76–95

Beat out 123 applicants to land this job. Met my customers' needs far beyond providing hundreds of product lines: delivered on every promise, listened to every concern, worked to make each customer more successful. *Payoffs:* When sales force turnover dropped to zero—and stayed there—this **territory became profitable fast and stayed that way.**

Strategy: *This candidate's successful entrepreneurial venture followed a lengthy career with Procter & Gamble. Now he's seeking to return to a corporate position. The storytelling style and quantifiable "payoffs" convey tremendous capability and potential.*

RESUME 98, CONTINUED

John R. Corley	**District Sales Manager**	334·555·5555

Found buying decision makers in our largest account and proved our products would generate more profits than their own house brands. **Built** our **market share to 62% in a year**. *Payoffs:* Sought out by my district manager **to train 35 other sales professionals** to duplicate my success.

Persuaded a busy store manager to let me design even more effective sales displays. *Payoffs:* My display—the largest for this product in the Southeast—**boosted his sales 50-fold**. He gave us two-thirds of his prime space, in an industry where visibility is everything.

Listened so well that I captured a major sale on my day off. Suggested a non-traditional use for one of our products to help a cotton farmer speed production. *Payoffs:* After he **bought a truckload of 1,200 units,** we began selling to a completely new market.

PROFESSIONAL DEVELOPMENT

❑ More than 40 hours of formal instruction a year from Procter & Gamble in areas like these: **increasing sales, communications that get results, leadership, customer service that builds ROI, serving diverse customers.**

AWARDS IN SALES

❑ **Recognized by our customers** above 125 more experienced professionals for the best customer satisfaction and sales performance, Procter & Gamble "Bulldog Award." 94

SERVING MY COMMUNITY

❑ Led the way to gain business support for local football and band booster clubs. Took time from the business day to show other businesses how they could also help raise funds. *Payoffs:* **Raised $52K** in four years and helped build new concession stands and facilities for our stadium.

❑ Suggested **a better marketing plan** when the friend of a cancer victim called on me for a donation. Designed, and helped execute, a fund-raising event. Then got the word out to our entire community. *Payoffs:* **Raised $1.5K in just three hours.**

COMPUTER SKILLS

❑ Proficient in Word, POS, and customer-contact software.

Licensed   **GLENN MORRISON**   Bonded

292 Pine Drive South, Bay Shore, NY 11706 • (631) 666-5555 • topcop@skymail.net

Private Investigation — Security — Surveillance — Loss Prevention

Law enforcement professional with a 25-year career track, exploring a position in the capacity of:

Chief Investigator

Select Skills, Strengths, and Accomplishments:
- Fifteen-year tenure with the New York City Police Department; retired as Sergeant.
- Extensively experienced across multiple branches of private investigation.
- Professionally trained in all aspects of Riot and Disturbance Control.
- Martial Arts and Firearms Expert/Trainer; conduct self-defense and weapons protection classes.
- Exceptional skills in the areas of research, analysis, strategic planning; program management, crisis intervention, conflict resolution; team leadership, training, evaluation.
- Awarded throughout career with medals and commendations for the resolution of difficult cases.

Maintain a broad scope of experience, education/training, and attributes well suited for:
- Development and implementation of safety, security, and loss-prevention programs.
- Management of loss prevention associates in areas of training, supervision, and motivation.
- Conducting thorough and comprehensive internal and external investigations.
- Procurement, implementation, and troubleshooting of sophisticated surveillance security systems.

Professional Experience — *Law Enforcement & Private Investigation*

Private Investigator   1992–present
Provide specialized investigative services for corporate, private, and high-profile clients

Undercover Criminal Investigations	Foreign and Domestic Arrests and Extradition
Background Checks	Fugitive Location and Apprehension
Fraud Investigation	Skip Trace / Missing Persons
Employee Dishonesty	Electronic Surveillance and Detection

New York City Police Department   1977–1992
Retired as Sergeant from earlier positions as Patrol Supervisor, Desk Supervisor, Bike Supervisor, Training Officer, Project Community Officer, Anti-Crime Officer (Plain Clothes)

- Briefed uniformed and commanding officers on cases, providing critical information and corrective action plans. Monitored precinct operations in the areas of prison control, fingerprinting, photographing, line-ups, physical searches, warrant checks, and incident-report verification

- Recruited officers and spearheaded training programs to orient new police officers in tactical procedures, criminal trends, firearms, bomb threats, hostage negotiations, and crisis intervention; integrated new officers into communities to facilitate neighborhood stabilization programs.

- Led a target team during bike patrol of assigned vicinities, maintaining a pulse on the community through enforcement of neighborhood stabilization programs. Successfully carried out ongoing investigations that relied heavily on the trust and cooperation of community members.

Education, Military Background & Licensures

United States Marine Corps Reserves, Special Operations, 1985–present
Bachelor of Science, Criminal Justice and Human Behavior, 1985
New York State Licensed and Bonded Private Investigator

Strategy: *To position a background well-suited to multiple disciplines, a combination format is used to showcase the candidate's strengths at a glance. This attractive one-page resume packs a lot of information and a lot of punch.*

RESUME 100: WILLIAM KINSER, CPRW, JCTC, CEIP; FAIRFAX, VA

MICHELLE M. ARNOLD

3451 Chandler Circle, Scranton, PA 18504
Cellular Phone: (570) 347-0195
michellearnold@aol.com

O B J E C T I V E : To achieve exponential growth for a small, closely held venture-capital firm.

FINANCIAL OPERATIONS MANAGER

Results-oriented professional with more than 14 years of experience in financial operations management. Adept at overseeing accounting functions in a variety of environments from start-up organizations to large corporate subsidiaries. Skilled in promoting organizational growth, controlling costs, establishing key accounts, and streamlining procedures. Significant experience in administering employee benefit programs.

AREAS OF STRENGTH:

• Accounting/Bookkeeping	• Leadership/Supervision	• Cost Reduction
• Budget Administration	• Account Management	• Staff Development
• Resource Utilization	• Strategic Planning	• Payroll Services

P R O F E S S I O N A L   E X P E R I E N C E

CYPRESS BENEFITS (Formerly ABC Benefits Services, The R.D. Kinsey Co.), Scranton, PA   1987 to 2002
Served a key role as one of four founders of a start-up company (R.D. Kinsey) providing enrollment and administrative services for employers under Section 125/Flexible Spending Account (FSA) plans. Participated in establishing the company as a turnkey benefit-administration outsourcing solution for corporate clients, with annual revenues of more than $7 million.

Chronology of Positions:
President, Pennsylvania Service Center (1997 to 2002)
    Supervised five vice presidents in the financial and administrative operations of the Pennsylvania Service Center, which administered benefit programs for more than 1,000 employers.
    Oversaw R.D. Kinsey's transition from an independent operation to an ABC Service Center.
Vice President of Administration (1992 to 1997)
    Researched the feasibility of diversifying services and served a key role in expansion planning.
    Implemented additional services including payroll and retirement-plan administration.
Account Coordinator/Benefits Administrator (1987 to 1992)
    Provided employee benefit consulting and administration, developing new accounts with employers.
    Performed in-house administration of benefit plans and served as the liaison to enrollees/employers.

Key Achievements:
- Generated annual revenues of more than $4 million and increased staff to 75 people by 1994.
- Facilitated increases in annual revenue by 75%, from $4 million to $7 million from 1994 to 1999.
- Served on a committee of key managers to evaluate a lucrative buyout offer by ABC Services.
- Coordinated all aspects of four office relocations, within eight years, to accommodate rapid growth.
- Implemented security measures to ensure proprietary data administration.
- Collaborated with a team to develop in-house software, eliminating all vendor software expenses.
- Oversaw all aspects of facility closure and transitioned services to the Georgia Service Center.

E D U C A T I O N

MBA, Pennsylvania State University, 2001
BS, Accounting, Carnegie Mellon University, 1985

Strategy: *Highly successful in her entrepreneurial venture, this manager sought a corporate position after she sold her business. A chronological format is preceded by a strong key-word summary that highlights her areas of expertise.*

RESUME 101: ILONA VANDERWOUDE, CJST, CEIP; RIVERDALE, NY

KEVIN STERLING

592 Third Avenue #3W • New York, NY 10017 • Tel: 212-200 2295 • Fax: 212-200-1556 • k_sterling@msn.com

TECHNOLOGY INDUSTRY EXECUTIVE

General Management ... Operations ... Negotiations ... Project Development

Highly driven, fast-track MIT graduate with track record of start-up, accelerated growth, turnaround, joint venture, international relations, and acquisition success. Built top-performing, award-winning integrated marketing agency servicing Fortune 100 and emerging e-commerce companies domestically and internationally. Captured market share within nation's top ten of transactive content integrators (Forrester Research, 1999) against rapidly emerging competition through expertise in:

- Competitive Market Positioning
- Operations Management
- Strategic & Business Planning
- Relationship Building
- Team-building & Leadership

- Internet Technology
- Marketing & Business Development
- Budgeting, Pricing & Cost Control
- Quality & Performance Optimization
- Contract Negotiation

Profiled in 30 industry-leading publications for expertise, leadership, and innovation
Finalist in Ernst & Young's "Entrepreneur of the Year" award, 1999
Published (co-)Author & Public Speaker

Professional Experience

MEDIA XYZ, INC., New York, NY—Chairman and CEO   1995 to 2001

Achieved rapid expansion within short timeframe after founding company in 1995. Built company from ground up to $12 million in 6 years with no initial outside funding. Core business entailed Web Content Creation, Interactive Advertising, and Systems Integration. "End-to-end" strategy positioned many Media XYZ clients as industry leaders within their field. **Representative clients included:** Microsoft, AlwaysOn Software, Worth Interactive, Ameritrade, Oracle, IBM, Lloyd Webber, American Express, Deutsche Bank, Swiss Bank, HIP, National Geographic, Sony, Pitney Bowes, iAnswers, and Janssen USA.

Team-Building & Operations Management
- Attracted and retained award-winning designers by building a collaborative and challenging organizational culture.
- Directed multi-site and international operations; capable of managing staff of up to 400.
- Developed and instituted management processes and procedures in all three offices, streamlining daily communications and operations, increasing efficiency, and ensuring project deadline compliance.
- Provided pro-active, decisive, and hands-on leadership within volatile industry.

Finance & Technology
- Introduced vendor bidding to cut overhead by 15%.
- Structured and negotiated strategic alliances and acquisition to further strengthen financial position and customer satisfaction through broadening of services and resources.
- Designed and implemented (then) cutting-edge "Media XYZ Client Extranet"; integrated project tracking and accounting system to accommodate international clients.
- Recognized for use of innovative Internet technology rendering competitive edge for clients.
- Served on Microsoft Internet Advisory Board from 1997 to 1998.

Strategy: *To position this executive for a technology-management position after the less-than-favorable sale of his company, this resume groups achievements under functional headings and leads with a very strong summary that includes notable industry awards and recognition.*

RESUME *101*, CONTINUED

KEVIN STERLING

Page 2 of 2

Marketing & Business Development
- Led high-powered negotiations with Microsoft for the successful award of launching Windows XY in 1996. Exceptionally innovative designs and aggressive approach played instrumental role in securing account. Project included high-impact, multimedia presentation to Bill Gates.
- Visionary talent with keen eye for new opportunities. Quick in identifying chance to redefine corporate strategy and capitalize on integrated services in response to increased competition from mainstream competitors. Implemented four-stage development methodology including cross-functional specialist teams and directed company through consequential accelerated growth, capturing a 73% annual growth rate.
- Instituted growth strategy comprising penetration of existing client accounts through cross-selling of additional services, favorably impacting bottom line and gross margins.

A & B INTERNATIONAL, Los Angeles, CA—Manager of Publicity ('94-'95); Auditor ('92-'94) 1992 to 1995
COMPACT, Houston, TX—Systems Engineer (secured employment following internship)   1988 to 1991

Consulting Engagements

INSIDE OUT, INC., Beverly Hills, CA   October 2001 to Present

Recruited by president as CFO with full P&L responsibility to manage fast growth and improve poor cash flow of pharmaceutical meeting- and event-management company.

Key accomplishments:
- Increased annual contracted revenue from $12 million for 2000 to $19 million for 2001 within 2 months.
- Remedied cash-flow difficulties by evaluating and renegotiating $8 million key contracts.
- Created new revenue streams by introducing new service offering and by negotiating and establishing joint venture.
- Successfully negotiated with banks to establish company's line of credit.

NY INVESTMENT COMPANY, LLC, New York, NY   April to October 2001
Project Manager for company with combined $5 billion fund.

TECH COMPUTER, New York, NY   Spring 1995
Frequent public appearances by conducting Internet Business Seminars. (Listing available.)

Education

Diploma: "The Birthing of Giants" (Executive Leadership Program), MIT, Cambridge, MA   2001
Degree: B.B.A., Emphasis in Business and Finance, Texas A&M University, College Station, TX   1991

Publications and Awards

Publications:
- Co-authored: Smith, A.M., "Chapter 3: Web Site Infrastructure and Hosting." *Buying Web Services: The Survival Guide to Outsourcing.* New York: John Wiley & Sons Publishing Co., 2000, pp. 85-123.
- Listing available of all company and personal publicity obtained.

Awards:
- Received 15 prestigious industry awards, including: Webby Award (2000); Ad Tech Award (2001); Golden Pencil Award (2001).

MICHAEL R. FEIDER

N234 W15005 Brookfield Drive
Sussex, Wisconsin 53082

Residence: (262) 840-3654
mrfeider@mail.com

SALES AND RELATIONSHIP MANAGEMENT
Pharmaceutical … Medical Device … Medical Technology

Entrepreneurial, hard-working, and results-oriented business professional with 7 years of successful outside, business-to-business sales experience. Solid interpersonal and written communication skills with effective relationship-building and sales-presentation abilities to individuals at all levels of the organization, including executives and other decision-makers. Strong analytical and creative abilities—can quickly develop strategies to solve business challenges. Well organized with excellent follow-through and follow-up skills. Core competencies include:

- Strategic Business Planning
- Market Research & Analysis
- Competitive Product Placement
- New Product Launch

- Key Account Management
- Client Relationship Management
- Presentation Development & Delivery
- Budgetary & Expense Management

PROFESSIONAL EXPERIENCE

MRF, Incorporated—Sussex, Wisconsin
A privately held manufacturer and distributor of the Gadget Lawn™ lawn tool.

June 1994 to Present

SALES AND GENERAL MANAGER

Operations and Business Start-up Accomplishments
- Conceived of product concept, engineered/fabricated initial prototype, and presented to capital investors.
- Created potential customer list and developed relationships with retail buyers and other large distributors nationwide.
- Developed sales presentation and delivered to corporate decision-makers. Presentation designed to capture interest very quickly with very targeted product information.
- Negotiated product specifications, secured order commitments, and coordinated delivery.
- Managed production and manufacturing with outside vendors: stamping, degreasing, heat-treating, plating, and packaging. Independently sourced all outside services/contractors.
- Coordinated legal aspects including trademark and patent with legal professionals.
- Prepared monthly and year-end financial reporting including sales forecast and projections. Handled bookkeeping and accounting records.

Sales Accomplishments
- Grew business from ground floor to 400% growth in 2 years. Delivered consistent 7–9% growth every year thereafter.
- Landed 40,000-unit account with Wal-Mart (5,000 products compete for every one item in its retail stores).
- Developed long-term, profitable relationships with Shopko, Stein Garden, QVC, Franks, and many other retailers. Distributed product internationally.
- Received no product back as unsatisfactory.

EDUCATION

B.S. in Management—Marquette University, Milwaukee, Wisconsin, 2001
Received Wisconsin Collegiate Entrepreneur of the Year Scholarship

Strategy: *This entrepreneur had a successful business but wanted to work fewer than 80 hours a week! The resume downplays his ownership of the business.*

RESUME 103: DEB DIB, CCM, NCRW, CPRW, CEIP, JCTC, CCMC; MEDFORD, NY

Gerald F. Hewlitt

Hospitality Industry Specialist
Senior-Level Operations Manager

Sales + Marketing + Owner Mentality + Technology + Daring Creativity = SUCCESS

Executive Profile

Over 20 years' experience in every facet of the hospitality industry in positions as general manager, consultant, and/or owner with a solid background in successful traditional and entrepreneurial venues. Use a real-world approach to problem solving and a deep well of experience to meet the challenges of this fast-paced, high-turnover industry.

- Have operated multiple restaurants accommodating 900+ patrons and managed events for up to 2,000 attendees while partnering with diverse management, overseeing a multitude of activities, and managing half-million-dollar budgets / P&Ls.

- Proven team-forming and motivational skills have delivered unmatched loyalty and a nearly unheard-of staff turnover rate of less than 25%, far below the 61% industry standard. Consistently develop cost-cutting and profit-building initiatives.

- Honed and demonstrated project planning and management skills in supremely high-stress scenarios where failure was not an option and the wrong decision could end a career and / or deliver substantial personal loss.

- Skilled at simultaneously supervising several restaurants and projects. Directed management of two separate restaurants, 20 miles apart, for five years. Worked 18+ hours concurrently managing early-morning renovations and late-night operations.

- Use life-long interest in computers / IT to enhance every business opportunity and activity from marketing, to inventory control, to menu preparation, to catering scheduling, etc. Hold Certificate in Computer Science from Adelphi University (2001).

- Strategic business sense, uncompromising work ethic, and natural sincerity have helped create consistent profits and have won loyal support and motivation of customers, employees, partners, managers, community leaders, suppliers, and local officials.

Summary of Qualifications

- multi-unit operation management
- multimillion-dollar P&L management
- facility management
- event management & promotion
- troubleshooting & change management

- project planning & systems development
- advanced IT knowledge
- risk management & inventory control
- purchasing & negotiation skills
- vendor sourcing & negotiating

- sales / product / market analysis
- food / labor / marketing cost controls
- customer relations and satisfaction
- human resources management
- team building & staff retention programs

Career Development

PRESTIGE FOOD AND SPORTS ENTERPRISE, INC. (PFS), OYSTER BAY, NY
1988 to present

President and COO
Partner / Manager

PFS operated two consecutive successful theme restaurants on Long Island. Original concept, Charlie's Big City Grill, opened in 1989 as an 800-patron sports bar restaurant much like The ESPN Zone restaurants.

- Charlie's grossed over $2 million in f/y 1990 and $2.4 million in f/y 1992 and 1993. Well-trained staff (only 25% turnover rate), value menu, and "almost as good as being at the game" mentality built a loyal customer base of young professionals, over-30 single clientele, families, and out-of-town guests.

- Restaurant was featured in numerous publications as a top sports bar/café and was one of the first sites in Metro New York to feature complete sports broadcast from satellite transmission, with Sunday NFL football afternoons attracting 1,500 guests.

In proactive response to increased competition from satellite dishes and sports-bar market saturation, renovated site and in 1995 transitioned Charlie's to the New Orleans Roadhouse, a Cajun menu "House of Blues"-style restaurant.

- Took only four months to plan and develop this restaurant / entertainment concept entirely new to Metro New York. Handled politicking / project planning necessary to get permits, plans, contractors, and equipment in place for summer renovation (slow season). Opened on Labor Day weekend 1995, two weeks ahead of schedule and below $750,000 budget.

- Negotiated with property-management company for an additional 10 years on lease and lower rent (both valuable assets for future sale). Fine-tuned, upgraded, and enhanced facility, adding handicap access, assessing risk management, and increasing venue flexibility. Planned menu, hired kitchen staff, developed company's first employee manual, created marketing plans, and booked live entertainment.

- Now a top rhythm & blues showcase and popular Cajun / Creole dining destination, the Grill was recently sold for a profit.

25 Bay Drive, Amityville, NY 11701
phone: 631-555-5555 ■ fax: 631-000-0000 ■ cell: 516-555-5555 ■ e-mail: GH.PFS@email.com

Strategy: *This resume focuses on the candidate's exceptional operations and marketing skills, as well as his profit-making and money-making accomplishments. As a result, potential employers can see that his entrepreneurial vision is easily translatable to a corporate position.*

Gerald F. Hewlitt / page two of three

Career Development, continued

Key Leadership Initiatives at Prestige Food & Sports Enterprise

Developed Successful Theme Restaurant in Highly Competitive Area

Developed and operated a major theme restaurant in Nassau County, NY. Created concept from emerging sports-bar trend, incorporated local venue elements into large-scale restaurant. Composed business plan and sought financing from U.S. Small Business Administration. Took possession of 10-year lease, construction, and physical development in less than four months. Driven by desire to succeed, took Charlie's Big City Grill from concept to creation in under a year.

Key Results:
- First year's gross sales exceeded $2 million with sales growing by more than 20% in next four years.

Reduced Staff Turnover in High Turnover Industry

Challenged with creating a strong team environment to reduce turnover of staff. Trained managers in "team management" principles, focusing on workplace pride. Compiled PC-based employee guidebook. Shared company's success with employees through annual bonuses, social gatherings, and benefit options.

Key Results:
- Delivered industry-low, 25% turnover rate, even keeping 25% rate during renovation closure.
- Retained competent and recognizable employees; increased sales by building repeat-customer / staff bond.
- Improved service quality and customer loyalty through better, more knowledgeable employees.

Managed Redevelopment and Construction of Successful Theme Restaurant

Challenged to co-develop and implement a new, next-generation theme-restaurant concept; to outperform, within five years, previous years' flat growth; to implement changes within a 90-day window; and to retain core customer base, as well as staff crucial to immediate success and profitability.

Identified key areas of planning and attention, set calendar, assigned management / partner responsibilities. Researched themes / concepts. Established $750,000 budget, developed project plan, and scheduled major construction for traditionally low-performing period. Renegotiated a lengthened lease, concessions for capital improvements, and lower rent. Established cooperative dialogue with town and county officials to expedite necessary permits and approvals.

Key Results:
- Completed construction of The New Orleans Roadhouse below budget and two weeks ahead of schedule.
- After renovation, year-one gross revenue rose to $2.6 million from $2.3 million.
- Reduced daily maintenance costs by 18%, energy consumption by 8%+, by updating infrastructure, HVAC, and layout.
- Achieved reduced insurance risk through facility changes that allowed full handicap accessibility.
- Retained market share, provided exposure to different market areas, and positioned firm for strong short-term growth.
- Booked live performances by top entertainers and expanded catering capacity.

Rebranded Local Restaurant to Attract New Customers

Challenged with marketing New Orleans Roadhouse without conveying rural image. Recognized traditional radio spots did not take advantage of new theme so explored and implemented 30- and 60-second local television spots with a major Metro NY cable television provider.

Key Results:
- Quarterly sales increased 21%. Ads generated qualified first-time customers and helped in rebranding.

Reduced Marketing Costs While Increasing Market Visibility to Targeted Customers

Challenged to develop effective, low-cost method of advertising to main customer base. Researched and implemented customer databases for direct-mail and target-marketing strategies, integrated direct mail software for in-house mail sorting, and added POSTNET bar-coding to meet USPS regulations. Appended 80,000-member database with phone numbers leading to telemarketing efforts. Eliminated manual removal of outdated customer information from database by using USPS National Change of Address files to automate process.

Key Results:
- Slashed direct-mail costs to 33% from $63,000 to $42,000. Reduced marketing budget to 15%.
- Realized 3% to 7% annual postage and labor cost savings by updating database with USPS.

25 Bay Drive, Amityville, NY 11701
phone: 631-555-5555 ▪ fax: 631-000-0000 ▪ cell: 516-555-5555 ▪ e-mail: GH.PFS@email.com

RESUME 103, CONTINUED

Gerald F. Hewlitt / page three of three

Career Development, continued

THE LINDEN TREE CAFÉ, BABYLON, NY   **General Manager & Principal**
1999 to 2000 & 1982 to 1995

The Linden Tree Café is a well-established neighborhood café located in a historical building in one of Long Island's largest downtowns, Babylon, an urban / suburban town attempting revitalization from ongoing effects of "mall creep."

- In 1982 identified closed café as a good prospect—surrounding area's demographics were upscale, community revitalization efforts were strong, and circa 1880 building matched current trend for historic charm. Successfully negotiated 10-year lease with option to purchase building within five years at 1982 value, with half of paid rent credited toward purchase price.

- Working with Town of Babylon officials, the Babylon Historical Society, and the Chamber of Commerce, renovated building's façade to circa 1880, funding 70% of work through state and federal historic preservation funds. Purchased fixtures with no money down.

- Opened in November of 1982 and quickly established a local clientele. Then marketed to non-local population using regional magazine advertisements, popular radio stations, and supplier co-op ads.

- Café steadily grossed over $700,000 annually in early '80s. Although maintaining an historic building with apartments was an ongoing challenge, in 1986, purchased building at 1982 negotiated price of $110,000 rather than appraised price of $225,000.

- Restaurant's revenues began to falter in the late '80s as national recession reached Long Island, mall creep continued to deflect downtown business, town's road and sidewalk repairs limited access for months, and the large summer beach crowd started to gather at bay-front restaurants close to the ferries, rather than in the downtown area.

- In 1990 planned complete building renovation including infrastructure, new kitchen, HVAC, handicap access, 100% fire sprinklers, increased dining area, and all-new outside dining area. To reduce effect on business, completed entire renovation in under four months. Kept core customer base informed of upcoming grand re-opening with a 20,000+ newsletter mailing and invited best customers and community leaders to menu tastings and mock service dining shortly before reopening.

- Renovation and new menu generated results above initial projection, but with unsteady growth. Decided to sell when a generous offer was received in 1994. Completed sale in 1995. Kept possession of building and separate real estate company; transitioned professional activities into new investment areas.

- New owners' establishment closed after only four years through owners' series of business-devastating decisions. Owners changed name and concept; invested heavily in fad, not trend; maintained business cash flow with questionable business practices; tarnished establishment's reputation; damaged property with brew-pub equipment; and drove away original clients.

- Determined to personally rebuild and reestablish business and then sell to a buyer or team who could maintain and enhance it. Repossessed property in winter of 1998, facing enormous challenges as landlord of a building in need of a tenant and as a member of a community that wanted to see / solicit a fine establishment in the area.

- Achieved this goal in less than 18 months with under $100,000 investment after reestablishing cordial community and business working relationships. Reopened in Spring 1999 with Chamber of Commerce celebrating the event with a party at the establishment in June 1999. In August 2000, business was sold for a profit and continues to develop.

Education and Certification

Bachelor of Science in Management, Adelphi University, Garden City, New York

Adelphi University, Garden City, New York
Certificate, 320 hours, Computer Science, 2001
Earned while running two businesses

CompUSA
MS Excel (2 days)
Advanced use of CorelDRAW software (2 days)

Hospitality Certifications
Food Service Managers Certificate, No. 92122, County of Suffolk Department of Health Services
Food Service Managers Certificate, Nassau County Department of Health

National Restaurant Association
Preventing Sexual Harassment in the Workplace
Restaurant Catering
Trends in Restaurant Design

New York Restaurant Association
Writing an Operation Manual (2 days)

25 Bay Drive, Amityville, NY 11701
phone: 631-555-5555 ■ fax: 631-000-0000 ■ cell: 516-555-5555 ■ e-mail: GH.PFS@email.com

APPENDIX

Internet Career Resources

With the emergence of the Internet has come a huge collection of job search resources for individuals returning to work. Here are some of our favorites.

Dictionaries and Glossaries

Outstanding information on key words and acronyms.

Acronym Finder	www.acronymfinder.com
Babelfish Foreign-Language Translation	http://babelfish.altavista.com/
ComputerUser High-Tech Dictionary	www.computeruser.com/resources/dictionary/dictionary.html
Dave's Truly Canadian Dictionary of Canadian Spelling	www.luther.bc.ca/~dave7cnv/cdnspelling/cdnspelling.html
Dictionary of Investment Terms	www.county.com.au/web/webdict.nsf/pages/index?open
Duhaime's Legal Dictionary	www.duhaime.org
High-Tech Dictionary Chat Symbols	www.computeruser.com/resources/dictionary/chat.html
InvestorWords.com	www.investorwords.com
Law.com Legal Industry Glossary	www.law.com
Legal Dictionary	www.nolo.com/lawcenter/dictionary/wordindex.cfm
Merriam-Webster Collegiate Dictionary & Thesaurus	www.m-w.com/home.htm

National Restaurant Association Restaurant Industry Glossary	www.nraef.org/pdf_files/ IndustryAcronymsDefinitions- edited-2-23.pdf
Refdesk	www.refdesk.com
Technology Terms Dictionary	www.computeruser.com/
TechWeb TechEncyclopedia	www.techweb.com/encyclopedia/
Verizon Glossary of Telecom Terms	www22.verizon.com/wholesale/glossary/ 0,2624,0_9,00.html
The Virtual Reference Desk-Dictionaries	http://thorplus.lib.purdue.edu/reference/
Washington Post Business Glossary	www.washingtonpost.com/ wp-srv/business/longterm/ glossary/index.htm
Webopedia: Online Dictionary for Computer and Internet Terms	www.webopedia.com
Whatis?com Technology Terms	whatis.techtarget.com
Wordsmyth: The Educational Dictionary/Thesaurus	www.wordsmyth.net

Job Search Sites

You'll find thousands and thousands of current professional employment opportunities on these sites.

GENERAL SITES

411 Jobs	www.411jobs.net
6FigureJobs	www.6figurejobs.com
America's CareerInfoNet	www.acinet.org/acinet
America's Job Bank	www.ajb.dni.us
America's Talent Bank	www.ajb.dni.us/html/atb_home.html
BestJobsUSA	www.bestjobsusa.com/index-jsk-ns.asp
BlackWorld Careers	www.blackworld.com
Canada WorkInfo Net	www.workinfonet.ca
CareerAge	www.careerage.com
CareerBuilder	www.careerbuilder.com
Career.com	www.career.com
CareerExchange.com	www.careerexchange.com
Career Exposure	www.careerexposure.com

The Career Key	www.careerkey.org/english
Careermag.com	www.careermag.com
CareerShop	www.careershop.com
CareerSite.com	www.careersite.com
Contract Employment Weekly	www.ceweekly.com
Digital City (jobs by location)	home.digitalcity.com
EmploymentGuide.com	www.employmentguide.com
Excite	http://careers.excite.com
FlipDog	www.flipdog.com
For Work	www.4work.com
Futurestep	www.futurestep.com
GETAJOB!	www.getajob.com
Help Wanted	www.helpwanted.com
HotJobs.com	www.hotjobs.com
The Internet Job Locator	www.joblocator.com
It's Your Job Now	www.ItsYourJobNow.com
JobBankUSA	www.jobbankusa.com
JobHuntersBible.com	www.jobhuntersbible.com
Job-Hunt.org	www.job-hunt.org
JOBNET.com	www.jobnet.com/philly
JobOptions	www.joboptions.com
JobsOnline	www.jobsonline.com
Job Source	www.jobsource.com
JobWeb	www.jobweb.com
Kiwi Careers (New Zealand)	www.careers.co.nz
Monster.com	www.monster.com
MonsterTRAK	www.jobtrak.com
NationJob Network	www.nationjob.com
NCOA MaturityWorks	www.maturityworks.org
Net Temps	www.net-temps.com
Online-Jobs.Com	www.online-jobs.com
The Riley Guide	www.rileyguide.com
Saludos Hispanos	www.saludos.com

SIRC Internet Resume Center	www.inpursuit.com/sirc
TrueCareers	www.careercity.com
US Resume	www.usresume.com
Wages.com	www.wages.com.au
WorkTree	www.worktree.com

ACCOUNTING CAREERS

American Association of Finance and Accounting	www.aafa.com
CPAnet	www.CPAnet.com
SmartPros Accounting	www.accountingnet.com

ARTS AND MEDIA CAREERS

Airwaves MediaWeb	www.airwaves.com
Auditions.com	www.auditions.com
Fashion Career Center	www.fashioncareercenter.com
Playbill (Theatre Jobs)	www.playbill.com/cgi-bin/plb/jobs?cmd=search
TVJobs.com	www.tvjobs.com

EDUCATION CAREERS

Academic360.com	www.academic360.com
Chronicle of Higher Education Career Network	www.chronicle.com/jobs
Council for Advancement and Support of Education	www.case.org
Education Jobs.com	www.educationjobs.com
Education Week's Marketplace Jobs Online	www.edweek.org/jobs
Education World	www.education-world.com/jobs
Jobs.EduFind.com	www.jobs.edunet.com
Teaching Jobs	www.teaching-jobs.org/index.htm
University Job Bank	www.ujobbank.com

ENTRY-LEVEL CAREERS

CampusCareerCenter.com	www.campuscareercenter.com
College Grad Job Hunter	www.collegegrad.com

College Job Board	www.collegejobboard.com/?1100
jobsource.com	www.jobsource.com
MonsterTRAK	www.jobtrak.com

HEALTH CARE/MEDICAL/PHARMACEUTICAL CAREERS

Great Valley Publishing	www.gvpub.com
Health Care Recruitment Online	www.healthcareers-online.com
HealthJobSite.com	www.healthjobsite.com
Health Leaders	www.HealthLeaders.com
HMonster	myh.monster.com
J. Allen & Associates (physician jobs)	www.NHRphysician.com
MedHunters.com	www.medhunters.com
Medzilla	www.medzilla.com
Nursing Spectrum	www.nursingspectrum.com
Pharmaceutical Company Database	www.coreynahman.com/pharmaceutical_company_database.html
Physicians Employment	www.physemp.com
RehabJobsOnline	www.rehabjobs.com
Rx Career Center	www.rxcareercenter.com

HUMAN RESOURCES CAREERS

Empty.Net	www.empty.net
HR Connections	www.hrjobs.com
HR Hub	www.hrhub.com
Human Resources Development Canada	www.hrdc-drhc.gc.ca/common/home.shtml
Jobs4HR	www.jobs4hr.com

INTERNATIONAL CAREERS

EscapeArtist.com	www.escapeartist.com
International Career Employment Center	www.internationaljobs.org
LatPro	www.latpro.com
OverseasJobs.com	www.overseasjobs.com

SALES AND MARKETING CAREERS

American Marketing Association	www.marketingpower.com
Job.com	www.job.com/jobsearch/ index.cfm?tid=search.cfm&us=226& catbox=53
MarketingJobs.com	www.marketingjobs.com
Rollins Search Group	www.rollinssearch.com

SERVICE CAREERS

Chefs at Work	www.chefsatwork.com
Culinary Jobs	www.pastrywiz.com/talk/job.htm
Escoffier On Line	www.escoffier.com
Foodservice.com	www.foodservice.com

TECHNOLOGY/ENGINEERING CAREERS

American Institute of Architects	www.aia.org
American Society for Quality	www.asq.org
Brainbuzz.com IT Career Network	www.brainbuzz.com
CareerShop	www.careershop.com
Chancellor & Chancellor Resources for Careers	www.chancellor.com/fr_careers.html
ComputerWork.com	www.computerwork.com
Computerworld Careers Knowledge Center	www.computerworld.com/ careertopics/careers?from=left
Dice	www.dice.com
IDEAS Job Network	www.ideasjn.com
IEEE-USA Job Service	jobs.ieeeusa.org/jobs/services/
Jobserve	www.jobserve.com
National Society of Professional Engineers	www.nspe.org
National Technical Employment Services	www.ntes.com
Quality Resources Online	www.quality.org
Resulte Universal	www.psisearch.com

| Techies.com | www.techies.com |
| Techsource | www.techsource.org/index.htm |

GOVERNMENT AND MILITARY CAREERS

Federal Jobs Net	www.federaljobs.net
FedWorld	www.fedworld.gov
FRS Federal Jobs Central	www.fedjobs.com
GetaGovJob.com	www.getagovjob.com
GovExec.com	www.govexec.com
HRS Federal Job Search	www.hrsjobs.com
Military Career Guide Online	www.militarycareers.com
PLANETGOV	www.planetgov.com
USAJOBS	www.usajobs.opm.gov

LEGAL CAREERS

FindLaw	www.findlaw.com
Greedy Associates	www.greedyassociates.com
Legal Career Center	www.attorneyjobs.com

SITES FOR MISCELLANEOUS SPECIFIC FIELDS

AG Careers/Farms.com	www.agricareers.com
American Public Works Association	www.pubworks.org
AutoCareers.com	www.autocareers.com
BrilliantPeople.com	www.brilliantpeople.com
CareerBank.com	www.careerbank.com
CEOExpress	www.ceoexpress.com
CFO.com	www.cfonet.com
Environmental Career Opportunities	www.ecojobs.com
Environmentalcareer.com	www.environmental-jobs.com
Find A Pilot	www.findapilot.com
International Seafarers Exchange	www.jobxchange.com
Logistics Jobs	www.jobsinlogistics.com
MBACareers.com	www.mbacareers.com

RAI: The Executive Search Firm	www.raijobs.com
Social Work Jobs	www.socialservice.com
Vault	www.vault.com

Company Information

Outstanding resources for researching specific companies.

555-1212.com	www.555-1212.com
Brint.com	www.brint.com
EDGAR Online	www.edgar-online.com
Experience	www.experiencenetwork.com
Fortune Magazine	www.fortune.com
Hoover's Business Profiles	www.hoovers.com
infoUSA (small-business information)	www.infousa.com
Intellifact.com	www.igiweb.com/intellifact/
OneSource CorpTech	www.corptech.com
SuperPages.com	www.bigbook.com
U.S. Chamber of Commerce	www.uschamber.com/
Vault Company Research	www.vault.com/companies/ searchcompanies.jsp
Wetfeet.com Company Research	www.wetfeet.com/asp/ companyresource_home.asp

Interviewing Tips and Techniques

Expert guidance to sharpen and strengthen your interviewing skills.

About.com Interviewing	www.jobsearch.about.com/business/ jobsearch/msubinterv.htm
Bradley CVs Introduction to Job Interviews	www.bradleycvs.demon.co.uk/ interview/index.htm
Dress for Success	www.dressforsuccess.org
Job-Interview.net	www.job-interview.net
Northeastern University Career Services	www.dac.neu.edu/coop.careerservices/ interview.html

Salary and Compensation Information

Learn from the experts to strengthen your negotiating skills and increase your salary.

Abbott, Langer & Associates	www.abbott-langer.com
America's Career InfoNet	www.acinet.org/acinet/select_occupation.asp?stfips=&next=occ_rep
Bureau of Labor Statistics	www.bls.gov/bls/wages.htm
CareerJournal (The *Wall Street Journal*)	www.careerjournal.com/salaries/index.html
Clayton Wallis Co.	www.claytonwallis.com
Compensation Link	www.compensationlink.com
Consultant Salaries	www.cob.ohio-state.edu/~fin/jobs/mco/salary.htm
Economic Research Institute	www.erieri.com
Health Care Salary Surveys	www.pohly.com/salary.shtml
Janco Associates MIS Salary Survey	www.psrinc.com/salary.htm
JobStar	www.jobstar.org/tools/salary/index.htm
Monster.com Salary Info	salary.monster.com/
Salary and Crime Calculator	www.homefair.com/homefair/cmr/salcalc.html
Salarysurvey.com	www.salarysurvey.com
Wageweb	www.wageweb.com
WorldatWork (formerly American Compensation Association)	www.worldatwork.org

GEOGRAPHIC INDEX OF CONTRIBUTORS

The sample resumes in chapters 4 through 15 were written by professional resume and cover letter writers. If you need help with your resume and job search correspondence, you can use the following list to locate a career professional in your area.

A note about credentials: Nearly all of the contributing writers have earned one or more professional credentials. These credentials are highly regarded in the careers and employment industry and are indicative of the writer's expertise and commitment to professional development. Here is an explication of each of these credentials:

Credential	Awarded by	Recognizes
CBC: Certified Behavioral Consultant	The Institute for Motivational Living and Target Training International	
CCM: Credentialed Career Master	Career Masters Institute	Specific professional expertise, knowledge of current career trends, commitment to continuing education, and dedication through *pro bono* work
CCMC: Certified Career Management Coach	Career Coach University	Training and expertise in career coaching
CECC: Certified Electronic Career Coach	Professional Resume Writing and Research Association	Expertise in job-search-related Internet technology and electronic communications

(continues)

Credential	Awarded by	Recognizes
CEIP: Certified Employment Interview Professional	Professional Association of Resume Writers and Career Coaches	Expertise in interview preparation strategy
CIPC: Certified International Personnel Consultant	National Association of Personnel Services	Expertise in staffing and placement
CJST: Certified Job Search Trainer	Career Masters Institute	
CMP: Certified Career Management Practitioner	International Association of Career Management Professionals	
CPC: Certified Personnel Consultant	National Association of Personnel Services	Expertise in staffing and placement
CPRW: Certified Professional Resume Writer	Professional Association of Resume Writers and Career Coaches	Knowledge of resume strategy development and writing
CRW: Certified Resume Writer	Professional Resume Writing and Research Association	Successful passage of all requirements of the Certified Resume Writer examination
CSS: Certified Search Specialist	Search Research Institute	Advanced knowledge of personnel law, recruitment, and placement
CWDP: Certified Workforce Development Professional	National Association of Workforce Development Professionals	
Ed.S.: Educational Specialist in Counseling	Accredited university	Graduate-level education
JCTC: Job and Career Transition Coach	Career Planning and Adult Development Network	Training and expertise in job and career coaching strategies
IJCTC: International Job and Career Transition Coach	Career Planning and Adult Development Network	Training and expertise in job and career coaching strategies
LPC: Licensed Professional Counselor	Individual states	Master's in counseling plus three years of supervised counseling experience
MA: Master of Arts degree	Accredited university	Graduate-level education

Credential	Awarded by	Recognizes
MBA: Master of Business Administration degree	Accredited university	Graduate-level education
M.Ed.: Master of Education degree	Accredited university	Graduate-level education
MFA: Master of Fine Arts degree	Accredited university	Graduate-level education
MS: Master of Science degree	Accredited university	Graduate-level education
M.S.Ed.: Master of Science in Education	Accredited university	Graduate-level education
NCC: National Certified Counselor NCCC: National Certified Career Counselor	National Board for Certified Counselors (affiliated with the American Counseling Association and the American Psychological Association)	Qualification to provide career counseling
NCRW: Nationally Certified Resume Writer	National Resume Writers' Association	Knowledge of resume strategy development and writing
Ph.D.: Doctor of Philosophy degree	Accredited university	Post-graduate education

United States

ALABAMA

Don Orlando, MBA, CPRW, IJCTC, CCM
Executive Master Team—Career Masters Institute
Owner, The McLean Group
640 S. McDonough St.
Montgomery, AL 36104
Phone: (334) 264-2020
Fax: (334) 264-9227
E-mail: yourcareercoach@aol.com

Teresa L. Pearson, CPRW, JCTC, Master in Human Relations
President, Pearson's Resume Output
16 Castle Way
Fort Rucker, AL 36362
Phone: (334) 598-0024
Fax: (503) 905-1495
E-mail: pearsonresume@snowhill.com

CALIFORNIA

Debi Bogard
Principal, The Write Resume
11835 Carmel Mountain Rd., Ste. 1304-175
San Diego, CA 92128-4609
Phone: (858) 592-9406
Fax: (858) 592-7271
E-mail: thewriteresume@san.rr.com
URL: www.itsthewriteresume.com

Nancy Karvonen, CPRW, CEIP, IJCTC, CCM, CJST
Executive Director, A Better Word & Resume
771 Adare Way
Galt, CA 95632
Phone: (209) 744-8203
Fax: (209) 745-7114
E-mail: Support@aresumecoach.com
URL: www.aresumecoach.com

Denise L. Lidell, MA
Principal, Career Crossroads
P.O. Box 421175
San Diego, CA 92108
Phone: (858) 560-8331
Fax: (858) 560-8341
E-mail: denise@careercr.com
URL: www.careercr.com

Denise Lupardo
President, Denise's Office Support & Resumes
22961 Mullin Rd.
Lake Forest, CA 92630
Phone: (949) 581-7901
Fax: (949) 581-7961
E-mail: Success@ResumeRelief.com
URL: www.ResumeRelief.com

Vivian VanLier, CPRW, JCTC, CEIP, CCM
6701 Murietta Ave.
Valley Glen (Los Angeles), CA 91405
Member, Phoenix Career Group
Toll-free: (800) 876-5506
Fax: (859) 236-4001
E-mail: info@phoenixcareergroup.com
URL: www.phoenixcareergroup.com

Pearl White, CEIP
Principal, A 1st Impression Resume Service
41 Tangerine
Irvine, CA 92618
Phone: (949) 651-1068
Fax: (949) 651-9415
E-mail: ckeys@cruznet.net
URL: www.a1stimpression.com

CONNECTICUT
Louise Garver, MA, CMP, JCTC, CPRW, CEIP
President, Career Directions, LLC
115 Elm St., Ste. 203
Enfield, CT 06082
Toll-free: (888) 222-3731
Phone: (860) 623-9476
Fax: (860) 623-9473
E-mail: TheCareerPro@aol.com
URL: www.resumeimpact.com

Ellen Mulqueen, MA, CRW
Vocational Counselor, Dept. of Rehabilitation
Services
The Institute of Living
200 Retreat Ave.
Hartford, CT 06106
Phone: (860) 545-7202
Fax: (860) 545-7140
E-mail: emulque@harthosp.org
URL: www.instituteofliving.org/rehab.htm

Debra O'Reilly, CPRW, JCTC, CEIP
President, A First Impression/ResumeWriter.com
16 Terryville Ave.
Bristol, CT 06010

Toll-free: (800) 340-5570
Phone: (860) 583-7500
Fax: (860) 583-9611
E-mail: debra@resumewriter.com
URL: www.resumewriter.com

FLORIDA
Laura A. DeCarlo, CCM, CERW, CPRW, JCTC, CECC, CCMC
President, A Competitive Edge Career Service
1665 Clover Circle
Melbourne, FL 32935
Toll-free: (800) 715-3442
Fax: (321) 752-7513
E-mail: getanedge@aol.com
URL: www.acompetitiveedge.com

GEORGIA
Lori Davila
President, LJD Consulting, Inc.
1483 North Springs Dr.
Dunwoody, GA 30338
Phone: (770) 392-1139
E-mail: loritil@aol.com

HAWAII
Peter Hill, CPRW
Distinctive Resumes
1226 Alexander St. #1205
Honolulu, HI 96826
Phone: (808) 306-3920
E-mail: distinctiveresumes@yahoo.com
URL: www.peterhill.biz

ILLINOIS
Sally McIntosh, NCRW, CPRW, JCTC
Advantage Resumes (of Illinois)
35 Westfair Dr.
Jacksonville, IL 62650
Phone: (217) 245-0752
Fax: (217) 243-4451
E-mail: sally@reswriter.com
URL: www.reswriter.com

Phaedra Winters
Principal, Professional Career Solutions
P.O. Box 9265
Naperville, IL 60567-9265
Phone: (630) 759-6615
Fax: (866) 686-3812
E-mail: winningres@att.net
URL: www.winningres.com

IOWA
Billie Sucher, MS
President, Billie Ruth Sucher & Associates
7177 Hickman Rd., Ste. 10
Urbandale, IA 50322
Phone: (515) 276-0061
Fax: (515) 334-8076
E-mail: betwnjobs@aol.com

KANSAS
James Walker, MS
Counselor—ACAP Center
Bldg. 210, Rm. 006, Custer Avenue
Fort Riley, KS 66442
Phone: (785) 239-2278
Fax: (785) 239-2251
E-mail: jwalker8199@yahoo.com

MAINE
Rolande L. LaPointe, CPC, CIPC, CPRW, CRW, IJCTC, CCM, CSS
President, RO-LAN Associates, Inc.
725 Sabattus St.
Lewiston, ME 04240
Phone: (207) 784-1010
Fax: (207) 782-3446
E-mail: Rlapointe@aol.com

MARYLAND
Sheila Adjahoe
President, The Adjahoe Group
Upper Marlboro, MD 20774
Phone: (301) 350-5137
Fax: (301) 324-7736
E-mail: sadjahoe@aol.com

MASSACHUSETTS
Wendy Gelberg, M.Ed., CPRW, IJCTC
President, Advantage Resumes
21 Hawthorn Ave.
Needham, MA 02492
Phone: (781) 444-0778
Fax: (781) 444-2778
E-mail: WGelberg@aol.com

Rosemarie Ginsberg, CPRW, CEIP
Employment Recruiter, Creative Staffing
Associates, Inc.
15 Michael Rd.
Framingham, MA 01701
Phone: (508) 877-5100
Fax: (508) 877-3511

E-mail: csadirecthire@aol.com
URL: www.creativeresumesnjobs.com

MICHIGAN
Jennifer Nell Ayres
President, Nell Personal Advancement Resources
P.O. Box 2
Clarkston, MI 48347
Phone: (248) 969-9933
Fax: (248) 969-9935
E-mail: info@nellresources.com
URL: www.nellresources.com

Joyce L. Fortier, MBA, CPRW, JCTC, CCM
President, Create Your Career
23871 W. Lebost
Novi, MI 48375
Toll-free: (800) 793-9895
Phone: (248) 478-5662
Fax: (248) 426-9974
E-mail: careerist@aol.com
URL: www.careerist.com

MINNESOTA
Linda Wunner, CPRW, JCTC, CEIP
President, A+ Career & Resume Design
4516 Midway Rd.
Duluth, MN 55811
Toll-free: (877) 946-6377
Phone: (218) 729-4551
Fax: (218) 729-8277
E-mail: linda@successfulresumes.com
URL: www.successfulresumes.com

MISSOURI
Gina Taylor, CPRW
President, Gina Taylor & Associates, Inc.
A-1 Advantage Resume & Career Services
1111 W. 77th Terrace
Kansas City, MO 64114
Phone: (816) 523-9100
Fax: (816) 523-6566
E-mail: GinaResume@sbcglobal.net
URL: www.GinaTaylor.com

MONTANA
Laura West, CCMC, CJST, JCTC
President, Orion Career Group
634 N. Birch Creek Rd.
Corvallis, MT 59828
Toll-free: (888) 685-3507
Phone: (406) 961-8366

Fax: (208) 460-5804
E-mail: laurawest@earthlink.net
URL: www.OrionCareerGroup.com

NEW HAMPSHIRE
Kirsten Dixson, JCTC, CPRW, CEIP
President, New Leaf Career Solutions
P.O. Box 963
Exeter, NH 03833
Phone: (866) 639-5323
Toll-free fax: (888) 887-7166
E-mail: info@newleafcareer.com
URL: www.newleafcareer.com

NEW JERSEY
Beverly Baskin, Ed.S., MA, NCCC, LPC, CPRW
President, Baskin Business and Career Services
6 Alberta Dr.
Marlboro, NJ 07746
Toll-free: (800) 300-4079
Phone: (732) 536-0076
Fax: (732) 972-8846
E-mail: bbcs@att.net
URL: www.baskincareer.com

Susan Guarneri, MS, NCC, NCCC, LPC, CPRW, IJCTC, CEIP, CCM, CCMC, CPRW
President, Guarneri Associates/Resumagic
1101 Lawrence Rd.
Lawrenceville, NJ 08648
Phone: (609) 771-1669
Fax: (609) 637-0449
E-mail: Resumagic@aol.com
URL: www.resume-magic.com

NEW YORK
Ann Baehr, CPRW
President, Best Resumes
122 Sheridan St.
Brentwood, NY 11717
Phone: (631) 435-1879
Fax: (631) 435-3655
E-mail: resumesbest@earthlink.net
URL: www.e-bestresumes.com

(Ms.) Freddie Cheek, M.S.Ed., CPRW, CWDP, CRW
Cheek & Cristantello Career Connections
4511 Harlem Rd., Ste. 3
Amherst, NY 14226
Phone: (716) 839-3635
Fax: (716) 831-9320

E-mail: fscheek@adelphia.net
URL: www.CheekandCristantello.com

Deborah Wile Dib, CCM, NCRW, CPRW, CEIP, JCTC, CCMC
President, Advantage Resumes of New York
77 Buffalo Ave.
Medford, NY 11763
Toll-free: (888) 272-8899
Phone: (631) 475-8513
Fax: (501) 421-7790
E-mail: 100kPLUS@advantageresumes.com
URL: www.advantageresumes.com

Salome A. Farraro, CPRW
Careers Too
3123 Moyer Rd.
Mount Morris, NY 14510
Toll-free: (877) 436-9378
Phone: (585) 658-2480
E-mail: srttoo@frontiernet.net

Andrea J. Howard, M.S.Ed
Employment Counselor, NYS Dept. of Labor
175 Central Ave.
Albany, NY 12206
Phone: (518) 462-7600, ext. 124
Fax: (518) 462-2768
E-mail: ah3@labor.states.ny.us

Linda Matias, JCTC, CEIP
Executive Director, CareerStrides
34 E. Main St. #276
Smithtown, NY 11787
Phone: (631) 382-2425
Fax: (631) 382-2425
E-mail: careerstrides@bigfoot.com
URL: www.careerstrides.com

Ilona Vanderwoude, CJST, CEIP
Career Branches
P.O. Box 330
Riverdale, NY 10471
Phone: (914) 376-4217
Fax: (646) 349-2218
E-mail: YourResumeWriter.com
URL: www.careerbranches.com

NORTH CAROLINA

Alice P. Braxton, CPRW, CEIP
President, Accutype Resumes & Secretarial
Services
635-C Chapel Hill Rd.
Burlington, NC 27215
Phone: (336) 227-9091
Fax: (336) 227-6548
E-mail: accutype@netpath.net

Billie P. Jordan
Advantage Resumes and Career Services
2362 Belgrade Swansboro Rd.
Maysville, NC 28555
Toll-free: (877) 563-2509
Phone: (910) 743-3641
Fax: (910) 743-0435
E-mail: bjordan1@ec.rr.com
URL: www.benchmarkresumes.com

John M. O'Connor, CRW, CPRW, MFA
President, CareerPro Resumes & Career Centers
3301 Woman's Club Dr., Ste. 125
Raleigh, NC 27612-4812
Phone: (919) 787-2400
Fax: (919) 787-2411
E-mail: john@careerproresumes.com
URL: www.careerproresumes.com

OHIO

Louise Kursmark, CPRW, JCTC, CCM, CEIP
Executive Master Team—Career Masters
Institute™
President, Best Impression Career Services, Inc.
9847 Catalpa Woods Ct.
Cincinnati, OH 45242
Phone: (513) 792-0030
Fax: (513) 792-0961
E-mail: LK@yourbestimpression.com
URL: www.yourbestimpression.com

Sharon Pierce-Williams, M.Ed., CPRW
President, The Resume.Doc
609 Lincolnshire Ln.
Findlay, OH 45840
Phone: (419) 422-0228
Fax: (419) 425-1185
E-mail: TheResumeDocSPW@aol.com
URL: www.TheResumeDoc.com

Richard B. Robertson, MBA
Principal, Target Interviews Resume Service
432 Landings Loop E.
Westerville, OH 43082
Phone: (614) 746-5890
Fax: (614) 794-7573
E-mail: rick@targetinterviews.com
URL: www.targetinterviews.com

Teena Rose, CPRW, CEIP, CCM
President, Resume to Referral
7211 Taylorsville Rd., Office 208
Huber Heights, OH 45424
Phone: (937) 236-1360
Fax: (937) 264-9930
E-mail: admin@resumetoreferral.com
URL: www.resumebycprw.com

PENNSYLVANIA

Jewel Bracy DeMaio, CPRW, CEIP
President, A Perfect Resume.com
340 Main St.
Royersford, PA 19464
Toll-free: (800) 227-5131
Phone: (610) 327-3202
Fax: (610) 327-8014
E-mail: mail@aperfectresume.com
URL: www.aperfectresume.com

Jane Roqueplot, CBC
President, JaneCo's Sensible Solutions
194 N. Oakland Ave.
Sharon, PA 16146
Toll-free: (888) JANECOS (526-3267)
Phone: (724) 342-0100
Fax: (724) 346-5263
E-mail: info@janecos.com
URL: www.janecos.com

Darren Shartle, M.Ed., CPRW, CEIP
President, Advanced CareerTools
318 S. Market St.
Mechanicsburg, PA 17055
Toll-free: (888) 233-9183
Phone: (717) 791-2730
Fax: (717) 791-9353
E-mail: darren@advancedcareertools.com
URL: www.advancedcareertools.com

TEXAS

Lynn Hughes, MA, CPRW, CEIP
A Resume and Career Service, Inc.
3402 A 34th St.
P.O. Box 6911
Lubbock, TX 79493
Phone: (806) 785-9800
Fax: (806) 785-2711
E-mail: lynn@aresumeservice.com
URL: www.aresumeservice.com

Gerald R. Moore, CPRW
Principal, Career Advantage
5536 Longview Circle
El Paso, TX 79924-1317
Phone: (915) 204-4192
Fax: (915) 822-8146
E-mail: jmoore@gwelp.com

William G. Murdock, CPRW
President, The Employment Coach
7770 Meadow Rd., Ste. 109
Dallas, TX 75230
Phone: (214) 750-4781
Fax: (214) 750-4781
E-mail: bmurdock@swbell.net

Ann Stewart, CPRW
President, Advantage Services
P.O. Box 525
Roanoke, TX 76262
Phone: (817) 424-1448
Fax: (817) 329-7165
E-mail: ASresume@aol.com

UTAH

Diana C. LeGere
President, Executive Final Copy
P.O. Box 171311
Salt Lake City, UT 84117
(also in Richmond, VA)
Toll-free: (866) 754-5465
Phone: (801) 550-5697
Fax: (626) 602-8715
E-mail: execefinalcopy@msn.com
URL: www.executivefinalcopy.com

VIRGINIA

William Kinser, CPRW, JCTC, CEIP
President, To The Point Resumes
4117 Kentmere Square
Fairfax, VA 22030
Phone: (703) 352-8969

Fax: (703) 352-8969
E-mail: resumes@tothepointresumes.com
URL: www.tothepointresumes.com

Jean Oscarson
3610 Plymouth Place
Lynchburg, VA 24503
Toll-free: (888) 808-6949
Phone: (434) 384-7488
Fax: (413) 294-7508
E-mail: JeanOscarson@aol.com
URL: www.career-resumes.com

WASHINGTON

Janice M. Shepherd, CPRW, JCTC, CEIP
Write On Career Keys
2628 E. Crestline Dr.
Bellingham, WA 98226
Phone: (360) 738-7958
Fax: (360) 738-1189
E-mail: janice@writeoncareerkeys.com
URL: www.writeoncareerkeys.com

WISCONSIN

Michele J. Haffner, CPRW, JCTC
Advanced Resume Services
1314 W. Paradise Ct.
Glendale, WI 53209
Toll-free: (877) 247-1677
Phone: (414) 247-1677
Fax: (414) 247-1808
E-mail: mhaffner@resumeservices.com
URL: www.resumeservices.com

Australia

Annemarie Cross, CEIP, CPRW
A.E.C. Office Services
P.O. Box 91, Hallam, Victoria 3803
Australia
E-mail: aec_office@alphalink.com.au
URL: aec-office.alphalink.com.au/
ResumeWriters.htm

Gayle Howard, CPRW, CRW, CCM
Founder/Owner, Top Margin Resumes Online
P.O. Box 74
Chirnside Park, Melbourne 3116
Australia
Phone: +61 3 9726 6694
Fax: +61 3 9726 5316
E-mail: gayle@topmargin.com
URL: www.topmargin.com

Canada

Martin Buckland, CPRW, JCTC, CEIP, CJST
President, Elite Resumes
1428 Stationmaster Ln.
Oakville, Ontario L6M 3A7
Canada
Toll-free: (866) 773-7863
Phone: (905) 825-0490
Fax: (905) 825-2966
E-mail: martin@aneliteresume.com
URL: www.AnEliteResume.com

Deborah Reaburn, CEIP, CCMC
President, Personal Marketing Group
3650 Marda Link SW, Ste. 107
Calgary, Alberta T2T 6G9
Canada
Phone: (403) 229-0424
Fax: (403) 209-0957
E-mail: careercoach@shaw.ca

INDEX

A

accounting career Web sites, 234
accuracy, 17
achievements, highlighting, 16
addresses, e-mail, 14–15
arts careers Web sites, 234
ASCII text files, 55–56
attachments, e-mail, 55
awards, 43

B

benefits, identifying, 4
boldfacing, 16
Bookman Old Style font, 15
bulleted format, 13
buzzwords. *See* key words

C

capitalization, 16
careers
    entering new, xv–xvi
    identifying interests, 4–5
    managing, xiv–xx
    objectives, xiii–xx
    resumes. *See* resumes
    summaries, 33–36
certifications, 36–38
chronological format, 12
civic affiliations, 45
cold calls, xix
colors, selecting, 17
combination resume format, 14
committees, 44
company Web sites, 238
comparing resume types, 60–61
components. *See also* formatting
    educational-emphasis resumes,
      22–24
    experience-emphasis resumes,
      25–26
    functional/skills resumes,
      20–21
confidence, 10
consulting, xix
contact information, 32–33
content
    highlighting, 16
    reasons to lengthen resumes,
      16–17
    resumes, 9. *See also* resumes
    standards, 11
contracting, xix
cover letters, 50–51
credentials, 36–38

D

dates, including, 48–50
dictionaries, 231–232
duties, 8–10

E

e-mail
    addresses, 14–15
    attachments, 55
    targeting, xviii
editing resumes, 17
education
    including dates, 50
    non-degree resume format,
      38
    resume sections, 36–38
    Web sites, 234
educational-emphasis resumes,
    22–24
electronic resumes, 54–56, 59
emphasizing typestyles, 16
employment trends, xiii–xiv
engineering career Web sites,
    236–237
entering new professions, xv–xvi

entry-level career Web sites, 234–235
equipment skills, 43
experience-emphasis resumes, 25–26

F

first-person writing style, 10
focus
    "big" things resume strategy, 8–9
    educational-emphasis resume, 22–24
    experience-emphasis resume, 25–26
    functional/skills resume, 20–21
    on job functions, 10
fonts, 15. *See also* typestyles
formatting
    chronological, 12
    importance of, 27–31
    resumes, 9, 12–14
        accuracy, 17
        bulleted format, 13
        combination format, 14
        e-mail addresses, 14–15
        educational-emphasis resumes, 22
        experience-emphasis resumes, 25
        functional/skills resumes, 12, 20–21
        graphics, 17
        page length, 16–17
        paper colors, 17
        paragraph format, 12–13
        sections. *See* sections
        type size, 15–16
        typestyles, 15. *See also* typestyles
        whitespace, 17
freelancing, xix
functional resume format, 12, 20–21

G

general job search Web sites, 232–234
Gill Sans font, 15
glossaries, 231–232
goals, identifying, 4–5

government Web sites, 237
graphics, formatting resumes, 17

H

health care career Web sites, 235
highlighting words, 16
histories, salary, 51
honesty, maintaining in resumes, 10
honors and awards, 43
human resources, 7, 235

I

identifying
    benefits, 4
    career interests, 4–5
    features, 4
    goals, 4–5
    objectives, 4–5
importance of resume formatting, 27–31
improving
    interviewability, 9
    resume readability, 9
in-person cold calls, xix
international career Web sites, 235
interviews, 8–9, 238
italics, 16

J

jobs
    focusing on job functions, 10
    general search Web sites, 231–232
    searching, xiv–xx

K

key words, 6–8

L

law career Web sites, 237
length of resumes, 8–9, 16–17

M

magazines, responding to ads in, xvii
maintaining honesty in resumes, 10
managing careers, xiv–xx
margins, 17
marketing, xvi, 236
media career Web sites, 234
medical career Web sites, 235
military career Web sites, 237

N

narrative styles, selecting, 10
networking, xvii
new professions, entering, xv–xvi
newspapers, responding to ads in, xvii
non-degree resume format, 38
numbers, highlighting, 16

O

objectives
    career, xiii–xx
    identifying, 4–5
"one to two page" length rule, 16–17
online job postings, responding to, xvii
online resumes, posting, xviii

P

page length, 16–17
paper colors, selecting, 17
paragraph resume format, 12–13
past performance, focusing on, 8–9
perception, creating, 5
performance, focusing on, 8–9
periodicals, responding to, xvii
personal information, 46
pharmaceutical Web sites, 235
phrases. *See also* key words
    to avoid, 11
    highlighting, 16
points, type size, 15
posting resumes online, xviii
presentation standards, 15
printed resumes, 53, 57
professional affiliations, 45
professional experience, 38–41
professions, entering new, xv–xvi
projects, highlighting, 16
proofreading resumes, 17
public-speaking skills, 44
publications, 44

Q

qualifications, 42–43

R

readability
    improving, 9
    type size, 15–16
reasons to lengthen resumes, 16–17
re-entering fields, xvi

referrals, xvii
requirements, salary, 51
responding to job postings, xvii
responsibilities
    avoiding phrases such as, 10
    focusing on the "big" things, 8–9
resumes
    content and structure, 9
    and cover letters, 50–51
    formatting, 12–14
      accuracy, 17
      bulleted format, 13
      combination format, 14
      e-mail addresses, 14–15
      educational-emphasis resumes, 22
      experience-emphasis resumes, 25
      functional/skills resumes, 20–21
      graphics, 17
      importance of, 27–31
      page length, 16–17
      paper colors, 17
      paragraph format, 12–13
      type size, 15–16
      typestyles, 15–16
    length, 8–9
    posting online, xviii
    presentation standards, 15
    proofreading, 17
    reasons to lengthen, 16–17
    rules, 10–17
    sections, 31
      career summary, 33–36
      certifications, 36–38
      civic affiliations, 45
      committees and task forces, 44–45
      contact information, 32–33
      credentials, 36–38
      education, 36–38
      equipment skills, 43
      honors and awards, 43
      personal information, 46
      professional affiliations, 45
      professional experience, 38–42
      publications, 44
      public speaking, 44
      teaching experience, 44
      technology skills, 42–43

targeting, xviii
tips, 47–51
types of
comparing, 60–61
electronic, 54–56
printed, 53
scannable, 54
Web, 56
writing, 3–4, 20
rules
"one to two page", 16–17
writing, 10–17

S

salaries, 51, 239
sales, 7, 236
scannable resumes, 54, 58
searching jobs, xiv–xx
sections, 31
career summary, 33–36
certifications, 36–38
civic affiliations, 45
committees and task forces,
44–45
contact information, 32–33
credentials, 36–38
education, 36–38
equipment skills, 43
honors and awards, 43
personal information, 46
professional affiliations, 45
professional experience, 38–42
public speaking, 44
publications, 44
teaching experience, 44
technology skills, 42–43
selecting. *See also* formatting
narrative styles, 10
type size, 15–16
"Sell It to Me..." resume strategy, 5–6
service career Web sites, 236
sizing type, 15–16
skills
equipment, 43
focusing on the "big" things,
8–9
technology, 42–43
standards
content, 11
"one to two page", 16–17
presentation, 15

strategies
confidence, 10
content and structure, 9
focusing on job functions, 10
focusing on the "big" things,
8–9
honesty, 10
identifying career goals, 4–5
key words, 6–8
resumes as interview tools, 9
"Sell It to Me...", 5–6
structure, 9. *See also* formatting
styles
chronological, 12
functional resume, 12
selecting narratives, 10
typestyles, 15
writing, 11
summaries, career, 33–36

T

targeting e-mail campaigns, xviii
task forces, 44
teaching experience, 44
technology skills, 42–43, 236–237
third-person writing style, 10
time not worked, accounting for, xv
Times New Roman font, 15
training experience, 44
trends, employment, xiii–xiv
types of resumes, 53–61
typestyles (fonts), 15–16

U

underlining, 16
URLs (uniform resource locators),
14–15

V

value of experience, creating, 5–6
Verdana font, 16

W–Z

Web resumes, 56
white space, 17
writing resumes, 3–5, 19–20
rules, 10–17
styles, 11
tips, 47–51